WOMEN AND DEATH

Recent Titles in
Contributions in Women's Studies

Women and Death

LINKAGES IN WESTERN THOUGHT AND LITERATURE

BETH ANN BASSEIN

CONTRIBUTIONS IN WOMEN'S STUDIES, NUMBER 44

GREENWOOD PRESS
Westport, Connecticut · London, England

Library of Congress Cataloging in Publication Data

Bassein, Beth Ann.
  Women and death.

  (Contributions in women's studies, ISSN 0147-104X ;
no. 44)
  Bibliography: p.
  Includes index.
  1. Women.   2. Women in literature.   3. Death.
I. Title.   II. Series.
HQ1206.B29   1984   305.4   83-8544
ISBN 0-313-23924-X (lib. bdg.)

Library of Congress Catalog Card Number: 83-8544
ISBN: 0-313-23924-X
ISSN: 0147-104X

First published in 1984

Greenwood Press
A division of Congressional Information Service, Inc.
88 Post Road West, Westport, Connecticut 06881

Printed in the United States of America

10 9 8 7 6 5 4 3 2 1

"Any woman's death diminishes me."
—Adrienne Rich

"Men know a lot about dying, but they don't know enough about living."
—Margaret Mead

"It is only by putting it into words that I make it whole; this wholeness means that it has lost the power to hurt me. . . ."
—Virginia Woolf

CONTENTS

———— PREFACE ————

This book deals with the image, aura, and actuality of death as they relate to women's lives both in literature and, insofar as art represents life, in reality as people know or define it. Because of the almost universal identification of women with sex and the historical tendency to see sexuality as their main or only function, the subject under discussion hinges on woman, sex, and death or, as situations vary, woman, love, and death.

Although the subject of love or sex and death has been studied extensively, it has rarely been treated under the broader subject of woman and death. Not many scholars have reacted on a reasonable or literal level, for example, to the Renaissance use of the phrase *to die* to mean *to copulate*.* Perhaps even fewer have brought reason to bear on Edgar Allan Poe's statements about the death of a beautiful woman being the most poetic subject imaginable, or have pondered just how their responses to women and death differ from those of Poe or other artists treating the subject. There are not a great many scholars who have analyzed the inevitable and "honorable" end, that of death, which until recent times was meted out to women in fiction who committed adultery.

By examining such links between women and death with an eye to their pervasiveness and the ways in which life does or does not dictate their inevitability or reinforce them, the scholar may gain insight into attitude-building and into how the arts and language

———————————
*This usage was popular slang or a pun during the Renaissance and is often documented by scholars and editors. See note 56 in Chapter I.

perpetuate thinking, emotional responses, and habits. It then may not seem entirely preposterous to venture a conjecture about such seemingly innocuous developments, for example, as the abusive "Fuck You!" which has recently been hurled at friend and enemy, male and female, with varying degrees of venom, to mean something closely akin to "Drop Dead!," an expression that previously served its popularity turn for a similar purpose.

This book seeks to go beyond this kind of quick and easy conclusion, however, and, by presenting an abundance of evidence exhibiting a prevailing obsession with the death of woman, it will show that an extremely deep-seated association between the two exists. The evidence presented in Chapter I centers on language and its capacity to reiterate the inevitable link. The following chapter focuses on traditional Christianity as a facilitator for perpetuating the tie between the two. The treatment of *memento mori*, which comes next, demonstrates that women can be highly tangible symbols of death. After these introductory chapters, an analysis is presented of a large and varied body of literature which, for the most part, takes the inevitable link between women and death for granted.

While this book furnishes evidence that a prevailing tendency to yoke women unreasonably with death exists, it also recognizes life-oriented writers who have not chosen to become involved with the subject or who have broken away from it to present women more realistically. Obviously, supporting the thesis that there is a special kind of death aura hovering over women does not call for extensive treatment of those writers who do not exhibit this tendency. The last chapter, however, will show how Adrienne Rich seeks new means of giving a full treatment of women. She would alter language that tacitly underscores brutality and death when related unreasonably to women. She would hope to dislodge the inseparable linkage of women, sex, and death and to free them from an automatic fusion.

For some, it may be tempting to speculate on whether there have been experiences in women's lives from the beginning that have somehow tied them closely enough to death to make what seems an exaggerated association a legitimate one. Although it is beyond the scope of this book to investigate to any extent the history of women's experiences with death or the death-producing (and quite likely a nearly impossible task since so little of women's history has been written and preserved), an appendix provides some information on this subject. It offers the tentative suggestion that until quite recently many of those who have written about women's actual lives have leaned heavily toward portraying woman's sexual side at the expense of much else, especially when death is the major focus.

It needs to be stated at the onset that this book does not deal to any degree with the frequency of death among women as compared to men. Obviously, it will imply that women are often thought to die under a different set of circumstances than men. While examining literary materials that purportedly are about life or form a part of it, the book centers on situations in which women are undergoing death or death-producing experiences.

Neither does the book dwell on the cliché that death is the great equalizer, for obviously the experience of death itself (and here is meant the few minutes in which breathing stops) in women seemingly cannot be vastly different from what it is in men. Nor does it question the fact that chance does not, in most cases, favor one over the other. Others have dwelt on such subjects as which sex undergoes these final few minutes with more courage, but it is not the intent here to argue this point one way or the other. Neither does the book advocate ways in which people can undergo these few minutes more meaningfully or peacefully. Rather, it deals primarily with the aspects of death which hover over life, reducing life to less than it could be and, as many will hasten to add, blighting it with crippling negativism.

Those who might assume that a special affinity between women and death develops only in the minds of the criminally inclined will perhaps find some surprises in this book. Certainly, the artist often finds the subject extremely interesting, as do many readers. Moreover, in giving his or her coloring to reality, the artist may ignore vast areas of personality which are highly significant. Consequently, when artists dwell on women and death, frequently the tendency is to give women only partial existence. Now when women are leading much fuller lives between the time when they are awakened sexually and when they die (years often left out of literature and historical treatments), many would think there seems to be much less reason for the inevitable link to persist. Yet, the

number of death-producing experiences, or depictions of death itself, still found in the arts when women are involved tends to suggest that the link has become much more pronounced during the
twentieth century, a time when advancements in medicine, if
nothing else, ought to make the death aura surrounding women
even more at variance with what happens in daily life.

This study began in what was perceived to be an unexplainable
irrationality, if not contradiction, in conceiving sex to be *la petite
mort* and in detecting an assumption in literature that a special affinity between women and death exists. The reader who looks into
the ramifications of this study may wish to search further into
prevailing attitudes toward women and/or death, both in and out
of the literary context and from a historical standpoint. The bibliography at the end of this book will help in this endeavor as well
as indicate sources to which this work is indebted.

WOMEN AND DEATH

I

LANGUAGE AS DIMINISHER AND DESTROYER

A strong death-orientation, not descriptive of death and the dead per se but of persons living, colors the English language. Not registering actuality but the capacity to fantasize and exaggerate, the language has a large vocabulary and repository of images that delineate partial destruction and annihilation and suggest that we tend to be preoccupied with diminishing and destroying apart from what actually takes place in our surroundings. This vocabulary and imagery feed into and emerge from fears about ourselves and attitudes we have about people. Many of our attitudes toward women, for example, are expressed in terms we inherit, and either these attitudes or those undergoing modification are given utterance in the mainstream of speech and writing. In investigating the subject of women and death, one discovers words and images occurring along a broad spectrum from submersion to extinction. In her submersion, woman is often imagistically seen as having some part, aspect, or quality missing or as having some part, aspect, or quality taken for her totality. In both cases, she is seen as less than complete. Between submersion and extinction is an area where she is invisible. She is present but she is not seen. At the far and ultimate end of the continuum, she is simply dead and diminished to nothing. Here she is spoken of as not existing in any sense, either as apparition or as visible form when, of course, her heart still beats, her muscles flex, and often she lives what from the casual observer's point of view may be a normal life. These three areas often blur into each other and may seem at times to be almost all of one piece, or at other times each may be subdivided within its category, positives at one point and negatives at another.

Language designates women as less than whole, less than total, less than complete. Woman becomes less than human, less than capable, less than male, less than reasonable, less than a citizen— the reader who has read misogynist or feminist literature knows how long the list can be. The misogynist denigrates woman by diminishing her. Example: "Women have little practical common sense and even less native ability."[1] The feminist is usually either combating what the misogynist has said or setting up a base on which to begin improvement. Example: "They all say that women as human beings are substandard: less intelligent; less moral; less competent; less able physically, psychologically, and spiritually; small of body, mind, and character; often bad or destructive."[2] Example: "It is said that women are less capable than men of doing any kind of work requiring a high degree of rationality, abstraction, and intelligence, because women are intellectually inferior and characteristically not given to rationality and logic."[3] Both the misogynist and feminist help stabilize or build vocabulary that is a vehicle for attitude or concept formation. It has been suggested that an aura of unreason surrounds the misogynist's thinking, while feminists see women more realistically; the extent to which this colors the language of each and the degree to which each uses language literally and figuratively are interesting subjects for speculation.

Those who determine what is whole, total, or complete skew reality to their perspective and thus, for others who agree with them, help create a skewed perspective. Aristotle epitomized the whole person in Book IX of *Historia Animalium* as male when he said, "the nature of man is the most rounded off and complete" and, consequently, in man various qualities and capacities are found in their perfection.[4] Woman, on the other hand, is deficient in reasoning capacity; in fact, many of her qualities and capacities come in smaller portions than they do for males.[5] The male has the capacity to reason perfectly, but the female does so imperfectly because her deliberative faculty lacks authority.[6] The parts of the soul are also present to a lesser degree in woman.[7] Discussing woman, along with slaves, children, and animals, Aristotle sees her as a misbegotten male, a partial or faulty replica of man. In dealing with the terms *masculine* and *feminine*, Simone de Beauvoir states that they are used "symmetrically only as a matter of form, as on legal papers." The relation, she says, of the "two sexes is not quite like that of two electrical poles, for *man* represents both the positive and the neutral, as is indicated by the common use of *man* to designate human beings in general; whereas *woman* represents only the negative, defined by limiting criteria, without reciprocity."[8]

For the most part debaters on whether or not woman had a soul came finally to conclude that she did possess one, although of a lesser quality. That the early Church Fathers came to allow her equality in at least possessing a soul was, according to Eleanor Commo McLaughlin, a "new ideal in the late Hellenistic world in which religion and philosophy often limited the heights of spiritual perfection to males."[9] McLaughlin also mentions the belief held by Aristotle and Aquinas that woman's less superior body worked "a deleterious effect on woman's soul."[10] Had the belief been entertained that woman was a total person in the eyes of most, and certainly in the eyes of God, these discussions regarding her soul obviously would never have occurred. Church literature thus exhibits some of the early examples of language used in connection with women that is reductive.

Alexander Pope's comment that women have no character at all, Schopenhauer's and Freud's discussions (along with those of several others) to the effect that she lacked a sense of justice, and her generally being relegated to the procreative function which eclipses all others all illustrate the tendency to spell out her identity with less-than-total terms. Books of proverbs and "wise" sayings from notable persons net us, for example, Napoleon's comments that woman is nothing but a machine for producing children and that she lacks rank. Shakespeare's pronouncement "Women, being the weaker vessel, are ever thrust to the wall" and Shaw's "Woman reduces us all to the common denominator" both point to woman in reductive terms. These long-standing "definitions" have been "effected by men primarily through control of social institutions that determine behavior and attitudes."[11] These opinions appear acceptable to many who act as if they were, but "The alien definition of women, even more extreme than it first appears, goes beyond merely the production and imposition of foreign images, beyond women's accepting these images as our own; it proceeds all the way to our accepting the status of not only less-than-standard humanity, but less-than-standard *being*."[12] Feminists, making it clear that woman has no past and no history, support their theses by calling attention to these uses of language, but their perspective is one that sees woman as a much more complete person. Other women assist in their own self-depreciation by always comparing themselves to what has been defined (most often by males) as ideal.[13]

The less-than-total language was given a tremendous boost when Freud pointed to woman's lack of a penis which he thought cut into her aspirations and potential in many areas. She is only an "homme manqué," a man with something missing.[14] Basing most of his notions on the acceptance of woman's passive role, Freud was certain she could not live with the kind of totality that the male does. The vagina was no match for the penis; that each has a special function seemed not to alter his way of considering them. He doubtlessly would have spurned a shovel over a bucket for picking apples, but he could not transfer such practical, reasonable notions to male/female equipment. He, and most noted sex-role theorists until very recently, worked from the premise that woman was *lacking*, a starting point that was bound to produce language to go in its wake. Often employing the word *natural* to describe women in the passive state and emphasizing nature's way as God's way, ideologies, with great credibility for many, lock in an expected behavior pattern. The amount of discussion that exists, however, tends to suggest that it has been difficult to accept these notions as foregone conclusions and remain silent. A constant barrage of depreciation has been necessary to keep up the illusion that women are lesser beings. As feminists become more and more aware of this barrage, they seek to position women so they can be accounted for as total beings and from all sides.

It is not difficult for females to realize that a penis could get in the way when it is not needed, but male values are taken to be universal and reality is skewed to the male perspective. In some cultures, men speak a language that the women are forbidden to use, while in ours women speak a language often not of their making. It was not so very long ago that it was felt a dangerous thing for women to learn because it might sap the energies needed for reproduction; remnants of this belief are found in our advocating different schooling for girls and boys. Never having access to language-building to the extent that the male has, she has basically been a helper in creating and maintaining the language of unreason that constantly bombards her.

Women, having been led to believe they cannot be whole alone, seek a wholeness through marriage. Thomas Hardy's Jude asks Sue: "Is a woman a thinking unit at all, or a fraction always wanting its integer?"[15] Una Stannard in *Mrs. Man*[16] has a chapter called "Dwindling into a Wife" about women with high goals who slip back into the stereotype, thinking that a true identity cannot be had without a husband. Publicly, she will be very little without marriage, and to posterity she is certainly less than a complete woman. It is significant that the feminist sees her as not whole while she is attempting to become what she thinks is whole; the peer pressure that pushes her into marriage demands she become whole while the feminist frequently sees her diminishing. She is caught from many sides and is asked to fill vacancies in her makeup. While all terms applied to the unwed woman carry a stigma unavoidably implying a denigrated or less-than-total state,[17] she, whether becoming a wife or mistress, may be looked upon as a thing or object, like a car or a private plane, to bolster the male ego. Women often also lower themselves to servant status to please men. As Simone de Beauvoir says, "She is defined and differentiated with reference to man and not he with reference to her."[18]

Another effect of the male appropriation of reality on language is to conceive of and describe a part of woman as representative of the whole. Most obvious in identifying her solely with sex, this way of thinking has made her come to mean sex; sex makes up nearly all of her totality.[19] If for any reason, sex is not a recognized part of her makeup, most of society reduces her to zero. My collection of words with which she has been tagged denoting only her sexual side is extensive, but very partial when we realize that woman's history would lead us to believe that she has basically been for the purpose of "relieving man's estate." Pause over babe, box, breeder, buxom blonde, coquette, concubine, courtesan, cunt, demirep, earth mother, femme fatale, floozey, harlot, hooker, lay, lizzie, muff, nymph, pickup, piece of tail, prostitute, punk, seat cover, seductress, skirt, sorceress, spread, stale, street walker, strumpet, tart, trollop, twat, virago, virgin, wanton, wench, white

slave, whore. All of these words call attention to sexuality and re-
fer to scarcely any other characteristic, attribute, or part. This
naming evinces a tunnel vision capable of thwarting all reason.

A list of words calling attention to other sides of the individual
can obviously be made (workers, both male and female, have been
called hands); char, gossip, grass widow, scatterbrain, shrew, spit-
fire, vixen, and wife all call attention to other aspects of woman,
but my list applicable to female sexuality in the previous paragraph has grown at a much swifter rate. A further aspect of this
language is that most of the words apply to woman's life from
birth to marriage, leaving the most productive years of her life
unspecified. Germaine Greer in *The Female Eunuch* says age thirty
is the limit beyond which women as people are recognized.[20] Ad-
vertising and most aspects of the media bear this out. The only
conclusion to draw then is that not only is she limited to sex, but
also her sex is limited once she is into marriage or has reached an
age when her sex no longer possesses desired qualities.

Because sexual overtones are used to degrade, many of the terms
applied to women obviously become invectives intended to diminish her. "Lower-class distrust of airs and graces has resulted in
the ironic application of terms like *madam, lady, dame* and *duchess*,
which is fair exchange for the loading of dialect names for women
with contemptuous associations, as in *wench, quean, donah, dell, moll,
biddy* and *bunter* (once a ragpicker, but now invariably a prostitute)."[21] Venereal disease added a set of terms expressing abuse and
hatred for women (fireships, brimstone, bawdy baskets). A low
regard for semen has made them receptacles for refuse as in the
term *bag*. All of these terms which pull woman down and victimize her rest on the demand that women will be/are less than complete and are preferred that way: "women are more conveniently
exploitable and indeed more sexually exciting when they are stripped
not only of clothing but of power, strength, assertiveness, and sense
of self."[22] Shulamuth Firestone summarizes: "A good portion of
our language is designed to degrade women to the level where it
is permissible to have sexual feelings for them."[23]

Perhaps as one of the legacies from Aristotle and others who
"reasoned" on woman's nature from observation of animals, another group of words links her to the less-than-totally human, the
animal: biddy, bird, bitch, brood sow, bunny, cat, chick, cow,

duckie, ewe, goose, hen, kitten, pussy. Menander tells us: "There are many wild beasts on land and in the sea, but the beastliest of all is woman." Like *babe*, these words link woman to the easily manipulated. Most of this list also have overtones of sexuality and call up just that part of woman. As Mary Daly indicates, women very much need to let "out the bunnies, the bitches, the beavers, the squirrels, the chicks, the pussy cats, the cows, the nags, the foxy ladies, the old bats and biddies, so that they can at last begin naming themselves."[24] Daly does not believe it is time for dialogue with those "who have stolen the power of speech and made all language a system of false words, having made the part stand for the whole. Rather it is time for men to learn at last to listen and to hear knowing that this is how . . . to discover at least the way to adequate speech."[25]

At this writing I have just read a short article in the local college newspaper which gives as a sales pitch for car pooling the coming to know that cute blond "you may have seen in biology class." The article does not mention any of the reasons for car pooling; no comments surface on saving our environment, or fuel supplies, or even our purses. Here the sexual part of woman is mistaken for the whole, and the sexual part of existence takes precedence over matters of great significance. To compound the problem of sexism in language, the writer of this article was challenged by a feminist on his language, and he dismissed the charge with the statement that nowhere in the article does the cute blond become a *she*.

Obviously, then, sex defines women for many. Yet, throughout history she has been taught to pretend she has no sex, to limit even that. If all she is is sex, and if she squelches it, then she is indeed very insignificant. Greer suggests that she becomes a eunuch, a partial being. Furthermore, this kind of hiding her quest for sex builds in her an inertia that spreads through her like a contagion. "No sooner does her pubic hair appear than she has to learn how to *obliterate* it . . . her menstruation strikes her as a hideous *violation* of her physical integrity." Her personality steadily *erodes*; she *represses* herself, *abandons* autonomy, and adopts the role of eunuch.[26] (My underlining in these statements calls attention to words Greer uses that suggest diminishing or giving up.) Freud backed up the repression of sex, firming up his arguments with "valid" clinical studies that made her incomplete since she lacked a penis and thus libido. This kind of conditioning to which the young woman is exposed causes her to want to lose a part of herself: her intelligence (frequently diminishing at puberty), her eyebrows, her underarm hair, her freckles. Even if she is pushed into a much applauded symbol, a personified abstraction, or a means of getting to God, she is still only partially defined.

The second category of terms along the continuum from submersion to extinction makes ghosts of women. They are there but no one can see them. Particularly in this terminology do we find users among feminists whose intent is to call attention to facts in order to remove them. Calling a woman a *cunt*, however, tends to suggest that the rest of her is not perceptible, not visible. Interestingly, when we consider how much space we take up, it may very well be more than that taken up by the average male, if we exclude the things he has manufactured. We are more in number, we sometimes grow rounder with age, and we have a great deal of apparatus in connection with child-bearing and -rearing. Certainly, our total space is nothing to be minimized, and we definitely can be seen with normal eyesight!

The language specifying invisibility often feeds into a culminating thrust: extinction. It also occurs, as does much of the language discussed here, any place where people are pushed down in order to raise others up. Ralph Ellison's *The Invisible Man* states that this tendency in people not to see others "occurs because of a peculiar disposition of the eyes . . . those eyes with which they look through their physical eyes upon reality."[27] He refers to a prejudicial, skewed perspective that causes one to be unable to recognize reality. If a person is invisible or some part is missing, this person is to the viewer not quite all there; he or she is regressing, diminishing, shrinking, or often on the way to going up in smoke. Definitely there is a kind of on-the-road-to-extinction language employed whenever the invisibility vocabulary takes over.

Robin Morgan's poem "The Invisible Woman" shows an asylumed woman who "sees others quite clearly" but thinks she is invisible—she thinks she is invisible because all around her suggests she is. The doctor goes around "talking and gesturing to nothing." Feeling compassion for him, she "pulls on a body" so to keep him from going insane.[28] Coming from a feminist, the poem quite clearly makes a point of the invisibility of women, save for their body (their sex) and the inability of the medical world to take into account the whole patient.

Cynthia Ozick thinks that any woman who believes she can make herself more visible by giving birth to a child has not examined the process and consequences or compared this kind of "creativity" to writing a great book or poem. In the first place, she says, the minute pregnancy begins, the rest is done not by the woman but for her. She is simply a parasite. *Home*, she says, and *Children, Homemaker*, and *Womanhood* have no reality, but are abstractions to give prestige to a fairy tale. They label just as *Muse* and *Mystery* label. Woman, a human being, is never seen as that. Looking at her she would be real, but looking aside and not seeing her, she is in the imaginations of those around her a myth.[29] What she truly is is a dishwasher, chauffeur, laundress. Living in a phantom world, she lacks reality.

Women sometimes find it easier to live in shadows, behind the scenes, not visible. Women novelists of the nineteenth century took masculine names to remain out of sight. About the shyness of young girls, Simone de Beauvoir writes: "The young girl feels that her body is getting away from her, it is no longer the straightforward expression of her individuality; it becomes foreign to her; and at the same time she becomes for others a thing; on the street men follow her with their eyes and comment on her anatomy. She would like to be invisible; it frightens her to become flesh and to show her flesh."[30]

Carol Smart indicates in *Women, Crime, and Criminology: A Feminist Critique* that women have basically been invisible to those making studies of crime. Categorized alongside juvenile delinquents and mentally abnormal offenders or in many cases not mentioned at all, their "existence is ignored." In discussions of crime, the pronoun *he* is always applied to the criminal, further making women "invisible."[31] "It is no surprise that our language and choice of words reflects the social 'invisibility' of women because in our culture, man is the centre of the universe and woman features only in her relation to him."[32] We could duplicate Smart's findings regarding crime in numerous areas such as politics, education, and commercial enterprises. What would it take to make women more visible? Kate Millett in writing about the bitter, honest, determined Lucy Snowe of Charlotte Brontë's *Villette* gives a partial answer: "She is no one, because she lacks any trait that might render her visible: beauty, money, conformity."[33]

Moving beyond submersion and invisibility into our third category of words, those specifying death, one finds it worthwhile to look at Betty Friedan's *The Feminine Mystique* which, according to its cover at the sixth printing in Dell paperback, was the best-seller that "ignited" women's liberation in the sixties. It should not be denied that images of death are powerful awakeners and that Friedan knew what she was doing in using them figuratively (even sometimes literally) to define the apathy many women were defining for themselves when she wrote. Neither should it be overlooked that this kind of power can be/has been used to erase women. Anyone seemingly dead while still living has a good many strikes against her! When we consider the number of novels written by men that show women dying because of adultery, the number of rapes that are a prelude to murder, the identification of sex and death, and the pervasive efforts through such practices as suttee, foot binding, witch burning, cosmeticizing, and medicine, to partially destroy or annihilate women, the motive behind the use of language delineating death in a work like *The Feminine Mystique* stands, however, in sharp contrast.

Certainly, Friedan's widely read and remarkable book did much to shape the language of the women's movement. Friedan did not invent the image of woman as a death-in-life figure,[34] and her basically figurative use of it, or quotation of others using it, may be a means of distinguishing her from those feminists who more recently think we have to change language simultaneously with finding freedom. Her heavy use of this imagery may have driven other feminists to seek a more varied, less self-annihilating, and more action-oriented way of speaking of women's problems as they make greater and greater efforts to move out of them. Certainly, the women's movement has caused many women to "come alive." It is interesting to speculate on how much we have gained since her book was published; if we have been able to replace the "dead" female with a live one, perhaps our gains are greater than some find who are working to pass legislation, get equal pay, or fund child care.

It will be well to pause over a number of passages in *The Feminine Mystique* to see how death imagery defined and brought into focus the situation surrounding women, how getting our mind around this situation may have been an initial step in finding ways to alter it. Friedan writes of one woman unable to express the nature of her problem except by sensing emptiness, incompleteness, and a feeling that she does not exist.[35] A Long Island woman just does not "feel alive."[36] Friedan wonders if some part of women is buried like Victorian women buried sex.[37] She senses that editors are growing tired of stories about women where suicide pills are found in the medicine cabinet.[38] Housewives, Friedan thinks, can readily identify with the living death of another person whether this person is dying of cancer or paralysis.[39] She states that women lack a private image; the public image created for them has great power because it causes them to have an identity crisis prompting their coming to a "strange, terrifying jumping-off point."[40]

In speaking of earlier feminist movements, Friedan tells of women who recognized that the law made married women civilly dead.[41] Lucy Stone, for example, kept her maiden name in fear that becoming a wife meant dying as a person.[42] Women of the past possessed a nothingness inherited from their mothers who were also "trapped."[43] Friedan sees how Freudian thought relegated feminists to "man-hating" phantoms; this she feels has a profound effect on women's desires to be more than part of a glorified femininity that persists in restricting their movement.[44] Women are trapped in "dead center" by some of the discoveries by psychologists and sociologists which should have helped free them.[45]

A Vassar study that came to Friedan's attention shows that girls stop growing.[46] When a woman is only a sex object, Friedan wonders if she does not experience a kind of "giving up, a kind of death, of her very reason for existence."[47] Women slash their wrists, hang themselves, and have no self-worth.[48] Women who do not question, who "adjust," are like those who walked to their death in concentration camps. They also may be like those who think the concentration camps did not exist.[49] Their own death can even be analyzed away.[50]

And in Friedan's third-to-last paragraph: "American women lately have been living much longer than men—walking through their leftover lives like living dead women."[51]

Friedan's imagery caught on and refuses to go away completely, as the examples that follow will indicate. Perhaps until many more women "come alive," it will be with us. However women feel about having their state likened to the state of the dead, it cannot be denied that Friedan's thrust was/is intended to bring about a positive response. Her heavy underscoring of recurring experiences of women coming to a realization, even if a painful one, is step one.

A special report called "The Unfulfilled Promise," which was brought to my attention from a state university, explains that affirmative action is not working. The university is still dominated by men, and many of the old excuses are still given for the failure to hire and retain more women, to make them more "visible." The writers of the report found through interviews that in the face of this failure a feeling of powerlessness among women on campuses prevails. This powerlessness leads to isolation, especially when a woman works alone among males. Turning to one another, a female faculty member in a male-dominated department called her friend to say, "You have to come over here and tell me I'm not crazy. I feel like I don't exist."[52] This almost exact duplication of one of Friedan's statements is not uncommon. A newsletter from another state school quotes a teacher of a Women's Studies course as saying, "To be a functioning human being, you [through history] had to be male. . . . To be female was to be dead."[53] Mary Daly in *Gyn/Ecology* spends much time explaining how women are "erased" from history. To give one instance among many, patriarchal scholarship, she says, has erased the massacre of millions of women as witches from the records. Speaking of "the State of Animated Death," she retains the powerful image, drawing on it often in her latest work. To her patriarchy is necrophilic.

For the most part, the uses of death imagery mentioned thus far buttress the feeling of uselessness and meaninglessness felt by women who have not found their identity or escaped a subordinate and undesired role. The legacy of an inactive life such as these women experience is sometimes augmented by overt efforts that women must make to keep out of sight. About the women who are not connected with a male by marriage and must either pretend their sex life does not exist or keep themselves hidden in order to protect wives from learning about them, Susan Kedgley and Wendy James in *Mistresses: The Free Woman and the Unfree Man* write:

Whether they like it or not, the majority of mistresses have to pretend they don't exist. They have to accept that their lovers deny their existence, at least to wives and colleagues, if not to close male friends. . . . Society might choose to mythologize the mistress in retrospect, but while she is alive and well and threatening, she simply does not exist. . . . In her role as mistress she is "persona non grata"—an isolated woman living on the fringe of society, neither recognized nor integrated into it.[54]

Changing lifestyles have altered this fringe existence somewhat, but the man who wants to maintain a wife and mistress still often insists that the mistress keep out of public view. Taking care of man's insatiable sexual needs is but one area where women are obliterated. Gaye Tuchman's *Health and Home: Images of Women in Mass Media*[55] tells how women are "symbolically annihilated" in television fiction. Either by having her greatly outnumbered by men, picturing her in stereotyped roles, or trivializing her role in the home, she is diminished or left out altogether.

This discussion has indicated that there is no paucity in our language of words and images that limit, devitalize, and wipe out women both in giving credence to reality and in picturing her according to a prejudiced notion. Except in the area of sex she is often not seen, and even here, there are limiting ways of describing her. That the infinitive *to die* has meant *to copulate*[56] and that *to copulate* is, except in limited circumstances, *to sin* surely gives summary credence to the notion that woman is involved with some of the basic activities of life but that she is, in terms of linguistic usage, neither reputable nor life-oriented.

One person who has sorted through the language of unreason connected with women and has come up with some substitutes is Adrienne Rich who makes extensive use of astronomical and topographical imagery in her poetic delineations of women. Dropping negatives, she shows expanding vistas opening up for them. As she tells us in "When We Dead Awaken: Writing as Re-Vision," language has trapped women, but it can also liberate them.[57]

NOTES

1. Quoted from The Inquiring Fotographer of the *New York Daily News* by Sheila Ruth in *Issues in Feminism* (Boston: Houghton Mifflin, 1980), p. 237.

2. Ibid., p. 96.

3. Ibid., p. 159.

4. Richard McKeon, ed., *The Basic Works of Aristotle* (New York: Random House, 1941), Book IX, 608b.

5. Ibid., Book I, 1367a.

6. Ibid., Book I, 1260a.

7. Ibid.

8. Simone de Beauvoir, *The Second Sex* (New York: Bantam, 1968), p. xv.

9. Eleanor Commo McLaughlin, "Equality of Souls, Inequality of Sexes; Woman in Medieval Theology," in *Woman in Western Thought*, ed. Martha Lee Osborne (New York: Random House, 1979), p. 81.

10. Ibid., p. 79.

11. Ruth, *Issues in Feminism*, p. 84.

12. Ibid., p. 85.

13. Ibid., p. 161.

14. Betty Friedan, *The Feminine Mystique* (New York: Dell, 1972), p. 106.

15. Thomas Hardy, *Jude the Obscure* (London: Macmillan Library Edition, 1951), p. 424.

16. Una Stannard, *Mrs. Man* (San Francisco: Germain, 1978).

17. Ruth,*Issues in Feminism*, p. 264.

18. De Beauvoir, *The Second Sex*, p. xvi.

19. Ruth, *Issues in Feminism*, p. 88.

20. Germaine Greer, *The Female Eunuch* (New York: Bantam, 1971), p. 131.

21. Ibid., p. 279.

22. Ruth, *Issues in Feminism*, p. 90.

23. Shulamuth Firestone, *The Dialectic of Sex* (New York: William Morrow, 1970), p. 67.

24. Mary Daly, *Gyn/Ecology: The Metaethics of Radical Feminism* (Boston: Beacon, 1978), p. 7.

25. Mary Daly, *Beyond God the Father* (Boston: Beacon, 1973), p. 174.

26. Greer, *The Female Eunuch*, pp. 84–87.

27. Ralph Ellison, *The Invisible Man* (New York: The Modern Library, 1952), p. 3.

28. Robin Morgan, "The Invisible Woman," in *Monster* (New York: Vintage, 1972), p. 46.

29. Cynthia Ozick, "Women and Creativity: The Demise of the Dancing Dog," in *Women in Sexist Society*, ed. Vivian Gornick and Barbara K. Moran (New York: New American Library, 1971), pp. 438–44.

30. De Beauvoir, *The Second Sex*, p. 288.

31. Carol Smart, *Women, Crime, and Criminology: A Feminist Critique* (London: Routledge and Kegan Paul, 1977), p. 177.

32. Ibid., p. 178.

33. Kate Millett, *Sexual Politics* (New York: Ballantine, 1969), p. 197.

34. Among others, Coleridge used the female death-in-life figure in "Rime of the Ancient Mariner."

35. Friedan, *The Feminine Mystique*, p. 16.

36. Ibid., p. 17.

37. Ibid., p. 28.

38. Ibid., p. 32.

39. Ibid., p. 46.

40. Ibid., p. 68.

41. Ibid., p. 76.

42. Ibid., p. 82.

43. Ibid., p. 93.

44. Ibid., p. 94.

45. Ibid., p. 117.

46. Ibid., p. 168.

47. Ibid., p. 258.

48. Ibid., p. 281.

49. Ibid., p. 294.

50. Ibid., p. 301.

51. Ibid., p. 363.

52. "Aurora Borealis," University of Colorado/Boulder *Silver and Gold Record* Monthly Supplement, December 18, 1979.

53. Women's Studies *Newsletter*, University of Missouri/Columbia, Winter 1980, p. 3.

54. Susan Kedgley and Wendy James, *Mistresses: The Free Woman and the Unfree Man* (New York: Bobbs-Merrill, 1975), p. 37.

55. Gaye Tuchman, "The Symbolic Annihilation of Women by the Mass Media," from *Health and Home: Images of Women in Mass Media*, reprinted in Ruth, *Issues in Feminism*, pp. 413–18.

56. Hyder E. Rollins and Herschel Baker, eds., "Glossary of English Words and Phrases," in *The Renaissance in England* (Boston: D. C. Heath, 1965), p. 932.

57. Adrienne Rich, *On Lies, Secrets and Silence* (New York: Norton, 1979), p. 35.

II

CHRISTIANITY AS FACILITATOR

An interesting study could be made of how the language of those exposed to Christianity proceeds from its dogma and the traditional ways Christians approach life. The purpose of this chapter, however, is to move into a different area of inquiry and to look at other aspects of Christianity that have preserved and perpetuated the link between women and death. Emphasis is placed on ways in which women are both consciously and unconsciously manipulated and influenced by the beliefs they and other Christians share. In examining those tendencies in Christianity that especially touch women as they attempt to shake free of excessive preoccupation and direct association with death, the aspects that seem most central as well as the most restrictive are its dichotomization which sets up mutually exclusive polarities like good and evil, its hierarchical master/servant structure, and its strong anti-life orientation.

Christianity sets the soul far out in front so that when the body asserts itself, it is beaten back with such vigor that, at some points in history, it literally was totally destroyed. Ironically, harnessing the body is the means to one important end which Christianity seeks, and, without the body to combat and become the source of sin, much of the whole edifice would crumble. The dichotomy of soul and body is perhaps more difficult to actualize than the numerous dichotomies that it spawns or gives support to: reason versus passion; God versus man; pain versus pleasure; the saved versus the damned; male versus female; virgin versus nonvirgin; the adulterous versus the nonadulterous. This is to say nothing about the conditioning implanted by an archetypal example that prompts people through dichotomization to thwart a generous and charitable approach toward variety and individual differences in such areas as whites versus minorities, heterosexuality versus other kinds of sex, the good life versus the bad life. The list could go on endlessly of areas where we put one person, philosophy, possession, or solution to a problem in a slot and its opposite (or alternate) in another without seeing how actuality often makes our fine distinctions merge.

The notion of the soul is puzzling to one not caught up in the possibility of its existence. Definitions and analysis never fully lift the haze. The body, however, is a very different matter. It is a tremendous outcome-of-a-growth-process that has the capacity to feel, appreciate, think. It has eyes that see hills, the people walking to school, the cars going off to work, the pages of a book; ears that hear music and the child singing as she jumps rope. It is an entity that functions rhythmically: eat, work, enjoy a respite—eat, work, enjoy a respite; an entity that can take a seed into a place where it will grow into another thinking, feeling, appreciating person; an entity that can produce that seed; an entity that has the strength to withstand and support, but also operate without plan or reason. All these tangibles speak to actuality while the soul is elusive, incomprehensible, and some have thought a means of negating the body. Even if one chooses to claim there is such a thing as the soul, it would seem to be just as well defined as part of this outcome-of-a-growth-process we recognize as the body, for few deny that the body is potentially various in its capacity. The polarity of soul and body which cuts us in two parts, one of which we cannot actualize, does not seem an essential to the functioning human who attempts to understand or act in a responsible way. Rather, it serves to fragment and dilute a single focus necessary to deep vision. Emerson in his "Brahma" plays down all polarities and seems to be approaching existence in a deep and generous way. His attitude takes on plausibility when it is realized that human nature and much of life are ambiguous and thus not polarized. This fact is surely borne out by history where rarely do we find anything ordered to a precise description or falling into a neat category.

Even if we think men and women to be opposites, it is not at all necessary to see one as better than the other. Church history, however, makes it clear that woman is considered evil and a sinful contaminator, except when virgin, of the much more worthy male. Even if we get caught up in Christianity, there is something very unfair and unforgiving about making Eve, who appears innocently unknowing, and her successors the embodiment of this much evil.[1] The Eve story illustrates the contradictory aspects of the dichotomization of soul/flesh, spirit/flesh, good/evil that lead to a judgmental posture and narrow vision, to say nothing of placing squarely on the shoulders of one sex the responsibility of inflicting pain, struggle, death, and damnation through all time. We would certainly shun putting this much responsibility on one so innocent in actual life.

It should be noted that in early biblical exegesis where not all philosophers and theologians indicated that women had a soul, those who did thought it to be of lesser quality.[2] Woman's efforts to achieve immortality were therefore made more difficult because she, thought to be a much more fleshly creature than the male, had correspondingly more denying and destroying of her fleshly part to perform in order to reach her heavenly goal. She naturally developed extreme self-hatred, made supreme efforts to reclaim herself in the eyes of God, often secretly renounced all earthly ties including that of her husband, and lived an almost totally vacuous life except for religious ritual that she thought would help join her to her God in death. She was even led to believe she must be like the male, and to do this, she should remain virgin whenever possible because to give birth was a vile thing in itself, and to engage in the sexual process was the way to pass on original sin. Obviously, remnants of all this self-victimization and denial of life are still with us.

As a result of the Christian effort to externalize the soul/body dichotomy, women gradually *became* flesh, and men repositories for the soul.[3] The destructive ramifications of equating woman with flesh, or simply sex, can be seen in these as well as earlier signs of making woman the scapegoat for man's guilt and fears, and in the latest rape/murder that many of us read about last night in our newspaper. One is reminded of David Berkowitz's moralizing against women's sexual side in the courtroom as he lashed out: "Stacy was a whore! I'd kill them all again!" That women are

nothing but body, and thus sex objects, thwarts progress in gain-
ing equal employment rights, preventing rape, cleaning up the
media, the porno industry, marriage, and countless other sexist areas
of life where we cannot get beyond one prescribed function for
half the human race.

With woman locked to sex, and much of the time to sex alone,
death constantly hovers over her in a variety of ways. Sex/woman,
representing sin, led many males—not just churchmen or even
necessarily always Christians, who on biblical authority[4] were li-
able to damnation because of their lust—to look upon woman as
destroyer. Sex/woman not only destroyed the soul but also came,
especially in the orthodox mind, to mean death. As a corollary to
this attitude, the physical/psychic aspects of sex per se were also
death dealing. In recent interviews with numerous men, Phyllis
Chesler found that *la petite mort*, which many men experience in
coitus, has been blamed on women. According to Chesler, women
become the repository for the feelings of depression, of being
trapped or choked, that men experience in sex; men can then say
that they themselves intrinsically do not have such feelings.[5]

The obsessive equation of sin and sex and the disproportionate
association of women with sex led to her becoming a person of
secondary importance and especially to her dismissal after losing
her virginity. Relegated to or below the level of the child and servants, she could be dealt with indiscriminately. The dichotomies
of virgin/nonvirgin and chaste/nonchaste led to adulterous/
nonadulterous. What was to be done with the adulterous wife?
"Kill her!" said Alexandre Dumas *fils*,[6] and through much of history the husband did just that, considering it his privilege. Many
would have agreed with him. The problem of losing one's virginity outside the bounds of "Christian" marriage resulted in much
infanticide and suicide. The story of the unwed mother becoming
the scapegoat for whole communities has been told and retold
seemingly with a kind of morbid pleasure and without creating
much alteration in the adherence to a religion which, because of
its so-called moral standards, spooked/spooks generations into
atrocities comparable, but never recognized as such, to plagues and
wars, to say nothing of hypocrisy and sadism.

Bertolt Brecht's "Concerning the Infanticide, Marie Farrar"
universalizes this situation by focusing on participant and audience

response jointly. The participant is involved in a horrible ordeal; the audience is begged to temper its wrath and scorn for the participant. Brecht's social criticism is strong, and his poem helps screw the image into our consciousness of a minor, an orphan, a poor janitor/laundress, coming to the realization that she cannot rid herself of a fetus, that agony and sickness accompany childbirth, that she is driven to beat her child to death with her fists, and finally that she must die in the penitentiary. Brecht seems to want the readers not to relegate the girl's plight to a realm not their own, not to leave their own world intact by doing so. He is also aware of the communal need for a scapegoat so pronounced in history.

The Christian perspective was one of blaming men in such a way as to create the Church/man polarity. Man, it was thought, then had to create the man/woman polarity to shift blame from himself. Always the woman was the one who destroyed man's image in the eyes of the Church. Heresy, like woman, had allurements and became identified with her, with both clad in scarlet robes. To have anything to do with either was a kind of idolatry not to be tolerated, and deaths due to heresy, which was much more a man's crime, were numerous. Worldly desires of any sort also came to be identified with woman and were funneled into her image. When man became more and more frantic about his salvation, he tended more and more to attack any possible threat. The object of man's temptation became "the cause of it; in other words, he projects his own weakness onto its object."[7]

Even when woman was idolized, men came to see both their "lower" and "higher" impulses in her. She could become the symbol of man's fall or the symbol of his salvation; Eve was the first woman to fall, but she was also the first to be led out of hell by Christ.[8] Even as some came to see love between man and woman as a necessary step to love of man for God, and man came to depend on woman to help him reach God, she was asked to be what, in most ways, she was incapable of being. She was raised to fall all the harder when she failed.

Given the ways in which we are pulled forward to a much freer approach to sex, yet held back by tradition, many would agree with D. P. Verene who states that "Sexual morality is a problem for us because we are inheritors of the Judeo-Christian tradition."[9]

Andrea Dworkin puts it much more strongly and links dichotom-ization with the death-producing sides of our nature: "The dual-ism of good and evil, virgin and whore, lily and rose, spirit and nature is inherent in Christianity, and finds its logical expression in the rituals of sado-masochism."[10]

Dichotomization makes for special and more pronounced prob-lems for women in that they are held responsible for their acts and influence in ways men are not. The polarizers could not see that the two sexes were cut of the same cloth, that "power and weak-ness flow into each other,"[11] and that what they took to be strength had inherent weaknesses; and what they took to be weakness was so, in great part, because there was not enough stamina left in woman after being malled about the arena of life to exhibit the converse. Had churchmen known this and voiced it, we might be further on our way to freeing sexual life of anger, violence, and misunderstanding. Vern Bullough thinks that the dichotomy be-tween the spirit and the flesh contaminated Christianity by steri-lizing its sense of creation, perverting the confession of evil, and promoting a narrowness of outlook.[12] Had these dichotomies not left a legacy of others and had people not come to dichotomize as a way of buttressing their own perspective, the means of devel-oping a more open approach to a diversity of arguments, theolo-gies, and systems would have been secured.

A hierarchy with God at the top, man under God, and woman subservient to man has long been a part of the Christian stance. A theory of the cosmos not seriously disputed until the eighteenth century stipulated that a chain linked God to all angelic and earthly creatures as well as all created things. Below God, the most high, were stationed all these entities in a graduated order of decreasing importance. Interestingly, when this scheme came to be seriously disputed, discussion focused on minerals or other substances, which also were given a precise place in the chain. It was difficult to graduate these substances because quality in one category, such as that of diamonds, would be an issue for judging position while quantity would be an issue in another, and both quality and quan-tity would play a role in still another. Establishing in rank order the absolute worth of most persons or things would, to say the least, be difficult. To have our worth, a controversial term itself, be determined on the basis of whether we are husband, wife, or child certainly smacks of a dubious system and one that does not take into account the ambiguous nature of life.

One theory connected with this scale, which was frequently re-marked upon, was that the married woman did not have a direct line to God but had to defer to her husband in matters of religion and make him her "lord." As Milton says, "He for God only, she for God in him." Another often-repeated "proof" for keeping woman in a prescribed place is that it is her "natural" place. *Troilus and Cressida, King Lear*, and other Renaissance works make it clear that if any person steps out of her/his assigned place and dis-turbs the "natural" order, the world will start crumbling and all will be chaos. Mad Lear on the heath, with lightning cracking the sky open, clearly exhibits the kind of catastrophe that will occur. He has moved out of his appointed sphere, that of king and fa-ther, by dividing his kingdom into parts to be given to his daugh-ters. Woman who moves out of her position is destined to have as hard a time as Lear, or so those who advocate keeping her at home would say. Two centuries later, Rousseau gives a typically romanticized version of this notion: "The obedience and the fidel-ity she owes to her husband and the tenderness and the care she owes to her children are consequences of her *position so natural* [italics mine] and easily sensed that she cannot without bad faith refuse her consent to the inner sentiment that guides her, nor fail to rec-ognize her duty if her inclinations are still uncorrupted."[13] And more than a century later the structure still remains, in many in-stances making an oppressive and sometimes dangerous situation for women. The God-over-man archetype is imitated by man over woman and by woman and man over children. An authoritarian model is thus inculcated in those who are/will be in the position of dominance; this hierarchy allows a man in our time to say when charged with the attempted murder of his spouse, "But she's my wife!"[14] Before mentioning other problems arising from this structure, it will be well to suggest why the notion of any stance being natural has problematical aspects, just as sharply defined di-chotomies that determine action do.

The term *natural* has become nearly valueless because it has been assigned so many uses. Christine Pierce points out that it is some-times used against women, sometimes to suggest that there is a "natural superiority" in women, and at still other times as a legal excuse in a case of passion shooting when jealousy is said to be natural. Pierce has nothing against a word serving more than one purpose, but she contends, rightly, that we ought to recognize diverse uses as we employ it. She further points out that *natural* is nearly always used to mean good, but that there is no reason to assume this is always so. The advantage acquired by breaking from a traditional or "natural" position might cut down on liberty and make for some inefficiency, but there is nothing wrong with a change which will improve one's overall life, even though some freedom and efficiency may be at times lost in having it. Pierce also notes that even if we do have a natural function, it is not always necessary to use it. To argue from the point of view that natural law or instinct is desirable, she states, is to argue for a determinism that we all would find difficult and self-defeating if carried to its logical extreme.[15] There is a long list of activities that have always been a part of existence, but always to do them may entail stifling the growth or liberty of the doers or creating an abundance where it is not needed.

Precisely because Christianity argued for a kind of set scheme, it became outgrown. Statistics gathered recently in England indicate, however, that 73 percent of the population believes in God, 53 percent believes in the afterlife, and only 52 percent thinks that the Church is "complacent, old-fashioned and out of touch."[16] Thus, in a country which is usually considered less religious than the United States, many people are still under the influence of a theology that helped wedge woman between her husband and her children in a position where she had/has little room to exercise her intellect or talent. Apparently, for the Christian to conceive of God at all is to conceive of a force or power that has some direct influence and hold on people's lives; this hold leads to a concept of what God does or does not tolerate. We are than back to the repressive structure we have been discussing. In a climate in which God is recognized, it is difficult to escape conceiving of a hierarchical structure, one that is copied in the typical household.

In the tight family structure, violence erupts. The husband murders the wife. The wife murders the husband. Records reveal that the wife is most often the victim throughout both history and at present. Now that efforts are being made to keep the police from ignoring the wife's pleas and more women are speaking out on why they have stayed with battering husbands so long or why they finally brought their problems to an end, we discover that when women do commit murder, it is usually when their rage at being so often the victim has reached such a peak they can no longer contain themselves. Frequently, this violence has escalated because the victim has learned that the police will give no aid while the offender knows he will suffer no charge.[17] Absence of legal recourse has greatly added to this frequency of violence ending in the wife's death. Examples abound of the father's violence toward the wife later being also inflicted upon the children, and of the children in turn inflicting it upon their children. A home that accepts male dominance rarely opens the opportunity for alternative ways of conducting relationships. John Stuart Mill makes it clear that it cripples the husband as well as the wife because "even a really superior man almost always begins to deteriorate when he is habitually . . . king of his company: and in his most habitual company the husband who has a wife inferior to him is always so."[18]

John McMurtry emphasizes that marriage underwrites "a literally totalitarian expectation of sexual confinement." Questioning how a satisfactory sexual arrangement can ever endure for any length of time except in very unusual cases, he further calls attention to destructive aggression, apathy, lack of spontaneity, bad faith, sexual fantasizing, perversion, fetishism, prostitution, pornography—all endemic to marriage. It is, nevertheless, indispensable to the capitalist order and exists as a "linchpin of our present social structure."[19] Political theorists have long seen the necessity of working through controlling agencies like churches or heads of households when groups need to be manipulated. The Church, having close ties with the state and shedding great influence on the family, has often been a tool in manipulating people as the state sees fit. Sometimes called the opiate of the masses, the Church is a part of a fabric which holds, except in more enlightened circles, to traditional approaches and looks down its nose at change or eccentricity, both of which are essential for growth and revivification. Needed change having to do with the masses may therefore be blocked in instances where it is needed the most. If the social structure happens not to look askance at aggression and tendencies toward violence, then it implicates both the Church and the populace in its questionable system. Failure to separate Church and state has involved both in less-than-savory acts of aggression and thus killings on a global scale.

> Nobody was better aware than Hitler of the services rendered by the Catholic Church to his ideology and he summed them up very succinctly when two German bishops, representing the entire German episcopate, visited him on April 26, 1933: "I have been attacked for the way I treat the Jews," he told them. "For 1500 years the Catholic Church has regarded the Jews as parasites and has confined them to the ghetto . . . I adhere to what has been done for 1500 years. I am perhaps rendering the greatest service to Christianity."[20]

Many German priests felt so close in their Jew-hatred to Hitler's followers that they asked the Vatican for permission to join the Nazi party.

As John Stuart Mill and others have pointed out, more than simply domestic spats is involved when we approach the problem of marriage. We are looking at a segment of the social structure with wide influence and a set of attitudes that are so deeply entrenched that they are inevitably carried into affairs beyond the home. If we could solve problems of aggression at home, we might eventually be better equipped to solve them abroad, for if we could build people who value equalizing advantage and opportunity at home, these people could exert influence beyond the narrow sphere of family life. Certainly, one who is a tyrant and slave driver at home has little on which to base his pleas for peace abroad. Women are involved in much domestic violence which at times ends in death as well as in indirect ways in war. Although the Church has sometimes been a minister of peace, it does not provide support for altering the structure of the family or altering attitudes conducive to eliminating change and to shrouding women in potentially cramping, if not dangerous, environments.

Christianity exhibits antilife tendencies by negating certain sides of life that, according to its concept of evil, would make immortality impossible. That the search for immortality exhibits a death orientation on the part of Christians would be arguable, on the basis of this search being for the purposes of countering death, if it did not seem quite probable that a preoccupation with avoiding death brings about an excessive and self- or life-defeating interest in it. Using up life for the purposes of insuring an afterlife that may be only a figment of the imagination can scarcely be justified.

To the outsider, it seems that Christians are forever eating their way through the great banquet of life with dessert always in mind. They are not caught up in the early courses but place all their antic-ipatory salivary pleasures on the last one. This pattern of behavior naturally sets some limits to what they eat prior to the longed-for delectables that grace the final course. It also throws considerable attention on the final course, which would be more evenly distrib-uted over the entire banquet if each of the courses was considered no more tantalizing than the other. However, this would show far too ambiguous a taste for many Christians who obviously have a yearning for what they have been led to believe is so supremely divine that they have in no way gained access to it previously. They do not eat a bit here, a bit there, until they are satiated and then just stop, whether to the dessert or not. Rather, they swiftly move over and dismiss much, to get what they have been told is cooling in the refrigerator. One can just see all those lovely salads, expen-sive cuts of beef, and buttered buns going back to the kitchen to be scraped into the garbage bin, as well as those clutched forks, tines tipped upward, in ready-set-go posture as the chiffon pie is trundled in.

One bit of fare relegated to the waste bin, in theory at least, is sex. As we have noted, sex is nearly interchangeable with woman; it is in connection with the denial of sex (and by extension, life) that Christianity is decidedly discriminatory toward woman and especially the one who wants to be a mother. Sex is off limits in traditional ways of thinking for the aspiring candidate for afterlife. Most churches are quite friendly toward children once they are born, but the act that sets them growing is strictly taboo. Pleasure in this act is an absolute no-no; even thinking about it can slow up the mere application for rewards in the afterlife.

It has been said that the reason sex cannot be tolerated is that, while involved in orgasm, the participants have totally abandoned God.[21] Their attention to any exterior stimuli or to divine guidance, control, or sympathy has been suspended by the very nature of the act itself. Certainly, the participants have stepped off the pulley that George Herbert, the seventeenth-century theologian and poet, said ran between us and God, our yearning upward with a supplicating glance and God yearning down with a paternal concern. Even if it is believed that human love can be a replica of divine love, the ecstatic sexual encounter is obviously not of this character. The moments of orgasm simply eliminate all reason, devotion, or receptiveness, and, except for pure ecstasy, nothing else matters. *God cannot tolerate a state where nothing else matters.* This is an interesting theory, but is it not true that humans engage in other activities, such as conducting a complicated fugue by Bach, where all else is lost except the experience itself? Would it not be necessary to condemn much that goes on in life, as sex is condemned, if this theory explains shrinking from sex?

There is little to substantiate the notion that sex has been taken lightly by Christians (or, of course, by many non-Christians). Male and female chastity has traditionally been applauded. Virgins are better than wives and become "brides" of Christ. This thinking aborts the development of a healthy sexual life in women and gives credence to Berkowitz's notion that women are whores. Dworkin emphasizes that "the worship of virginity must be posited as a real sexual perversion, crueler and more insidious than those sex models condemned by the culture as perverse."[22] Being elevated to sainthood or to the position of Jesus necessitates being cleansed of any taint of sex. Until Jesus was crucified, he is reported to have talked of his brothers, who are mentioned in the gospels, but in order to be associated with an unsullied mother, by the fourth century his brothers were dropped from tradition and became cousins.[23] Mary was thus denied her generative powers and motherhood, and Christ his family, in order that original sin not taint the legend. God engenders those whom He wants to sit next to Him in an incestuous community, and by so doing supports a hierarchical caste that must be the envy of all those who want their family to stay in powerful positions of state. Because it is meritorious to be celibate, whole groups of clergy "burn" (to quote Saint Paul) in order to some day join the incestuous clan. To get there, of course, was/is no snap because the hardest of all vows to keep was/is chastity. One could never accuse God of not having high standards, and His criteria for a passing grade are certainly tough enough. These standards did, indeed, drive females to suicide and infanticide. Furthermore, they drove most women to think of life or "things of this world" as vile and to be passed through as soon as possible. Copulation could only produce more people to be sent into a world one should try to escape. Thus, whether approached as a horror or as an experience one must get beyond, death is a central focus.

Christianity is weak in supporting humans in their most intense and productive area of life. When there are exceptions to the rules that only an ascetic could live by, it appears to be just that, an exception, or of cult proportions. In Brazil, for example, there is a flourishing cult of the pregnant madonna, the madonna of the egg, and Brazilian husbands slip a crucifix under their wives during intercourse to insure conception.[24] Vestiges of "paganism" also enter, especially in Southern Europe, but these remain on the fringe of the predominant focus, that of emphasizing sex as the most pronounced sin.

Women have long been thought to be extremely vulnerable to Christianity, but as Simone de Beauvoir says, in discussing the female as religionist and mystic, their susceptibility is evidence of a profound need.[25] Their "basic inferiority" can be mitigated by their remaining children in the eyes of God. They can overcome the "advantage of the penis"[26] and any feelings of inferiority through a sincere faith. The child-woman, thinking she has found in God a refuge from men, will claim that her denial of sex is the first step on the road to God. "The women who abandon themselves to the joys of the heavenly nuptials are legion, and their experience is of a peculiarly emotional nature."[27] She does not need to touch or feel God at her side; she can worship fervently a transcendent absolute from afar. There seems to be an inevitable underlying confusion between man and God in many cases, and God performs as any ideal prince: he takes the initiative in love, he loves passionately, he communicates secretly, he is jealous and imposes punishment, and he is mystically inconcrete. She in her fervor loses all liberty and strives to obliterate her body. She neither sees nor feels; all aspects of her ego and personality are annihilated so to transform her suffering into her glory. "The mystic will torture her flesh to have the right to claim it; reducing it to abjection, she exalts it as the instrument of salvation." Excesses indulged in by female saints include drinking the water lepers have washed their feet in and cleaning up with the tongue the vomit and excrement belonging to the patient. In thus masochistically degrading the flesh, she believes she will save the flesh as Christ did. Catherine Emmerich, for example, longed to suffer a crown of thorns, and she is supposed to have sweat and spat blood. Woman's long history of being the victim may very well be underscored and explained by the fact that "of the 321 persons bearing stigmata recognized by the Catholic Church, only 47 are men."[28] There seems to be considerable evidence that women have appeared to be especially susceptible to a life-denying kind of existence that in many instances presupposes a tropism toward death.

Victorian prudishness also dictated the desexualizing of women so that they might help their husbands control their own sexuality. Men were to master their desires. Women were thought to have very little desire to master, but religion helped them to sublimate just as work helped men. Annie Besant, who later became a well-known secularist associated with William Bradlaugh, the well-known atheist and member of Parliament, was at first an excellent example, according to Peter Cominos, of a sublimated Evangelical. Her response to the early Christian martyrs was so vehement that she fancied she was tortured on the rack, flung to the lions, and burned at the stake. She said she had no knowledge of evil and was innocent of any passionate feelings except those associated with her mother and Christ.[29] Fortunately, she was to break with these early preoccupations.

The world of unreason that these women inhabited cut them off from real life, stifled their development, and often ended in failure. Unless such fervor can be transformed into some social goal, which throws them back into life, they continue to be absorbed in destruction and death. There have been some striking celibate women who have helped humanity; in some cases, the very fact that they did not have children made it possible for them to accomplish what they set out to do. Their accomplishments, however, do not counterbalance the denial of life which their celibacy proclaimed and which in its traditional focus left a legacy of "sin" and counterproductive moralizing that severely cripples young women and makes of men hypocritical searchers after scapegoats.

There is probably no other major area of our social structure which concentrates as heavily on death as the religious segment does, with the possible exception of the military. One can think of numerous other ways in which Christianity shrouds us in death besides those mentioned here. Christ pictured bleeding on the cross is a modern-day *memento mori* which many carry on their person or use to decorate their houses. Believers take seriously predictions about the end of the world. Easter celebrations, though balanced by those of Christmas, are part of a ritual which includes the death emphasis. Elaborate burial arrangements in Christian countries speak for themselves. It should also be noted that by putting taboos on sex, the defiant have been driven to greater excesses than if the taboos had not been placed; this kind of defiance compounds the sexual problems already existing and undercuts our quality of life and development as balanced humans. As with outwitting death, efforts in this area to defy are often counterproductive.

It would appear that efforts to ease the inevitable make the inevitable a tremendously greater burden by constantly keeping it in focus. The complex fabric of Christianity defeats itself by dichotomies that sacrifice diversity for absolutes, by establishing an elitist hierarchy, and by emphasizing antilife tendencies that diminish and degrade women's functions as well as victimize her as an all-too-willing "servant" of God. When looking at this complex fabric built to alleviate long-dead fears, it is difficult to see how it could be reshaped to serve present needs, but, obviously, many attempt to do so. However, scrapping the Church altogether would disorient a numerous and varied population—so numerous, it seems, that any effort to do so would be fruitless. A gradual playing down, however, of its world of unreason and replacing this emphasis with enlightened efforts to treat humans as thinking, working, creating entities, not naive and inferior supplicants, is necessary if the grip of tradition is to be broken. What so many people do not realize is that people can have a very decent meal without chiffon pie.

NOTES

1. Barbara Smoker, "Women and the Patriarchal God," *New Humanist* 90, no. 8 (December 1974): 263–66.

2. See discussion of Aristotle, pp. 4–5 of this book.

3. Joan M. Ferrante, *Women as Image in Medieval Literature* (New York: Columbia University Press, 1975), pp. 17–19.

4. Saint Paul: Galatians 5:16.

5. Phyllis Chesler, *About Men* (New York: Simon and Schuster, 1978), p. 226.

6. Quoted by Simone de Beauvoir, *The Second Sex* (New York: Bantam, 1968), p. 113.

7. Ferrante, *Women as Image in Medieval Literature*, p. 21.

8. Ibid., p. 25.

9. D. P. Verene, "Sexual Love and Moral Experience," in *Philosophy and Sex*, ed. Robert Baker and Frederick Elliston (Buffalo: Prometheus, 1975), p. 109.

10. Andrea Dworkin, *Woman Hating* (New York: E. P. Dutton, 1974), p. 73.

11. Sheila Ruth, *Issues in Feminism* (Boston: Houghton Mifflin, 1980), p. 246.

12. Vern L. Bullough, *The Subordinate Sex*, with a final chapter by Bonnie Bullough (Urbana: University of Illinois Press, 1973), p. 106.

13. Jean-Jacques Rousseau, *Emile or On Education*, intro., trans., and notes by Allan Bloom (New York: Basic, 1979), p. 382.

14. U.S. Commission on Civil Rights, *Battered Women: Issues of Public Policy*, January 30–31, 1978, p. 235.

15. Christine Pierce, "Natural Law Language and Women," in *Women in Sexist Society*, ed. Vivian Gornick and Barbara K. Moran (New York: New American Library, 1971), pp. 247–52.

16. "Do Humanists Count?" *New Humanist* 95, no. 4 (March 1980): 127.

17. U.S. Commission on Civil Rights, *Battered Women*, p. 247.

18. John Stuart Mill and Harriet Taylor Mill, *Essays on Sex Equality*, ed. Alice S. Rossi (Chicago: University of Chicago Press, 1970), p. 234.

19. John McMurtry, "Monogamy: A Critique," in *Philosophy and Sex*, pp. 171–75.

20. Reuben Ainstein, "Anti-Semitism in Catholic Poland," *New Humanist* 89, no. 8 (December 1973): 264.

21. Wayland Young, *Eros Denied: Sex in Western Society* (New York: Grove, 1964), p. 200.

22. Dworkin, *Woman Hating*, p. 73.

23. Young, *Eros Denied*, p. 201.

24. Ibid., pp. 207–8.

25. De Beauvoir, *The Second Sex*, p. 585.

26. Ibid., p. 586.

27. Ibid., p. 630.

28. Ibid., pp. 635–37.

29. Peter T. Cominos, "Innocent Femina Sensualis in Unconscious Conflict," in *Suffer and Be Still: Women in the Victorian Age*, ed. Martha Vincinus (Bloomington: Indiana University Press, 1972), pp. 155–72.

III

WOMEN AS *MEMENTO MORI*

Sir John Suckling (1609–1642) gazes at a woman only, he says, to see what kind of a death's head she will be once her skin and flesh have fallen away.[1] Drawing on the tradition of keeping *memento mori* on hand to curb riotous living which might net one hell instead of heaven, he joins all those haunted by notions of the dance of death or possessed by a "strange preoccupation with putrefaction"[2] especially pronounced during the Middle Ages, the Renaissance, and the Baroque period. Of special interest to this study is the claim that women represent death, that behind every so-called seductive temptress lies a grinning skull to haunt the onlooker and remind him of his own, once his flesh has fallen away.

Verse, woodcuts, musical compositions, and a polished skull (the death's head) were reminders of impending death as early as the fourteenth century when a morality poem featured a dialogue between death and representatives of all the classes from the Pope downward. By the fifteenth century, pictorial representations with verse illustrations were common. Death in the form of a skeleton or a corpse leading his victims was painted in churchyards and cemeteries. A set of seventeen woodcuts accompanied by verses was painted in Paris in 1485. Contemporary with Suckling is John Donne (1572?–1631) who combines violence, death, and sex in poems that startle and titillate, just as the skull might, and have much the same effect. In scanning a group of essays about Donne's works written in our time, one cannot help but be struck by comments on his explosive beginnings, heavy pounding rhythms, catatonic furies, harsh and grotesque language, thrashings about, and knife-like purpose. Anger, rant, energy, force, scandal, revulsion, cursing—all are words Donne himself uses. Even in his religious poems there is a strong masosadistic element: "Batter my heart, three-personed God . . . break, blow, burn, and make me new." We recall Samuel Johnson's definition of Donne's image: a violent yoking together of heterogeneous elements.

In one of his misogynistic poems, woman becomes "mummy"; in another she is murderer: "When by thy scorn, O Murdress, I am dead." His mistress makes him into a walking corpse and he will, he says, get vengeance on her in afterlife. "The Funeral" and "The Relic" are as distinctly macabre as they are sensual. In the first he hopes to get even with his mistress by burying a wreath of her hair (like the skull often designated as *memento mori*) around his arm, since, he says, "you [in life] would save none of mee, I bury some of you."[3] In "The Relic," he first calls attention to woman's capacity to entertain more than one man in bed, and he then proceeds to ask again that those breaking up her grave leave untouched the "Bracelet of bright haire about the bone" which, he says, will indicate the nature of their friendship.[4] Donne did not need the leap of imagination some of us do to connect woman, sex, and death; for him there was a neat sequence, for "we have a winding sheete in our Mother's womb, which grows with us from our conception, and wee come into the world, wound up in that winding sheet, for wee come to seeke a grave."[5]

Donne's obsessive interest in death is combined with sublimated eroticism which is parallel to those ecstasies he would like to have had in his relationship with God. Using the word *sex* for the first time in the modern sense, his works also have the ingredients of modern pornography, that is, women and violence, plus considerable concern about his soul—none of which has lessened his popularity with twentieth-century readers. In fact, the dance of death theme persisted through the eighteenth and nineteenth centuries and into our own day. Thomas Gray's "Elegy Written in a Country Churchyard" and other works by writers of the graveyard school have some of the same flavor. Laurence Sterne and Byron were said to drink with their cronies from skulls. Goethe wrote a ballad on the theme called "Der Todtentanz," and Saint-Saens' *Danse Macabre* is well known. August Strindberg's *The Dance of Death*, which centers on a tortured male-female relationship, is one of the most striking examples of this preoccupation. There is also Rachmaninov's *Isle of the Dead* based on Arnold Boecklin's painting, *Toteninsel*. Salvador Dali's *Shirley Temple* shows a young girl sitting poised over a wasteland of bones, skulls, a shipwreck, and a bat.

In Suckling's poem "Farewel to Love," woman is very like what we have defined *memento mori* to be, an object that reminds onlookers of death. Women served as *memento mori* to men in at least three ways: sexual experiences with her took their strength and brought on early death; she represented lust and for the sinner was the destroyer of the afterlife; and she was simply a rotting piece of matter already putrefied as she moved about adulterating the "more clean." Women have been *memento mori* for centuries, and remnants of this history of fantasized despicableness still exist in objects on which men (women have taken much less interest in such) fixate, that is, those found in pornography and literature.

It should be noted that among other symbols of death are the very old and sometimes even babies when they are seen to be that which those nearing death return to, namely the innocent or the childish. One thinks of Father Time and the simple talk of the senile. Making women into such symbols or more concretely into *memento mori* does, however, have one clear difference: women become these symbols when they are in the prime of life, while this is clearly not the case for either of the two examples just mentioned.

It was once believed that so much vital strength was spent when semen was lost to a woman that death would come sooner. This is the origin of the notion found in medieval and Renaissance literature that each session of intercourse takes one day off a person's life. John Donne's "The Canonization" tells how the speaker and his mistress "dye by it." The word *climax* suggests the ultimate, "the most" as we are currently saying, the "death" that comes at the end of struggle. The denial of pleasure and sex which lies at the heart of the Christian picture of the world[6] dictated asceticism, and asceticism dictated curbing, if not eliminating, sex, one of the arguments against it being that it was part of a wasting-away process. Comparing Eastern and Western cultures, Andrea Dworkin says "The loss of semen, and the feeling of weakness which is its biological conjunct, has extraordinary significance to men. . . .

For those Western men for whom orgasm is simultaneous with ejaculation, sex must be a more literal death, with the mysterious, muscled, pulling vagina the death-dealer."[7] Add to this male fears of venereal disease, which, according to most accounts, woman is always responsible for spreading, and she becomes death itself. The pox was an ineluctable reflection of hell, a disease which, like God, would carry the sinner off to the fire. Penicillin did away with such an important part of the structure of religious belief that hell itself, Wayland Young says, could thereafter be called in question.[8] Freudian interpretations of Poe's "Berenice" indicate that it was thought the vagina was equipped with castrating teeth.[9] For the unreasonable, it is easy to see that woman when she crossed man's path was a strong reminder of death like the skull or picture or poem; her effect becomes what she is in the world of unreason, a world that those who cannot get beyond their fears inhabit.

Beyond this biological death is the death of the soul that she caused/was. A destroyer like Eve who was the "ruin" of Adam or like Jezebel who did the same for Ahab, she is the repository of all the evil that keeps man from God. All malice originates in woman, she stands for lust, and she is held responsible for it. Tertullian said she destroyed God's image, man, and to save man, Christ had to be destroyed. She is then responsible for the destruction of both Adam and his successors as well as Christ. Roger de Caen, a French monk who died in 1095 is supposed to have said: "If her bowels and flesh were cut open, you would see what filth is covered by her white skin. If a fine crimson cloth covered a pile of foul dung, would anyone be foolish enough to love the dung because of it? . . . There is no plague which monks should dread more than woman: the soul's death."[10] As Dworkin indicates, the Christian emphasis on pain and suffering as the path to transcendence and salvation is "the very meat of most sadomasochistic pornography."[11]

Men's disgust with women's body odors leads them to link her with rotting corpses. With their persistent phobias about dirt, both men and women have hangups about any discharges from the body's apertures, and since woman has "one 'dirty' aperture too many," she is considered excessively filthy. As a result she is forever trying to clean herself.[12] Her putrefaction seems to set in with birth, and to know her is to be reminded by her foulness of death.

Thomas Nashe in *Christ's Teares Over Jerusalem* (1593) denounces woman's pride by visualizing her at death:

Nothing els is garish apparraile, but Prydes vlcer broken forth. . . . As many iagges, blysters, and scarres, shall Toads, Cankers, and Serpents make on your pure skinnes in the graue, as nowe you have cuts, iagges, or raysings, vpon your garments. . . . Your morne-like christall countenaunces shall be netted ouer and (Masker-like) cawle-visarded with crawling venomous wormes. Your orient teeth toades shall steale into theyr heads for pearle: of the ielly of your decayed eyes shall they engender . . . young. . . , O, what is beauty more than a wind-blowne bladder, that it should forget whereto it is borne? It is the foode of cloying-concupiscence, lyuing, and the substaunce of the most noysome infection, beeing dead.[13]

Shakespeare's Sonnet 130 also tells of a mistress reeking. Using the well-known weapon of the eighteenth-century satirist to align the person being satirized with filth, Swift in a similar way calls attention to how woman stinks and how she tries to cover it even as she has one foot in the grave. His "The Lady's Dressing Room" shows Celia's dirty smock, the container for her "spits" and "spues," and her smelly towels. Strephon seems shocked that women defecate; thereafter, he links all women with the despicable Celia.[14]

Woman is thought to be especially unclean when menstruating, a function associated by many with defecation and urination. In numerous cultures she is made to live in solitude so as not to contaminate, and menstrual blood is thought to flow from a supernatural wound which is the result of an attack by a bird, snake, or lizard. It is frequently connected with injury, illness, and death; the "wound" is therefore mysterious, and the danger from the blood that flows from it is often the origin of numerous taboos. The Wogeo people of South Australia, for example, believe that if a man has contact with a menstruating female, he will die from a disease for which there is no remedy. In the Hebrew tradition, if a male and female copulate during menstruation, the penalty is death for both. If a menstruating Uganda Bantu woman puts her hand on her husband's weapons, he will be killed in his next battle. Often the taboos are just as strong surrounding pregnancy, and here also the woman's organs are dangerous and death dealing. Ambivalence reigns in attitudes, however, because when menstruation ceases, women frequently are cast aside.[15]

Fear, envy, and hatred of woman seem to underlie pervasive concerns about her unclean state; remnants of this preoccupation persist in pornographic literature which is overwhelmingly concerned with crushing, violating, and punishing women. To pay them back for their defilement, they are made to bleed; they are bound, gagged, whipped, tortured, and murdered for the titillation of those who need extreme violence to be aroused or satisfied sexually.[16] Disgust at her defilement is one of the blinds that sexual arousal hides behind.

Inducing some of the same effects as *memento mori*, pornography, defined as "wishfully linking fucking with ecstasy-to-death,"[17] is fixated by the viewer just as women's legs, lips, and vagina are, and just as the skull or poem or musical composition is by those who luxuriate in fantasies arising from desires to experience the "pleasures" of pain. Those who view pornographic materials fixate on pain and cruelty being inflicted on others in order to have arousal bolster their ego and assure potential success in conquering a victim. The image of brutality ending in death (pictured so well in a popular album cover that shows a woman, with all of her body except her legs, head downward in a sausage grinder) presented in pornography is a stimulant needed to maintain masculinity. Moreover, "pornography and its effectiveness is telling us that we needn't have a real, living, breathing, female with us to respond sexually."[18] The picture will do, and a woman who asks more of a relationship than sex is, above all, not wanted or needed for an erection and, of course, is often pushed aside.

The Objectification/Fixation/Conquest trio has become standard practice in pornographic materials,[19] and all it takes is the generalization of woman into a concept, a thing, a nonindividualized category. Then by fixating on parts of her anatomy, the action having been greatly assisted and trained by the TV camera's eye on breasts and hips, the viewer is led to stimulation which can be recaptured and augmented later by recollections of the same or, if these are not strong or vivid enough, pornography or artistic renderings of women's parts will assist in achieving the desired effect, an erect penis. Society, which places high value on conquering, contributes to involvement with the kind of sex that must include mastery; as the desire to conquer grows more apparent, the need to be sexually aroused becomes more urgent. Pornography is a crutch for those who cannot otherwise be stimulated, and it constantly resets the norms by accelerating the power of the stimulant which will lead to a conquest. As capacity to be aroused weakens, the stimulant must be progressively more and more extreme to accomplish the desired end, which either through outright wish or inevitability can only bring death at its acme.

The multimillion dollar pornography business caters to these needs. Photography is a hobby which may serve the same function and save the purchaser from the stigma of buying pornographic materials. Interestingly, Susan Sontag says that all photographs are *memento mori* because to take a photograph is to participate in another person's "mortality, vulnerability, or mutability."[20] Emphasizing the aggressive sides of photography, she looks upon the one photographed as a victim whose image can often be used to induce sexual arousal. Language underscores the fantasy of conquest by making the camera a gun: it is loaded, aimed, and shot. To photograph people is "to violate" them.[21] Calling attention to Michael Powell's film *Peeping Tom* (1960), she illustrates how necrophilic photography can be. In this film, a Peeping Tom kills women with a weapon inside his camera which photographs the victim as she is in the throes of death. He is not interested in experiences with living women but just the photos of them which he later screens in his home for his private pleasure. Only shots of women undergoing death interest him.[22]

Moving into the public arena, we find that propagandistic uses are made of materials designed to convince viewers of the horrors of abortion and the crimes of the mother who seeks the abortion. Adrienne Rich refers to pornographic anti-abortion literature that shows images of fetuses "who will never disturb a mother's sleep," the "fetishism of tiny fingers and toes," and the "callously death-dealing mother."[23] In response, feminists may show pictures of the coathanger. Those on both sides of the issue display images of violence and death that serve as reminders of mortality.

There seems to be a distinct parallel between the motives for

fondling a skull and for becoming engrossed in pornographic materials. Either can bring sexual stimulation. Should it be thought
that only the most "deviant" become aroused by a skull, note that
among those addicted to this kind of *memento mori* as a spur to
pleasure, along with others mentioned above, is the seemingly
distinguished and in some ways appealing Baron in Isak Dinesen's
"The Old Chevalier" who in his *fantaisie macabre* holds the skull
of his one-time imagined lover. Unlike Suckling, however, he is
less open about woman's despicableness and is perhaps reliving an
earlier largely fantasized experience.

The common strand running through all this evidence of the need
to take into the hands objects that arouse is the inseparable triad:
woman, sex, death. While crematoriums and relatively guarded
burial sites now keep us from excessive fondling of skulls, we have
substitutes in pornography and the arts. Given our lengthened life
span compared to that during the Middle Ages and, it is hoped,
our greater capacity to think clearly, we ought to be able to exorcise death from our psyches, and possibly even the tendency to
handle its tangible images and symbols. Most pressing of all is the
need to pry apart the unreasonable link between women and death.

NOTES

1. A. Hamilton Thompson, ed., "Farewel to Love," in *The Works of
Sir John Suckling* (London: George Routledge and Sons, 1910), pp. 37–38.

2. T.S.R. Boase, *Death in the Middle Ages* (New York: McGraw-Hill,
1972), p. 106.

3. Herbert J. C. Grierson, ed., *The Poems of John Donne* I (Oxford:
Clarendon, 1912), p. 59.

4. Ibid., pp. 62–73.

5. Typical passage from his sermons.

6. Wayland Young, *Eros Denied: Sex in Western Society* (New York:
Grove, 1964), pp. 191–96.

7. Andrea Dworkin, *Woman Hating* (New York: E. P. Dutton, 1974),
p. 136.

8. Young, *Eros Denied*, p. 295.

9. Marie Bonaparte, *The Life and Works of Edgar Allan Poe* (London:
Imago, 1949), p. 218.

10. Quoted from *Carmen de Mundi contemptu* by Julia O'Faolain and Lauro
Martines, eds., *Not in God's Image* (London: Temple Smith, 1973), p. xiii.

11. Dworkin, *Woman Hating*, p. 73.

12. Lawrence S. Kubie, "The Fantasy of Dirt," in *Sex Roles in Literature*, ed. Mary Beth Pringle and Ann Stricker (New York: Longman, 1980), p. 106.

13. Ronald B. McKerrow, ed., *The Works of Thomas Nashe* II (New York: Barnes and Noble, 1966), pp. 138–39.

14. Harold Williams, ed., *The Poems of Jonathan Swift* II (Oxford: Clarendon, 1958), pp. 524–30.

15. H. R. Hays, *The Dangerous Sex* (New York: Putnam, 1964), reprinted in Sheila Ruth, *Issues in Feminism* (Boston: Houghton Mifflin, 1980) under the title, "I Am Unclean," pp. 101–7.

16. *The Guardian*, September 26, 1979.

17. Young, *Eros Denied*, p. 291.

18. Jack Litewka, "The Socialized Penis," in *Feminist Frameworks*, ed. Alison M. Jaggar and Paula Rothenberg Struhl (New York: McGraw-Hill, 1978), p. 71.

19. Ibid., pp. 68–71.

20. Susan Sontag, *On Photography* (New York: Dell, 1978), p. 15.

21. Ibid., p. 14.

22. Ibid., p. 13.

23. Adrienne Rich, *On Lies, Secrets and Silence* (New York: Norton, 1979), p. 15.

IV

POE'S MOST POETIC SUBJECT

Charles Baudelaire pronounced Edgar Allan Poe's attitude toward women chivalric, and scholars have repeatedly done likewise, even within the past three decades, without finding chivalry incompatible with his proclamation that the death of a beautiful woman is the most poetic subject to be found. Even when seeing his life and works as inextricably bound together, writers generally look upon what they consider his chivalrous approach as the accepted mode for a Southern gentleman and seem to have no special misgivings about his statement on what is suitable subject matter for poetry.[1] With a similar blind spot, educators who may condemn extremes in twentieth-century literature and life do not flinch at making Poe's poetry and fiction required reading in our schools. Others who regard death as the ultimate terror find his stories highly entertaining. When looking at Poe's own immediate predecessors and contemporaries, it is obvious that he was not unique in his interest in dead females. Other writers with similar interests can be found, and crime statistics, among numerous other sources, bear out this fact. What has escaped many is that his skills as a poet and fiction writer, his theories regarding art, beauty, and pain, and the enthusiasm of his audience have all helped perpetuate a view of woman that identifies her with the most passive state occurring, that of the dead, and thus creates negative conditioning for generation after generation of vulnerable readers. That Poe's works emerged from

---

This chapter was read before the Colorado Seminars in Literature held at the University of Southern Colorado, Pueblo, on November 6, 1982.

and fed into the much-read Gothic tale, which often makes woman a victim, goes without saying.

Anyone separating out the definitions of chivalry as Poe's critics use it, as history hands it down to us, and as Poe practiced and/or wrote about it would have to take into account varying circumstances and diverse customs. A rigid definition of the term would be difficult to formulate, but some valuable generalizations can be made about it. The element that Poe adds to the custom of chivalry may be viewed as contradictory to it, or as the other side of a coin that poses as one thing while participating in another. The reading of his tales given here will produce evidence in support of the latter view.

The linkage of women and death is not an absolute in the traditional chivalric pose. Chivalry often praised woman for her beauty and intelligence and sometimes for her faithfulness and chastity. Its purpose was ostensibly to protect the woman from ravishment or other types of harm. When the relationship between the knight and lady was adulterous, the woman adored was most often well stationed, independent, and capable of performing courtly rituals. Sometimes the two lovers vowed faithfulness until death, and their dual death functioned symbolically as the consummation of love.[2] For the most part, however, the relationship purported to spur the knight into performing deeds of valor and motivated women to perform an active role in court life. Problematical as we may now think the lady's role to be, she was a life-oriented person, and her lover was not totally obsessed with viewing her in the throes of death.

Death either as cancellation or as a spectre in woman's path would seem to add to her sense of hopelessness and make her doubt her own worth or that of any kind of productive action. As we see love and death becoming more closely allied in Romantic writers, the result makes for a negative outlook, but this coupling of love and death contains less of the one-sided obsession Poe depicts in his works. To label Poe chivalric in his attitude toward women is obviously to gloss over a special set of negatives which his depictions contain. As this discussion will illustrate, numerous works by Poe are not the product of a chivalric attitude that places women on pedestals and leaves them there. Instead, they picture her as annihilated, as a plague upon man, and simply as a catalyst for a deep-seated obsession wherein there are no reciprocated benefits for her.

Many efforts have been made to explain why Poe linked women and death. But of far greater significance are those aspects of his works that would shape the impressionable reader's concepts of women, aspects that relegate her to a kind of vehicle for imaginatively carrying both Poe and his readers into the throes of death, thereby limiting the woman to a death-oriented function. Some would even have us believe that Poe worshipped woman even as he imagined her undergoing death. Rather, one suspects that whatever courtesy and adoration Poe exercised before woman fell away as he worked himself into an empathetic death orgy over her expiration. To clothe him in chivalry is to shroud the negative with a positive that can only deceive the unwary.

It is possible to see Poe's works merely as his life rewritten; it is also possible to label and dismiss him as a case study in necrophilia or misogyny and to put him on the shelf with the peculiar. Much in his approach, however, suggests a sweeping attitude stretching much before and beyond his time, an attitude that takes lightly literature made up of nine parts satisfaction at the death of the female and one part (at most) courtesy and adoration. Poe is but one of many who accept an extremely exaggerated and totally unreasonable coupling of women and death, to say nothing of taking satisfaction from finding her so overcome.

Medicine is only one example of a nonliterary field in which beauty and death have a special titillation. Several articles in *Blackwood*'s magazine, which Poe read, coupled woman's beauty with disease. Margaret Alterton thinks Poe may have caught the suggestion for choosing his "most poetic topic" from medical articles found there. In "The Diary of the Late Physician," which incidentally "touched a chord of interest" in London, he could have found the suggestion that a greater thrill will result from diseased conditions if beauty is added. According to this article, more morbid pleasure can be produced if disease works on a beautiful woman.[3] With fascination the doctor describes developing cancer, calling attention to an eminent medical writer who thought the most beautiful women were usually the ones afflicted with this disease. Later, he is also fascinated with catalepsy in women:

"Beautiful, unfortunate creature!" thought I, as I stood gaz-
ing mournfully on her, with my candle in my hand, leaning
against the bed-post.[4]

Poets and thinkers on an artistic level and nearly contempora-
neous with Poe mingled pleasure and pain. Keats finds beauty in
melancholy; Coleridge's "Rime of the Ancient Mariner" features
life-in-death as female; and the conservative Edmund Burke in his
"On the Sublime and Beautiful" says beauty in distress is the most
affecting kind.[5]

Poe spawned much interest, but one suspects the attraction to
him sprang from like preoccupations, already rooted. In England,
the Pre-Raphaelites were impressed not just by his style but by the
pictures of his heroines. Dante Gabriel Rossetti stated that when
he set out to write "The Blessed Damozel," he had to go beyond
Poe's treatment of grief on earth, that he had "to reverse the conditions, and give utterance to the yearning of the loved one in
heaven."[6] Swinburne and Morris showed Poe's influence, and later,
Wilde and Beardsley exploited the chaste and ethereal coupled with
cruelty.

It was in France, however, that Poe inspired the most emula-
tion. Baudelaire translated Poe's tales in 1856 and 1857, and their
impact was felt all over Europe, even in Russia. Poe's influence is
found in the *Contes Cruels* of Villiers de l'Isle-Adam, in the writings of Barbey d'Aurevilly, and especially in the character of des
Esseintes, the hero of J. K. Huysman's novel, *À Rebours*. Huysman read and absorbed Poe. Hints of incest, the depiction of the
horrible along with asexual and learned women, and death-in-life
agonies in Poe's fiction all interested him and found their way into
his works.

French poetry was greatly influenced by Mallarmé's translation
of Poe's poems in 1875. After previously having been attracted to
Poe's "The Raven," Verlaine and Rimbaud spoke of learning English as they read Poe. The influence went south to Italy to be found
in D'Annunzio's plays and novels, and to Russia to appear in Dos-
toevski's *The Idiot*. The double; the blending of love and death;
the neurotic, pleasure-loving, aesthetic hero; insanity; the use of
drugs; pleasure sharpened by pain; hallucinations—all are found in

writers subsequent to Poe.[7] He was obviously not alone in his morbidity.

Some scholars explain Poe's interest in dead women by cataloging the deaths that occurred during his lifetime and by attempting to show how these affected him. The list is so extensive that we are left wondering how he could have escaped becoming blasé about death. His mother, Elizabeth Arnold Poe, died when he was three, having been deserted in July 1810 by Poe's father, who apparently disappeared at this point never to be seen again. Her husband's departure, her incipient tuberculosis, her being pregnant with Poe's sister, and her attempt to retain her glory on the stage brought her to death in December 1811. Acting as long as her strength lasted, she finally was bedridden:

> All the while her little son and her baby daughter were with her, hearing her cough and moan, witnessing her tears at the knowledge that she must soon leave them . . . on the aware, sensitive mind of her intelligent three-year-old son, the sights and sounds of the sickroom . . . the mother's despair and anguish, the gradual change in the familiar face, must have left their unforgettable mark.[8]

According to Frances Winwar, Poe's association with Jane Stanard, the mother of one of his friends, when he was fifteen did much to solidify his conception of the ideal of romantic womanhood. Jane is thought to have resembled Poe's mother and to have embodied for him a kind of purity and spirituality that evoked adoration. Poe seems to have thought Jane would guide him toward greater and greater heights as a poet and would stop any excesses that might pull him down. When she suddenly died in April 1824, he was distraught and for many weeks visited her grave every night.[9]

Frances Allan, his foster mother, died in 1829; his brother Henry in 1831 of tuberculosis; his grandmother Poe in 1835; and, probably most distressing of all for its lingering duration, his child-wife Virginia Clemm in 1847. Many believe that all these experiences with death colored his relationships with other women—Sarah Royster, Mary Devereaux, Frances Osgood, Helen Whitman, and Annie Richmond—by causing him to develop a strong dependence upon them, epitomized by his association with his Aunt Maria Clemm who often nursed him back to health or sobriety. He developed an acute fear of losing the person upon whom he depended, causing him to reenact her death repeatedly. It is believed that sexual passion was not part of these relationships to any extent, if at all. Intelligence in these women interested him sporadically and often only slightly. Death came to define nearly the whole of his concept of female reality. Other men have limited woman to sex, breeding, or dissembling, but most women would prefer these functions to being thought of as a vehicle for experiencing death. Poe makes *memento mori* of women. He forces, up out of his being, fictional character after fictional character in the throes of death. He handled death like a jeweler absorbed in his merchandise. His reading of the graveyard poets, Keats and Coleridge, his interest in mesmerism which he sees as a death-like state, his preoccupation with calling the dead back to life, his belief that contemplating beauty is a high challenge which must be done in the presence of death, his tendencies to elevate his dead mother into something which she was not—an English lady—along with strong melancholy tendencies, all helped establish around him an aura of death that seemed to obsess and nourish him. The character, of course, that most obsessed him and most often moved from life to cadaver was woman. A look at a number of these women is a meaningful trip into a source of woman's crippled self-image.

The death woman appears in Poe's best known poems, and in "Romance" he claims to have met her in his youth when "I could not love except where Death/Was mingling his with Beauty's breath."[10] He would have Lenore, the "queenliest dead that ever died,"[11] be alive, but the intensity of his sorrow and his requests that the Raven tell him if he will be united with her overwhelm the reader to such an extent that little life shines through. He returns to the tomb of his lost Ulalume and wonders if a demon has tempted him there, seemingly to suggest that it is a fiend in the tomb which holds him in its grip, not woman. A thousand roses in "To Helen" give out, "in return for the love-light,/Their odorous souls in an ecstatic death—."[12] Annabel Lee's highborn kinsmen bear her away from him, and he goes to lie in her tomb.[13] In these poems sound gives a compelling gloss to the corpse of woman. Almost all of us can remember reciting these poems at an early age.

In Poe's tales, however, the death woman gets much fuller treatment. We can assume that his statement about the most poetic topic also held for fiction. In "Berenice," Poe reduces his heroine to teeth just as street language has long turned woman into just a part of herself by designating her cunt, skirt, or any of dozens of other epithets most often suggestive of sexuality. Berenice's agility and beauty make little impression on the protagonist until she becomes emaciated by disease. Then her teeth hop out at him from a face that has lustreless, pupil-less eyes, a placid pale high forehead, and shrunken lips. Just as street language gives exaggerated efficacy to woman's sexual side, the protagonist speaks of the "sensitive and sentient power" of the teeth that can carry moral persuasion and restore peace to him.[14] So determined is he to have these teeth that he opens her tomb, only to find her alive.[15] His guilt, of course, shows on his spade and his clothes. We assume he got the teeth at the expense of her life.

Marie Bonaparte and other Freudians played into Poe's sadism when, in connection with this tale, they discussed the sadistic, castrating vagina, once thought to be equipped with teeth.[16] One does not have to follow their thinking to see the protagonist's lukewarm, if not rejecting, attitude toward woman who is energetic and attractive, and his preference for woman in a diseased and finally dead state. If Poe had a chivalric attitude toward women and if by that is meant respect for them, it does not spill over into his depiction of the protagonist in this ugly little tale, either as a pose or with some degree of sincerity.

In "Morella," the heroine tastes of intelligence and fathoms the unearthly so subtly that she terrorizes the protagonist. Her erudition includes determining that one's identity persists beyond the tomb. She dies but not before leaving him a daughter to take her place; even if both have separate and different identities, neither is palatable because of an exaggerated intelligence, which is as much a part of these women as teeth were for Berenice. All erudition and no passion, the first Morella can only give birth to "the most hideous."[17] As his wife's end approaches, the protagonist longs for her death. Fiendishly he prompts the death of the child by calling her by her mother's name, the sound of which is death-producing. His "long and bitter laugh" at the end is a "mad" and sinister I-got-ya-this-time response, perhaps because there will be no future child to trouble him as there had been when the mother died.[18] In this tale we find little chivalry.

"The Assignation" and "The Oblong Box," like the poems "Annabel Lee" and "For Annie," are about meeting the beloved in death. In "The Assignation," there is a kind of telepathic union when two lovers take poison. Evidently unable to see the Marchesa Aphrodite except under the stress of rescuing her child, the male lover retrieves the infant which she has let slip into the water. Although this woman seems to fit better than Berenice or Morella the goddess-to-be-worshipped stereotype (and her lover a brave knight doing a good deed), we scarcely see her enough to realize her nature since she is at a distance from her lover whom we constantly see in the company of the male character who tells the story. She, "the adoration of all Venice,"[19] is adulterous, as many women in the early chivalric tradition were, but she seems to have more in common with adulterous female sinners, much written about before and after Poe in nineteenth-century fiction, who have no choice but death. The tale is told from a male perspective, and it is mostly about males; the woman's role has its focus in death.

"Ligeia" presents an extravagant picture of woman's beauty, intelligence, and devotion, but even as Poe begins his laudatory description of this heroine, he seems to undercut the idealization, when he mentions the "ill-omened" marriage she has with the protagonist. Ligeia has some "strangeness" about her.[20] Like most of Poe's women, she gives but receives little from others; what she gives is a sense of the importance of will which, if exercised with strength, she thinks can save one from death. If this were Poe's only tale and if we read only the passages leading up to her illness, we might think Poe worshipped woman and took great pleasure in her vitality of spirit and mind. However, not only Ligeia but also Rowena, the new wife, dies in order that Ligeia may live again and in order, it would seem, that the protagonist may relish not one, but two, journeys into necrophilia. In opium fantasy and influenced by the phantasmagoric effect of a new abbey, he is able to will Rowena's return from death prior to willing her change into Ligeia. The night he spends with Rowena, who lapses into death and returns to life alternately and finally into Ligeia, is a rich orchestration of the death process that Poe employs often but nowhere with such prolonged intensity as in this case. Poe's most deeply felt and intense writing is not on woman alive but on woman experiencing death.

"The Fall of the House of Usher," like other tales, does not point to a conventional chivalric attitude toward women, nor does it make the death of a beautiful woman anything more than what it often is—a terror-producing experience. Poe's first-person narrator has another necrophilic adventure; the whole story appears to be a trip into a grave. The narrator visits a house of "excessive antiquity" reminiscent of "some neglected vault."[21] His cadaverous host Roderick Usher, whose lips have a "surpassingly beautiful curve,"[22] makes him aware of his "tenderly beloved-sister" who, as was also the case with the Marchesa Aphrodite, is never seen for more than a few seconds and who is never revealed as more than a tortured victim who is buried alive. We learn that she had been wasting away for some time with a lingering disease that had baffled the skill of doctors. Called a life-in-death symbol by various critics, she, like Poe's mother and wife Virginia, dies a slow death. Bonaparte, for example, who sees a very close link between sex and cruelty, says she was "a mother symbol to Poe Usher."[23] Provisions are made to have Madeline's corpse put in a vault within one of the main walls of the building, and the two men see to its being put there:

> The vault in which we placed it (and which had been so long unopened that our torches, half smothered in its oppressive atmosphere, gave us little opportunity for investigation) was small, damp, and entirely without means of admission of light; lying, at great depth, immediately beneath that portion of the building in which was my own sleeping apartment.[24]

The night they discover they have buried Madeline alive is one of "singular" terror and beauty.[25] Missing in this tale is an element that is not altogether absent in Poe, excessive mooning over the loveliness of woman. A sickly smile quivers on the host's lips as he discovers that he has buried his sister; guilt and "madness" seize him, and when Madeline does come forth alive only to fall heavily upon the person of her brother, she becomes the instrument of his death. Madeline is given no feelings, or for that matter much substance as a human being; she is victim–destroyer. Poe spends greatly less time on Madeline than he does on his two male characters. That he does not allow either the sister or the brother to live suggests that they were perhaps involved with the mysteriously "terrible": incest likely in the manner of that in Byron's *Manfred*. This tale clearly shows why the Freudians found so much in Poe, as well as why Leslie Fiedler insisted that American literature was basically a homosexual one written by authors incapable of depicting a realistic woman.[26]

"Eleonora" treats the innocence and decline to death of a woman whom the protagonist comes to love. Poe here blends transitions from childlike love to the delirious bliss of ardent passion with changes in nature. Their love is sharply cut off from the outside world and is soon darkened by impending death: "she had been made perfect in loveliness only to die."[27] Vowing fidelity after her death, he then watches nature become sterile in her absence. The Spirit of Love absolves him of his promises, and we learn that Ermengarde will take Eleonora's place. This tale was written when Virginia's health had worsened, and Poe apparently realized a certain uselessness of vows. Eleonora is as ephemeral as the daisies or the asphodel. At the end of this tale Poe is without any pretense to chivalry and is down to his own basic needs.

"The Oval Portrait" is of special significance because here Poe might be indicating that he realizes artists exploit women in the throes of death to produce art and that sadism and art are closely allied. In this work, the artist's canvas grows to perfection; his wife, the model, shrinks to death. She waxes pale and weak as her strength and beauty are transferred to the portrait. The painter grows "wild with the ardor of the work" and rarely removes his eyes from the canvas, "even to regard the countenance of his wife."[28] Standing proudly over his accomplishment, he proclaims it Life, but when he turns to his wife, she is no more. When we watch the mounting obsession and pleasure in the artist, we become more and more aware that a woman is being used to produce that pleasure and ultimately profit. How much Poe felt this exploitation also explained his art is not clear; had it made much of a dent in his makeup, he might have written more on the subject than is found in "The Oval Portrait," a slight four-page account.

Anyone searching for relief from the death woman in Poe's tales should not turn to "The Murders in the Rue Morgue" where Madame L'Espanaye is mutilated and decapitated and her daughter is killed and stuffed head downward in the chimney; or to "The Mystery of Marie Rogêt" where a girl's corpse is found in the Seine after a rape-murder; or to "The Black Cat" where the wife is axed to death by her drunken husband as she stays his hand when he is about to kill the cat with which he is obsessed; or to "Scheherazade" where the main character stalls death by talking, but in the end is done in as we might expect. Scheherazade's destroyer, incidentally, is a certain monarch who "having good cause to be jealous of his queen" put her to death and made a vow "to espouse each night the most beautiful maiden in his dominions, and the next morning to deliver her up to the executioner." When Scheherazade enters the picture, he had fulfilled his vow for many years "to the letter, and with a religious punctuality and method that conferred great credit upon him as a man of devout feelings and excellent sense."[29] This fellow, whom we hope is just a figment of the imagination used at least somewhat satirically, might find a parallel in the seventeenth-century Countess Elisabeth Báthory, who in the Carpathian Mountains put to death 650 virgins. Their slaughter aroused her sexually, after which she would bucket up their blood to bathe in, ostensibly to improve her complexion.[30]

If Poe had the conventional chivalric attitude toward women with the attendant sincerity that many of his critics thought he had, this attitude is not much in evidence in his poems and fiction. That he did exploit the death of females is quite apparent in his works. The life-orientation of chivalry does not seem to be compatible with his noticeable emphasis on death. If all women had to read was a steady diet of Poe, they would likely develop so keen a sense of their demise that they would have only a negative approach to life. If women believed that Poe's attitude toward women was chivalric, then they would come to think of chivalry as something having to do with graves, gasping their last breath, and coming alive again. They would soon unmask chivalry, as the term has recently been used, as a ritual that elevates women in order to topple them with a more pronounced thud. It goes without saying that many people still do not view chivalry in this light, although the number that do has increased sharply.

The thoughtful reader would want to have little to do with Poe's works or any literature exploiting similar stereotypes. However, given the abundance of Gothic romances written by women, apart from all those written by men, and given the number of female readers of those Gothic tales, it can be said that repulsion from the stereotypes that the Gothic tale perpetuates is not as strong as one would wish it to be. Interestingly, during periods of low emphasis on women's freedom, such as the fifties and early sixties, the publication of Gothic romances tends to increase. Perhaps the Gothic tale is thought to be necessary to uphold, through the support of identification, female capacity to go on in a victimized and subservient position.[31]

Poe does not, of course, hold up the entire weight of the Gothic tradition, for it existed long before him and branched into areas that he never treated. He did have considerable influence on this tradition, however, and it is time we addressed the question of what the legacy of that tradition has done to the image of women. It is important to analyze Poe's antagonisms,[32] his sexuality or lack of it, the influence of the deaths in his family, the American literary preoccupation with death, or whatever caused him to write as he did. Since we can neither alter Poe nor his works, we should concentrate on what his pictures of women have done and will do to the self-image and aspirations of generations of readers. If attitudes are to be changed, we need to school ourselves in how they are shaped. It would be good to label him more according to what he was and to read him with full awareness of literature's power to mold thought and action. All that Poe has done to relegate women to the world of the dead must be exorcised.

NOTES

1. Lois Hyslop and Francis E. Hyslop, trans. and ed., *Baudelaire on Poe* (State College, Pa.: Bald Eagle, 1952), p. 110; Edward Wagenknecht, *Edgar Allan Poe* (New York: Oxford, 1963), p. 25; Edd Winfield Parks, *Edgar Allan Poe As Literary Critic* (Athens: University of Georgia Press, 1964), p. 62; and Arthur Hobson Quinn, *Edgar Allan Poe, A Critical Bi-*

ography (New York: Cooper Square Publishers, 1969), especially his discussion of Poe's "The Philosophy of Composition." While these writers equate chivalry with protection, courtesy, and adoration or the show of same, others such as Kate Millett see it as sugar-coated lip service to placate the oppressed. Susan Griffin calls it an old protection racket that could not exist without rape.

2. Wayland Young, *Eros Denied: Sex in Western Society* (New York: Grove, 1964), pp. 211–14.

3. Margaret Alterton, *Origins of Poe's Critical Theory* (New York: Russell and Russell, 1965), p. 24.

4. Ibid., p. 25.

5. Edmund Burke, "On the Sublime and Beautiful," *The Harvard Classics* 24 (New York: Collier, 1909), Section IX, p. 94.

6. Jerome Hamilton Buckley and George Benjamin Woods, eds., *Poetry of the Victorian Period*, 3d ed. (Chicago: Scott, Foresman, 1965), Notes, p. 505.

7. Frances Winwar, *The Haunted Palace: A Life of Edgar Allan Poe* (New York: Harper, 1959), pp. 387–88.

8. Ibid., p. 24.

9. Ibid., pp. 54–57.

10. James A. Harrison, ed., *The Complete Works of Edgar Allan Poe* (New York: AMS Press, 1965), VII: 164.

11. Ibid., p. 53.

12. Ibid., p. 107.

13. Ibid., p. 118.

14. Ibid., II, p. 24.

15. Ibid., V, p. 256. Poe indicates in "The Premature Burial" that being buried alive is believed to be the most horrible death possible.

16. Marie Bonaparte, *The Life and Works of Edgar Allan Poe* (London: Imago, 1949), p. 218.

17. *Complete Works of Edgar Allan Poe*, II, p. 28.

18. Ibid., p. 34.

19. Ibid., p. 111.

20. Ibid., pp. 249–50.

21. Ibid., III, pp. 276–77.

22. Ibid., p. 278.

23. Bonaparte, *Life and Works of Edgar Allan Poe*, p. 249.

24. *Complete Works of Edgar Allan Poe,* III, p. 288.

25. Ibid., p. 291.

26. Leslie A. Fiedler, *Love and Death in the American Novel* (New York: Criterion, 1960), pp. 325–45.

27. *Complete Works of Edgar Allan Poe*, IV, p. 240.

28. Ibid., p. 248.

29. Ibid., VI, p. 79.

30. Gabriel Ronay, *The Truth About Dracula* (New York: Stein and Day, 1973), pp. 93–145.

31. Janice Radway, "Dialogue: Is Popular Culture Social History?" in *Humanities* 1, no. 1 (January–February 1980): 14.

32. Fiedler, *Love and Death in the American Novel*, p. 413. Fiedler thinks that Poe was in flight from woman when he died.

V

ADULTERY AND DEATH

CLARISSA

Clarissa, Emma, Maggie, Anna, Tess, and Edna all die, like thousands of other women in fiction, because, in accordance with the well-worn stereotypes and morality of their times, their sexual lives dictate that they must; because they are wrenched into existence by authors who see death as the end best fitting the demands of their fiction or as the one they are best equipped to display; because the masochism or brutality of authors finds an easy outlet in their works; or because authors are catering to a public that seeks emotional release by watching "good" women go to "God" where death has no sting and helps assuage guilt even as it builds for those left behind an atmosphere of horror that nullifies the will to work and live, a prerogative that those of an egalitarian turn of mind believe should be at everyone's disposal.

These six women have many sisters: women who commit suicide; women who are thrown into unbearable isolation by those closest to them; women who murder their tormentors—all warped to fit archetypal patterns and thus deprived of a totality possessed by their counterparts in life. Whether they are angel women pitted against devil men, or willful transgressors of female codes of behavior, they represent truth in minuscule form and lead unwary readers to believe they have before them all there is to woman, or in other words, a female who measures up to her society's expectations—as standard behavior dictates that she must. It is a well-known historical phenomenon that novel after novel has been published feeding the reading public's seemingly insatiable appe-

tite for the sexual assault on the virgin or the punishment of the
woman who breaks established behavior codes. The power of these
women to mold the reader's estimate of woman's totality can best
be realized if we recognize that their fictionalized lives have been
accepted as something close to a paraphrase of parts of the Bible
itself. Dorothy Van Ghent quotes a Dutch Mennonite divine who
said that if Samuel Richardson's *Clarissa* (1748) had formed "one
of the canonical books of the Bible, it would have furnished proof
positive of divine inspiration."[1] One has only to ask an average
group of students to define sin to realize that sin and sex are so
inextricably bound together in the thinking of most people that,
even when speaking to the irreligious, the association will automatically surface. In puritanical Christian mythology the devil is
obsessed with sex, which becomes the greatest evil and the most
stringent fear. This inevitable focus draws woman in its wake, and
she becomes the springboard for damnation or, as the case may
be, the ascension to something higher. Unfortunately, in both cases
this focus comes to shroud women with death and the death-producing.

Historians tell us that wherever Christianity found a safe home,
especially with the middle class, the myth of the deflowered or fallen
woman had tremendous hold on human emotion and mentality
whether treated by the artist or those addicted to power and cruelty, that is, the successors of the Marquis de Sade or the local wife
beater. With both artist and layman, woman can be seen to usurp
the power of Christ as she absorbs the sins of those around her.
Christ does indeed seem gradually to slough his charge of assuag-
ing guilt as women simultaneously gain more and more capacity
to shake off their subordination. Can it be that in order to counter
change in women's affairs, Christ's maleness has to assert itself by
shedding the capacity to absorb guilt? Is it possible that the image
of the male sufferer is so demeaning to the male ego that, for many,
he slips out of the picture? Obviously woman, like the suffering
Christ, tantalizes those addicted to brutality; much of the literature that readers have found most appetizing exploits her "crucifixion" with special vigor.

Some kind of death pervades the archetypal pattern to which the
six women mentioned above belong: Proserpina goes to the un-
derworld, Philomela is transformed into a nightingale, Lucrece takes

her own life; versions of the sex-leading-to-death motif occur in the stories of Tristan and Iseult, Phaedra and Hippolytus, Dido and Aeneas, and Antony and Cleopatra. Joining these women is *Clarissa* and all the works that this novel and others like it spawned; add to these the pornography and the cheap film fare on which billions of dollars are currently being spent to nourish our taste for brutality, and we have a tremendous body of materials that yoke women excessively with death. Although we have listened for a long time to historians of literature who tell us how *Clarissa* influenced writers like Diderot, Rousseau, and Goethe and how it set up the standard language and plot of the seduction novel, few of us have considered assessing the damage the emphasis on death found in this novel may have had on the mental and emotional makeup of women.

Instead, we have persistently applauded innumerable well-known authors, labeling their works our best literature when obviously these works are built on the same subject matter and themes as found in pornography. Our applause has helped make these works legitimate and worthy of a respect of the highest order when an examination of their conditioning power relegates them to a stockpile of brainwashing materials that need at the very least to be seen for what their effect can be. Remnants of the myths on which these works are built appear around us in various forms from slick magazine cover girls to outright pornography where the fun comes almost exclusively from seeing women brutalized, to the works of Norman Mailer and others discussed elsewhere in this work.

When one evaluates *Clarissa* as a conditioning force, it should be remembered that reading it is an endurance test of considerable magnitude. Its 2,200 pages in the Everyman four-volume set has taken all my spare time for three months. The action is slowed down by being presented in the form of letters and by the reader having to read several persons' reactions to the same event in order to arrive at the truth as to what is going on. The very act of reading it spells the kind of entrapment women find themselves in who are led to believe woman's role must include suffering and death. The process of working oneself through this tedious tale is bound to have impact on the susceptible reader; that this book was at first read widely suggests that people had a compulsion of un-

reasonable proportions to vicariously experience woman undergoing death, especially if associated with her sexuality. Still with us,
this compulsion needs to be exorcised from our systems if woman
is to be seen in her total reality and treated as more than victim.

The depiction of seduction and adultery so colors and limits the
image of women in literature that readers, even when allowing for
woman's generally subordinate state throughout history, rarely get
a picture of her total life span or any notion of the variety that her
life contains. The pronounced tendency to shroud her in death or
death-producing experiences, beyond those that are the lot of
everyone, by showing her violation or her transgression of accepted codes of behavior at the expense of other roles she plays in
life, presents the reader with partial truths and a kind of conditioning that builds false expectations in the reader and demoralizes
her/him. Certainly, much literature works as hard at this unreasonable stigmatization of people as does pornography, though literature often works more insidiously. Both evade reality, set up
constructs that feed our tendency to enjoy suffering, and perpetuate addiction to the kind of personal relations that build passiveness in women.

A look at how death colors the existence of Clarissa and Lovelace and how what we have come to call normal love and marriage are for the most part absent in Richardson's long, slow dirge
to a dying woman (which incidentally covers only a little more
than a year of Clarissa's life) will clarify the nature of the conditioning the novel produces in the reader. The book is, of course,
an effective conditioner both for what it leaves unsaid and for what
it makes explicit. The core of this novel and many of the other
books similar to it is a liaison between a male and a female which
invariably limits woman to those years of her life when she is
thought most appealing sexually, omitting almost all others. In
order for the heroine to be brought low, she may start out with
potential, the kind of potential often found in tragic characters. Any
aberrations from the norm, especially if these aberrations suggest
individuality or the capacity to think for herself, may be added to
her list of attributes to be pushed under, if not destroyed, as she
undergoes seduction.

Actually, Clarissa has some claims to being a "new" woman,
although these claims like all of her other positive attributes come

to naught in the face of her harassment, first by her parents and then in a much more complete way by Lovelace when he rapes her after having her drugged. That she endears herself to Anna Howe, whose ideas about men and marriage are perceptive, if at times too general, suggests she might have been able to let intelligence rule much of her life. Evidence of this intelligence comes through in comments like these to Anna: "what a degree of patience, what a greatness of soul is required in the wife, not to despise a husband who is more ignorant, more illiterate, more low-minded, than herself!"[2] She realizes her brother has no more right to control her than she him,[3] and she questions whether she will ever be free to follow her own judgment.[4] Anna tells Belford after Clarissa is dead that Clarissa had at one time said: "All that a woman *can* learn . . . above the useful knowledge proper to her sex, *let her learn.*"[5]

We also read of Clarissa's capacity to endear herself to others besides Anna (Clarissa has been especially favored by her grandfather who, because she has been the delight of his old age, leaves her his personal estate), of her honesty, generosity, stoicism, and charm, but these attributes have no positive outlet in the course of the narration except as she, on her deathbed, is able to influence a few people to think more circumspectly. For *herself* there is nothing but pain and suffering which prompt much thought on a way out through death. No sooner do Richardson's thousands upon thousands of readers get Clarissa's tale launched than we hear her saying she would rather die than face the solicitations of the odious Solmes[6] whom her family is insisting she marry. Only a few pages later she states that she would rather be buried alive than be associated with him.[7] Finding herself caught between Solmes and Lovelace, she fears the murder of Lovelace by her brother. "To avoid that," she again says, "I would most willingly be buried alive."[8] Persisting in her rejection of Solmes, she tells Anna she would choose death "in any shape, rather than that man,"[9] and a little later she again vows: "I will never be the wife of that Solmes— I will die first!"[10]

These are just the preliminaries; the reader continues to be bathed in the prospect of death. Clarissa dreams of being stabbed and thrown into a ready-dug grave by Lovelace.[11] She is ill and sometimes unable to write before the end of the first volume,[12] and after being spirited away from her home by Lovelace, she is fatigued to exhaustion.[13] Lovelace's "vile" treatment of her (which is delayed endlessly to make it extremely enticing to the voyeurs, as well as the readers who watch it take place) is delineated in Volume II and culminates with her screaming "Kill me! Kill me! if I am odious enough in your eyes to deserve this treatment." She would be thankful to be free of the burden of life, she says, and "wildly looking all around her" exclaims: "Give me but the means, and I will instantly convince you that my honour is dearer to me than my life!"[14] This scene draws an indelible picture of Clarissa into focus which tends very much to underscore a denial of life and to make the defense of honor the one most emphatic (and to us the most limiting) reason for existence that women had in the eighteenth and nineteenth centuries.

Clarissa later orders her own coffin, and it is learned that those around her keep knives away from her. References to death multiply as she gets nearer to it, and as she sees death as the only way out of her predicament, her death-wish becomes more pronounced. Since the illness of Lovelace's uncle prohibits his being in town near Clarissa, Belford writes him in specific detail about her diminishing state. Caught up in Clarissa's problems completely, Belford reveals his feelings so explicitly that Lovelace often reminds him of his addiction to dwelling on death. In Volume IV her coffin, which she has in readiness in her room, is frequently mentioned, and her demise occurs well before the end of the last volume, leaving plenty of time for dwelling extensively on how her death chastises those who have been cruel to her and elevates others such as Belford, who have undergone some reformation because of their association with her. The last volume wrings the spurious sentimental victory from defeat which doubtlessly kept the innocent reader tied to the page and to a negation of life that the archetype transmits.

This absorption in death is, of course, precipitated by the isolation to which Clarissa is driven by her family, her own poor judgment at some points with regard to Lovelace, and Lovelace's machinations and trickery. She is a young woman possessed of infinite "virtues," and had she been left alone, they might have come to important fruition. This "most excellent woman on earth"[15] has great capacity to give and forgive as well as inspire the same in

others. Richardson states that he did not intend to make her flawless, but save for mistaking Lovelace for a friend and often being
frightened by him or the predicaments he has led her into, she
proves that she can move with grace and caution as she responds
intelligently to the situations in which she finds herself.

That Clarissa has no other option for "repairing her honor" than
to marry Lovelace, once he has drugged and raped her, is perhaps
to the modern reader the most startling aspect of her situation. The
game Lovelace is playing gathers its significance from the belief
that sexual penetration will alter her permanently; from his point
of view, this belief transforms his monstrosities into his notion of
victories. That she is restricted to marriage only with Lovelace
might seem improbable were he not made up wholly of fantasies
of power and dominance (for example, he plots raping a whole
boatload of women) and possessed of the kind of egotism and in-
flated self-image that finds his own tricks and games an amusing
pastime. He is relentless, and there seems to be no way to evade
him. He is convinced women are "made to bear pain," Eve having "entailed upon all her succeeding daughters" that curse.[16] When
Clarissa does try to elude him, he finds he must "make use of power
and art" to prevent her escape and must, whenever he likes, act
above the law. He loves the triumph that subduing brings,[17] and
in the case of Clarissa, to subdue her, he says, would be a triumph
over the whole sex.[18] Her scorn only augments his pursuit, and
his own "greatness" is sustained by her failure to yield to him.
Unlike the Harlowes, Lovelace is not much interested in money;
dancing people on wires seems to attract him more. Intruding
himself into the presence of others when he is unwanted is another
of his most trying habits.

In order to make it seem probable that Lovelace is the primary
cause of Clarissa's death, Richardson works hard to show an underlying murderous intent in his character. In his letters to Belford, we find Lovelace saying men sometimes find themselves in
situations where they must commit a murder.[19] He calls attention
to games that he and other boys played as children where a bird
is toyed with until it dies, and he boasts of always being able to
devise means of achieving what he wants when he is thwarted.
Clarissa also writes a story about a lady who befriended a lion that

then turned on her—a story that parallels her own befriending Lovelace.[20]

Lovelace is not likely to give up or do anything so culpable as commit a quick murder. His method is much more of a war between two offending parties (the imagery of which he often uses) that will go on until Clarissa is too weak to struggle any longer. Comparing him to beasts and birds of prey, Anna finds him "infinitely less excusable." He, she says, is simply "vile, barbarous, plotting, destructive" and "destroys through wantonness and sport" what the animals and birds take for hunger and necessity.[21] Although some scholars believe Lovelace is honest except in his dealings with women, I find this argument holds little weight. Constantly involved in scrapes with women and plotting others, he has little time for this honesty to bear fruit, especially when one sees how he lords it over all his male friends and when one takes a look at his own avowal that he is not often honest for any length of time.[22] Even in his advice regarding Belford's finding a wife, he is not reliable.[23]

Many writers easily transfer the imagery of death used in connection with the hunter or the warrior to the pursuit of women. To overcome a proud woman is always a great triumph for the masculine ego; she seems often to be used as a testing ground for triumphs during the hunt or on the field of battle. Richardson is not the first to couch a tale of pursuit of woman in the language of the hunter and warrior where death is coveted and proclaimed a victory. Step by step, Lovelace "stalks his prey" until Clarissa achieves a kind of triumph over him by her firm rejection of his advances and her death.

Lovelace falls apart after Clarissa's demise, and he begins his own downward movement to death (which is predicted at intervals in the book by statements indicating he cannot live without Clarissa and by certain indications of his recklessness). So he, too, both in his "stalking" Clarissa and in his defeat, helps make Richardson's book a long hymn to death. As the primary instrument in Clarissa's catastrophe, he also can claim that she caused his own, and those readers who find him attractive would probably claim this notion to be valid.

Some readers also believe that Clarissa was in love with Lovelace, and Richardson does drop some not-totally-convincing hints that she "could have" loved him.[24] She, however, recognizes in him traces of foppery, effeminacy, and the coxcomb which, if carried too far, she says, can become "the scorn of one sex, and the jest of the other."[25] Lovelace's avowed contempt for women and desire to get "revenge upon as many of the sex as shall come" into his "power"[26] render him about as desirable a lover as a hungry rattlesnake, which, in fact, is what Clarissa labels him at one point.[27] Mixed with his desire to capture and control are, of course, many pathetic sides that make him incapable of sustained decisiveness, a satisfying sexual relationship with any woman,[28] maintaining his sanity once his fantasies of power break down over the reality of Clarissa's death, and any true understanding of women (although he thinks that by raping them he can reveal their true nature). Childishness takes over when he begs Belford for whatever comfort he can give him at the moment, be it more and faster letters, Clarissa's heart once its beating has stopped, or finally the renunciation of his own (Belford's) reform at having been led to a better life by Clarissa. It takes someone with the goodness of Clarissa, however, to pity Lovelace; and his cavalier attitude toward sex, his maudlin talk of his offspring, his going into mourning when a woman dies in childbed illness from giving birth to his child, his always going to the funeral of the children he has sired, and his finally plotting to begin all over again with a new escapade[29] make his psychosis contemptible even to most of those who could pity him. Perhaps his most disgusting feature is his gaiety that seems so much a part of his prefabricated conscience. Even so, his life is a tragedy just as Clarissa's is; he hides behind an artifice that crumbles around him only to leave him pathetic. It needs, of course, to be added that the stereotyping of the male here is exceedingly damaging to the individual male's concept of what life is.

Especially does one marvel at the "religious" intent of the book and at its being prescribed for the edification of young girls when one realizes there is no love in it except as it is conceived to be physical violation. Lovelace, whose name means loveless, proclaims early that other things besides love such as stratagems and contrivances make intrigue fascinating.[30] Declaring his love for Clarissa more intellectual[31] than he ever thought it could be, that is, making his responses more in the realm of intrigue, ingenuity, and quickness of wit than in love, he seems unable to come to a decision to marry that is honest or mutually agreeable to a woman. At one point he envisions a society where marriage partners would be exchanged every year. He finds durability of love especially absent in men: while women "bemoan themselves for their baffled hopes, we can rant and roar, hunt and hawk; and, by new loves banish from our hearts all remembrance of the old ones."[32] The emotional life connected with love is definitely submerged in the book, thereby diminishing both Lovelace and Clarissa to less than total depictions. Irrational as it may seem, *Clarissa* would appear to underscore the notion that sexual intercourse means death for the heroine and a passport to heaven, not joy or a means of producing new life.

Neither is sex interesting to Lovelace: "More truly delightful to me the seduction progress than the crowning act: for that's a vapour, a bubble!"[33] He sums it up early by declaring that he loves revenge but hates love.[34] Raping Clarissa while she is drugged negates the whole idea of sex for, except for its exhibitionistic aspects, he might as well be conquering a corpse. Sex and death are so pervasively equated in this novel that not only love and marriage are negated but also life itself.

Clarissa repeatedly tells her family and Lovelace that she prefers a single life to any marriage she foresees in her near future. She seems capable of sustaining lasting allegiances with women and of managing problematical situations such as her will and her funeral, as long as she is not hindered. Although she wavers, she is capable of renouncing marriage, for it may, she thinks, bring trouble, vexation, and a path strewn with sharper and sharper thorns.[35]

In Clarissa's world, marriage with love, apart from the possibility of her own, seems to count for very little. Clarissa's family sees lack of love as unimportant in her arguments against marrying Solmes; they set themselves against the language of the heart, and they subject feeling to the demands of economic gain and power. Her two uncles are bachelors, and her mother and father do not love one another; the father has far too much interest in current financial settlements and previously in the money his wife brought to their union. He, in his illness, tyrannizes over his wife who has no will left. The Howe and Hervey households offer nothing in the way of a satisfactory marriage, and although Clarissa's siblings James and Bella marry after Clarissa is dead, James finds that he is constantly involved in legal attempts to procure the estates his wife ostensibly had claim to, when he married her; and Bella is unhappy because she was tempted into marriage by a man more interested in her fortune than in herself. Bella and her spouse have so "heartily hated each other, that if either know a joy, it is in being told of some new misfortune or displeasure that happens to the other."[36] Only Anna and Hickman stand much chance of a mutually helpful relationship.

It is in the degree to which women and men accepted (and do accept) the pictures of Clarissa and Lovelace to be what women and men ought to be that our interest lies. Obviously, the book presents a very limited picture of both sexes in these two characters. People in life situations have a larger scope; moreover, a great number of moral problems arise in this work, one which many have assumed squared with sound morality. Clarissa's goodness results in her destruction, and her honesty is turned into a weapon to be used against her. Clarissa is a means to an end: Lovelace uses her for pleasure, and others around her in her last hours actually take joy from her death.

As prototype, Clarissa is a crippled woman on her way to death, and we see only part of her totality. Although possessing many more desirable qualities than Lovelace, the fact that these qualities mean nothing in life makes for a kind of negativism that thwarts women's rise out of passiveness. About Lovelace we can say "Oh, he's not every man; there are many men of conscience," and speak truth, but about Clarissa we have no reason to make a similar statement. She has many desirable qualities, but they cannot be brought to any use in life. As Mark Kinkead-Weekes indicates, both Clarissa and Lovelace are not as we find people in life, but Lovelace is more the playactor who enjoys the performance and Clarissa the one most put upon with his "playing a stage-part he thinks is real."[37] Our problem lies with the knowledge that many think both he and Clarissa are "real."

By her lack of assertiveness, by her fear of going alone to London, and by her inability to compromise, Clarissa proves herself typical of many women: honest, winning, and incapable of subterfuge. In so doing, she becomes a magnet for the innocent female reader who is drawn into her reasoning and plight; her road to death is glazed over with the slippery, and to follow her there is as easy as skating down an incline. Her "victory" in death is the bane of our existence, for it negates life.

Although Emma, Maggie, Anna, Tess, and Edna are never "victorious" in the sense that Clarissa is, their stories are no less damaging to woman's sense of self-worth and no less restricting in that they present only partial truths about women's lives, leaving the rest unvoiced or relegated to the unimportant. We get caught up in their dramas, but in the process we are pulled into preoccupation with the greatest of all negations, death. The same amount of time spent on activities oriented toward life would not only get us closer to the truth but would also help us build the stamina needed to reach our full potential.

EMMA

Gustave Flaubert joins a large group of novelists and readers who are drawn to the victim burdened beyond capacity to survive with all the catastrophic problems that chance, fate, science, religion, passion, and the normal growth process can produce. Propelling victims to their demise under the weight of their inner drives and conflicts, as well as uncontrollable forces beyond these, is the primary subject matter of innumerable works of fiction and dramas. These works have been much read, and one assumes they bring either pleasure or pain, or a combination of both, to an extent sufficient to make them of perennial interest. The writer may use the victim to underscore, exploit, or exhibit larger concerns regarding the capacity to destroy oneself or another, to exploit the reader's tendency to enjoy emotional extremes, to exhibit a preoccupation with death, or to elevate one ego at the deflation of another. The victim can thus be seen to be useful to creativity, to venting the author's spleen, and to drawing into focus ways in which people move up the ladder on the backs of others. That the victim is often woman goes without saying.

Flaubert in *Madame Bovary* (1857) condemns his main female character to a despicable, ugly, and drawn-out death without being either compassionate or dispassionate toward her. He seems to loathe the people of his time and to have attempted to concentrate in Emma many of their loathsome qualities. Although he does place before the reader representatives of larger segments of society— the religious, medical, and legal—his focus is basically on Emma who suffers not only the corruption of these but also the worst that chance and fate can deal her. As Jean Rousset indicates, Emma's life is constantly a prelude to her end: he thinks her joys are all followed by a small death that foreshadows her final demise.[38] Jean Pierre Richard comments about the book in a similar way when saying her death is prefigured in sensation, love, and sleep.[39] That her horrible death was thought by many readers to be just punishment for the kind of life she led implicates a wide group of participants in art and its effects. Emma is one of scores of heroines whose adultery made her into a kind of monster to spook generations of women and critically damage their concept of self.

Henry James tells us that *Madame Bovary* shocked public morality and that Flaubert was hounded as an indecent writer.[40] The primary objection was to linking religion and sex, although this link seems to us neither new nor very pronounced, especially in view of Flaubert's rather firm stand against the unconventionally religious. The attention paid to the work because of its "immorality" drew interest to it and doubtlessly increased its readership immensely. Its fame has been its shame from a feminist point of view.

A good case could probably be made for Flaubert's contempt for women being much greater than that for men. His central victimized character in *Madame Bovary* is a woman and the male characters who surround her are generally less contemptible and seemingly less deserving of punishment than she. A look at the way his contempt emerges and how several critics have evaluated his depiction of Emma will suggest that he was not eager to take a concerned approach to women's problems or aspects of their nature beyond the usual set of conventional clichés. In 1857, Charles Augustin Sainte-Beuve said that Flaubert spared nothing to show Emma's despicableness, denouncing her overrefinement as a child and her flirtatiousness as a girl as well as her overindulgence in fantasy.[41] Sainte-Beuve also believes that the author is exceedingly cruel in his depiction of his heroine, that virtue is "too absent" from the book, and that the reader feels more tolerance for Emma than for Flaubert.[42] Indicating that Flaubert's manner is "scientific, experimental, adult, powerful, a little harsh," he questions why he did not write of a woman who, in Emma's place, might have taken on the care of needy children in her neighborhood, becoming a public benefactor. She could have schooled them in practical as well as moralistic matters. Such a woman would have elevated and consoled while broadening one's view of humanity.[43] We can question Sainte-Beuve's placing excessive moral responsibility on women without questioning his point that Flaubert neglected to balance Emma's bad sides with qualities one could appreciate, or failing that, allow another major female character with less contemptible sides to come into the novel. Henry James, who can be credited with understanding depictions of women, also thinks Flaubert left a good deal out of the portrayal of women.[44] Percy Lubbock states that Flaubert has no illusions about Emma but persistently thinks her worthless.[45] Not all critics, however, see Emma in a totally negative light. Albert Thibaudet, for example, said in 1935 that women recognize in Emma "their inner beauty and their inner suffering,"[46] but he fails to recognize that few women of his age, or even of Flaubert's time, could find much inner beauty in Emma because her creator had failed to implant any in her that they could identify with. Thibaudet's remark seems to be made out of little understanding of women's identification with such heroines and out of a vision that stigmatizes women as death dealers possessed with the capacity to destroy themselves and leave a string of hardships in their wake. One would guess that of all the areas where it would be difficult for a male to feel as women feel, the area of female identification with other females would be the hardest to comprehend.

Flaubert's letter to Louise Colet (with whom he was on friendly terms until after the publication of *Madame Bovary* when they became bitter enemies) shows his contempt for women in the aggregate. Flaubert tells of spending an hour watching women at their bath and finding it a "hideous sight." From this experience, he concludes that the human race must have become totally moronic to have lost its elegance in such a manner. "Nothing is more pitiful than these bags in which women encase their bodies, and these oilcloth caps! What faces! What figures! And what feet! Red, scrawny, covered with corns and bunions, deformed by shoes, long as shuttles or wide as washerwomen's paddles." Amidst these ugly creatures are "scrofulous brats screaming and crying." And beyond them are old women knitting and old gentlemen reading newspapers; these look up occasionally as if in approval. The total sight made Flaubert want to leave Europe for the Sandwich Islands or Brazil. "There, at least, the beaches are not polluted by such ugly feet, by such foul-looking specimens of humanity."[47] Flaubert could see lots of the foul, decayed, and putrid here as if he were looking upon that which reminded him of death.

Baudelaire among others seems to interpret Flaubert's relationship to Emma as one of identity and to see his description of her as masculine[48] as evidence of this identity. In view of Flaubert's pervasive disgust with Emma throughout the book, it would seem as likely that in so describing her he is simply sneering at her another time. Masculinity in women has always been subject to ridicule. One should note that the main facet of her masculinity is a strong sexual appetite. Now that we freely admit that women may have as great a sexual appetite as men, we would not label Emma masculine for such a reason. Flaubert was simply using a traditional way to insult a woman, and critics have doubtlessly misinterpreted this fact to mean that he saw himself in Emma or conceived of her as androgynous.[49] Such commentaries need to be held against the stereotypic interpretation of female sexuality that prevailed at the time they were written.

Flaubert does not seem to be able to free himself from his ties to Christianity which makes adultery an abominable crime. Hinting that Emma may be what she is because she does not adhere to the teachings of the Church,[50] he further indicates his distaste for the unbeliever by revealing the mean sides of Homais, the pharmacist, who questions religion. Besides slandering the nearly helpless blind man, Homais might be credited with making it easy for Emma to get to the arsenic. Had Flaubert not thought Christianity had some worth, he likely would not have withheld it from these two. There is no suggestion that Emma will be forgiven in heaven; in fact, her abode is doubtlessly hell since she corrupts from beyond the grave.[51] There is not even a lesson to learn by those near Emma; not one of the persons close to her goes on to profit from her experience. Thibaudet indicates that Emma's death was a damnation.[52] Harry Levin states that this damnation was a "triumph for the community, a vindication of the bourgeoisie."[53]

Obviously, for death by poison to be deserved, Emma must be made despicable. Flaubert manages to do this so thoroughly that this reader has little tendency to identify with her or to see her as representative of the large group that Flaubert doubtlessly thought she represented. We pity Emma but not because Flaubert has helped us by his depiction to do so. We pity her because she lives in a world as hostile and unhelpful to her becoming a total human being as Flaubert is. Already, when less than one-third of the way through the book, Flaubert speaks of Emma as if he stands apart from her in order not to be soiled: she is a woman consumed with desire, hate, and rage. Her dress covers a tormented heart, and a "dark shapeless chasm" is certain to open within her soul.[54] Levin indicates that Flaubert detached himself from those whom Emma repudiated and those who repudiated her.[55]

Emma's life is made up of troughs and waves that grow ever more extreme until finally when her financial entanglements prove too much for her and she has nowhere to turn for help, she goes under, never to surface again. She is almost totally an other-oriented person; all of her private actions are designed to make her public stance more attractive or compelling in order that she may get a hold on those who will satisfy her lust. Drawn back to herself she does, when less mature, have her imagination to propel her into the realm of make-believe, but later, when drawn back to herself, it is to inner passions or deceits which ultimately make her so desperate that she takes her own life. The book is an onrush of events showing her stepping hopefully outward toward fulfillment and then receding back to her miserable self. Flaubert thus locks her in to defeat and degradation from which no amount of wishful thinking on the part of the reader can rescue her.

One gathers that enthusiasm bubbled around her when she first went to the convent school, but soon her whims led her out of the nuns' grip; when she left no one was sorry. Once home, she takes pleasure in ordering the servants around but then grows disgusted with the country and misses the convent.[56] When her mother dies, she shows extreme tendencies to mourn and asks to be bur-

ied in her mother's grave, but her emotions soon subside.[57] Before her marriage to Charles, she thought she was in love, but the
happiness she felt, in imagining this to be so, failed to be actual-
ized in reality.[58] Discovering that Charles is not as ardent in his
passions as she would like, she begins to search for "highs" away
from home. Every return to Charles is a "low" and a premonition
of the final one. The ball at the chateau of the Marquis d'Ander-
villiers keeps her at a higher pitch for some days, but it, too, fades,
leaving only a wistful feeling for a life unlike hers.[59] Sometimes in
her depression, she yearns to live in Paris; at even lower levels,
she yearns to die.[60] At home she wants Charles to be much more
ambitious[61] and imagines him so only to discover him impervious
to change. (Although Charles is not painted as a tremendously
striking person, Flaubert draws our sympathy more to him than
to Emma. Flaubert does not make his dullness or any circumstances surrounding him legitimate excuse for Emma's actions.) She
takes up music, drawing, and embroidery and drops each. She
grows capricious and dares the elements by living with the win-
dows open. She orders dishes for herself and then does not touch
them.[62]

When Emma and Charles move to Yonville, Emma counts it a
new beginning, and there are "highs" here unsurpassed before, the
chief being her association with Léon. Emma's adulterous desires
cause her to soar in fantasy, and she makes attempt after attempt,
each renewed with variety and greater vigor, to attract him, and
at the same time devise new methods, each more devious than the
last, to please Charles and keep him unaware of her stratagems.
As her lust grows for Léon, her hate multiplies for Charles whose
"very gentleness would drive her at times to rebellion." Domestic
mediocrity urges her to wild extravagance, "matrimonial tenderness to adulterous desires." Emma would have liked for Charles
to hit her so she might have a better excuse to hate him and get
revenge against him.[63] She even entertains going to church so that
she can lose her self by humbling her soul.[64]

With the advent of her very pronounced adulterous passions, she
feels pressures on her that seem greatly more out of her control
and cause her troughs and waves to fluctuate much more sharply.
She makes purchases of unneeded household adornments and

clothing, and feels the sting of her extravagance. She feels drawn to her child and then repulses her. When Léon leaves, she becomes even more vulnerable to her passions. When she and Rodolphe carry through a clandestine courting game and finally seduce one another; there has been a series of "highs" for Emma when she has been near him, and "lows" when separated. Realizing that something stronger than herself draws her to him,[65] she is "alive" when in his arms and "dead" at the thought of separation. Flaubert relentlessly propels her to her end. She loses Rodolphe, gains Léon back, loses Léon, and finally finds herself so in debt that she must do something to ward off prosecution and losing every possession she and Charles have. Realizing there is no one who will help her, she takes poison, having finally descended to a level she had thought of many times but never before reached.

Flaubert's novel shapes the reader's reactions on the subliminal level both by the rise and fall of events, each of which parallels Emma's life and death, and by constantly speaking in terms of death. We are not surprised that Emma takes her own life; not only has she threatened to do so but she also appears through Flaubert's chain of events, language, and imagery to constantly be *in process* toward that end. His depiction of her would seem to bear out his claim that every time he looked at an attractive woman, he thought of her skeleton.[66] While at times he does speak of her beauty, it is as an element associated with death, not as a compensatory virtue. Women, sex, and death certainly merge in *Madame Bovary;* Flaubert seems to conceive of the three inseparably.

Flaubert has two references to death in his first chapter and both of these have to do with women. Charles Bovary's mother is "on the lookout" for the death of the old doctor at Tostes whose place she wants Charles to take. Later, his mother finds him a wife ("she was ugly, as dry as a bone, her face with as many pimples as the spring has buds") who is so peevish that she thinks that if anyone returns to see her, this person has come to see her die.[67] In Chapter Two, she dies, freeing Charles to pursue Emma. In Chapter Five, Emma ruminates over the first wife's wedding bouquet which she finds in her conjugal bedroom and wonders what would happen to hers should she die.[68] In a flashback to the years before her marriage, Flaubert dwells on Emma's seemingly feigned morbidity at her mother's death[69] and speaks of Emma's clandestine readings in the nunnery which did not omit death, but rather included scenes of postillions being run down and killed along with their horses.[70]

Flaubert identifies Emma with death in images of the elderly and depraved; the first of these is the Duke de Laverdière, the Marquis' father-in-law. At the Marquis' ball, she notices this old man "bent over his full plate . . . his napkin tied around his neck like a child . . . letting drops of gravy drip from his mouth . . . eyes . . . bloodshot, and . . . hair in a little queue tied with a black ribbon." To show what produces such a sight, Flaubert says he lived a life of dissipation and was involved in duels, gambling, elopements. He had lost his fortune and made his family fearful. Emma cannot get her eyes off this old man who she knows led a licentious life at court.[71]

In Chapter Nine, still in Part One, Flaubert sums up Emma's "progress" with statements on her wanting to die but also wanting to live in Paris.[72] At this point she has plenty of energy to have new adventures, and one side of her wants to do that, wants to go to Paris, but this mood alternates with giving it all up. Flaubert drops the passage just quoted amidst various other wishes, without further explanation. No one is on hand to give Emma any help, psychiatric or otherwise.

In warm weather, Emma has fainting spells. Sometimes on Sundays she is sad and listens to the vesper bells dying away over the fields. She closes herself up, goes all day without dressing, and is careless about her health: she drinks vinegar to curb her weight, coughs, and loses her appetite.[73] In all these small ways, Flaubert portrays her as having an attraction/addiction to things conducive to death or diminishing. She says she has come to love novels that frighten and rush from one breathless moment to another.[74]

Once headed toward adultery in her first association with Léon, agonies begin to merge with sex: passionate desire, exaggerated greed, and melancholy all blend into suffering of great intensity which she makes no effort to put out of her mind. Rather she seeks means to prolong and revive the pain.[75] These comments and others that follow suggest that Flaubert thought of women, certainly Emma, as specimens that remind one of death, or as *memento mori*. With regard to this tendency, note the following where he shows her standing on her doorstep appearing so sad "she looked like a winding-sheet spread out before the door."[76] Another instance of Flaubert's use of the old custom of having reminders of death at hand occurs after Rodolphe has walked out of his adulterous relationship with Emma. Here Flaubert says her soul had drowned in the intoxication of her voluptuousness and become shriveled up "like the duke of Clarence in his butt of Malmsey."[77] Flaubert seems far more carried away with his death/woman imagery than would be necessary if his only goal were to make his ending credible.

Clouds come in black swirls, she carefully stirs the dying embers, her projects to find happiness crackle in the wind like dead boughs, and as "passion burnt itself down to the very cinders," no help comes; night surrounds her and she is engulfed by the "terrible cold that pierced her through."[78] As Charles, the physician, laments that woman's nervous system is much more fragile than man's,[79] Emma becomes ill and refuses help from other doctors. She is "pale all over, white as a sheet; the skin of her nose [is] drawn at the nostrils, her eyes [have] a vague look." When discovering her hair graying, she talks of old age.[80] Like the old Duke de Laverdière, except at the other end of the social scale and closer to Emma's, a frightened and shrunken old lady comes into Emma's view at the agricultural fair, her face more wrinkled than a withered apple.[81]

Adultery with Rodolphe is consummated at this agricultural fair as a result of Emma's prolonged nearness to him, and in less than a page Flaubert creates a woman-sex-death vignette that had become a stereotype in depicting woman in literature, and, of course, a way of limiting her to one function and making her association with death a necessity. This act, which for both Flaubert and most of his readers assumes disproportionate qualities, takes place, as we might expect, when the "shades of night are falling," suggesting diminishment, not fulfillment. Scattered on the ground in luminous patches are feathers of hummingbirds—either, we assume, as they have plucked them from themselves or been dispersed when killed. Something sweet, probably sickeningly sweet, comes from the trees. Emma has "abandoned" herself to Roldophe and momentarily we learn that her heartbeat returns, and the blood courses through her flesh "like a river of milk." Sex as *la petite mort* and as vehicle for procreation are clearly implied, but more clearly in

connection with Emma than her partner. Rodolphe, smoking a ci-
gar, is mending one of the broken bridles with his knife. What
nonchalance! And how handy he is! Once on their way after their
first sexual encounter, Flaubert allows Emma moments of unqualified beauty as if sex could make it flower. On the horse,
seeming slender and upright, her knees against the horse's mane,
her face slightly flushed by the air at sunset, she *is* attractive, but
such beauty is brought about by her involvement with Rodolphe
and Léon, who are vehicles for carrying her downward but who,
unreasonable as it appears to this writer, never equal her in guilt
and degradation.[82]

Out walking one morning shortly after her first sexual encounter with Roldophe, she runs head-on into Captain Binet's carbine
set to shoot ducks. He warns her that she could have been shot,
that she should have called out. With this incident the premoni-
tions of death are stepped up vigorously. It should also be noted
that Emma scarcely has any control over this incident, and the
reader is reminded that, added to Emma's tendencies to destroy
herself, there are the difficulties that chance or fate can bring. The
totality of the death-producing agents working against Emma grows
more and more astounding. The progress downward is made explicit with Rodolphe's rejection, Emma's near attempt at suicide,[83] her brain fever which almost kills her,[84] her mourning her
father-in-law's death, her liaison with Léon,[85] the lapse of his interest, her reading lurid novels with scenes of violence, orgies, or
bloodshed[86] and her spells of crying out that she will be driven to
something desperate.[87] All of these incidents document Flaubert's
obsessive preoccupation with woman in the throes of death and
build a reliable brainwashing device that could make the reader as
tolerant to such a device as Flaubert himself.

Like the old Duke de Laverdière and the old woman at the agricultural fair, the "wretched creature on the hillside" near the end
of the novel plays a significant role in drawing death into focus
for the reader, as well as shows Homais' meanness and total lack
of compassion for the pitiable. Emma first sees him upon return-
ing from a clandestine meeting with Léon: "A mass of rags covered his shoulders, and an old staved-in beaver hat, shaped like a
basin, hid his face." With hat off he reveals "two gaping bloody

orbits" in place of eyelids. The flesh hangs in red strips, and from his eyes flows a congealed liquid that runs down his face. He keeps sniffing convulsively.[88] To speak he throws his head back and lets forth an idiotic laugh. Then his rolling blueish eyeballs rub against his head wound. As he follows the carriages he sings a song Emma hears and will hear again when in the throes of death. When he first appeared before Emma as she was riding along, she drew back with a cry. His song lingered and was so distant and melancholy that it filled Emma with foreboding.[89] Emma is subtly linked with all three of these decrepit people who prefigure her end. At one point Flaubert links Emma with the blind man by describing her as having a diabolical determination in her burning eyes.[90] As D. L. Demorest indicates, he "becomes the incarnation of Emma's Nemesis."[91] Obviously, Flaubert does not limit himself to a few cursory sentences in order to spread the aura of death over Emma's life. In a letter of June 25–26, 1853 he claimed that Emma's death and funeral and her husband's grief would take at least sixty pages.[92] In the Norton edition the number of pages devoted to the period from her request for rat poison to the end amount to only twenty-six pages, but even so, the time spent on Emma's death and responses made to it, is greatly more than Kate Chopin spends on Edna's suicide (in *The Awakening*), where a few pages suffice.

Flaubert takes Emma through one of the most painful of deaths. The fact that she is amidst her people adds to the horror of it, because their response is not casual. She vomits blood, screams horribly, tortures Charles by confessing love for him, frightens her child by frequently wishing to have her near her, and takes communion from the priest whom Homais compares to ravens attracted to the smell of death.[93] Just as her death rattle becomes stronger, the blind man's song reaches her ears from the street and she begins "an atrocious, frantic, desperate laugh," thinking she sees the hideous face of the wretch looking out of the darkness and menacing her.[94] The old fellow has become her mirror.

Flaubert will not let Emma rest in her grave; her effects, negative as they are, persist in Charles' becoming blasphemous, drawing back in horror at the sight of her dead face, sparing nothing to give her a "decent" burial, and suffering the torture of listening to the hammer resound against the wood as her casket is being built. He seems now to imitate Emma in his financial involvements. Every night he dreams of her, but she falls away into decay in his arms. His distress helps bring on his own sudden death. Young Mademoiselle Bovary fares poorly also, coming to spend her days working in a cotton mill.

Emma Bovary surely tops the list of hideous women who stand as the embodiment of all that tradition has deemed evil and at the same time are viewed by some as possessing "inner beauty." Just as early churchmen equated women with sin, Flaubert sees her as a vile contaminator. Other men have shown their hatred of women and depicted them as responsible for undoing others, but few have been able to put this kind of debilitating image of unreason into a "classic" and have so remarkable and varied an audience shelve it among the greats and applaud its virtues loudly.

Albert Béguin states that one of Flaubert's "main qualities is that he suggests more than he says";[95] Sartre states that *Madame Bovary* is "more complete, more total" than life as Flaubert knew it.[96] Béguin's statement indicates the danger of Flaubert's work, that it be taken as more pervasive and universal than its face value presents it to be, while Sartre's statement points to the exaggeration and overstated quality of most works of art; he sees that their concentratedness suggests a greater portion of experience has been squeezed into focus than reality dictates. Both the elevation into a universal and the falsification of reality that such works exhibit do for Flaubert's readers what Emma's readings in the convent did for her: make her reach for what does not exist and in so doing make her go down to defeat.

MAGGIE

Death plays a major role in all literature, but women and men are depicted quite differently when they are subjected to death-producing experiences or to death itself. As has been noted, one of the chief differences is that the sexual side of the woman is far more often responsible for her death than it is for the male.

In writing the tragic story of Maggie Tulliver, George Eliot is quite aware of the differences between the way society looks upon women and men, as well as the differences that evolve in their growth processes as a result of society's differentiation between the sexes. That Eliot did not have Maggie die by other than accidental means perhaps suggests that she did not believe death to be the inevitable result of the female committing adultery, being seduced, or eloping. Certainly, that Maggie's death appears accidental sets *The Mill on the Floss* (1860) apart from tragedies that show death arising from an interrelated number of forces within and without a character. It is true that in the course of Eliot's novel the reader is often made aware of the possibility of death by drowning, but as U. C. Knoepflmacher observes, "Maggie's one act of willfulness, itself blamed on the hypnotic influence of her seducer and on her Tulliver blood, is unrelated to the cataclysmic circumstances of her death."[97]

Rather, Eliot seems to place Maggie in a predicament from which she, as writer, cannot extricate her except by ending her life; not having built a character who is essentially death-oriented, Eliot must utilize a means of bringing her novel to an end which does not arise out of character or situation as it does, for example, in Richardson's *Clarissa*. Reducing Maggie to the level where any choice she makes will hurt others or interfere with her responsibilities toward people who form a part of her past, Eliot chooses to call on a catastrophic natural event to draw her tale to a close, while Clarissa wills her own death not long after we meet her and is helped to bring it about by the people around her.

We know that Eliot had faced a comparable dilemma to the one Maggie faces with Stephen Guest when she formed a liaison with George Henry Lewes, and that she could and did subsequently have a full life and perhaps a great measure of happiness because of this decision. Therefore, it appears that when Eliot does dwell on death, or uses it as a means of extricating her heroine from a predicament, she is resorting to expediency and/or is being urged on more by her desire to create tragedy and perhaps hint at the *femme fatale* synthesis than by a desire to create a character out of her own experience.

That Eliot's efforts bore interesting fruit goes without saying, for in this novel she came into her own as a psychological and sociological novelist, and it stands high on any list of important fiction. Her work is outstanding, even though it feeds the reader's already sharpened susceptibility to the notion that it is futile to allow women's intelligence, initiative, sensitivity, and charm to combine and come to full flower. Even though *The Mill on the Floss* can be called high art, its stature does not negate the opinion that it, like hundreds of other similar and well-known works, relegates women to an unrealistic position in which death continuously hovers near and strikes them down when they are at their peak of accomplishment, thus depriving them of the best years of their lives. Neither does it suggest that Eliot was unaware that books such as hers tended to negate women's achievements. She tells her readers that she is attempting to depict the medium in which her characters move as thoroughly as she is depicting her characters themselves; and she makes it very clear that the medium in which Maggie moves is definitely prone to negate the development of the unusual and talented woman. Having been chastised by members of her own family for her relationship with Lewes, Eliot was well equipped to tell this part of her story from life. Had she stopped short of the catastrophe of the flood, she would have written closer to her actual experience and saved us one more bath in that death hovering unreasonably over women in literature. Her view of the way society crippled women was such, however, that she did not mind our condemning this society as the agent that drove Maggie to the Jakin house beside the river, reducing her to a *level* where angry waters best perform the disastrous act that brings on death, or in other words, perform the deed for which people in Maggie's social milieu had set the stage. Tom dies at the same time as Maggie, but unlike Maggie the reasons for his being in the wake of the flood obviously cannot be traced back to a relationship with a lover.

Clearly, works like this one rarely offer the female reader any incentive to accomplish anything other than the ordinary. This fact is at the heart of my thesis that, until we can bring reason to bear on women's lives, we will go on living in a realm of make-believe that is damaging to the development of strong women.

A look at how Eliot's remarkable heroine is crippled for having been born female, at how society turns its back on her, and finally at how she exists in a death-like atmosphere will demonstrate that *The Mill on the Floss* adds to the pervasive aura of death surrounding women in literature. Eliot's work is perhaps the saddest book ever written about a young woman; not uncommonly, readers weep long upon finishing it. Although Eliot has great sympathy for Maggie and shows us what the world does to women, her picture of this potentially great woman is bound to cultivate in the susceptible reader a sense of hopelessness. The danger zone, of course, lies in the area where the reader begins to conclude that women's lives cannot be other than shrouded in death.

Maggie, the unruly haired, dark-skinned child, is not appreciated by her mother who is "healthy, fair, plump, and dull-witted"[98] or by her blond, exacting brother Tom. In fact, throughout her childhood both mother and brother most often respond to Maggie with condemnation. Family criticism has the negative virtue of teaching Maggie to be sensitive to pain and to inflicting it upon others. Only her father finds her "cute" and "clever." His attention is not marked with any educational plans for her future; in contrast, he would like to see Tom sent to a school that would equip him to become a man of business in St. Ogg's.

We learn early that Maggie is much more quick-witted than Tom, for "he's slow with his tongue . . . an' as shy as can be wi' strangers."[99] Maggie, of course, reads everything she can get her hands on and can "make stories to the pictures" with ease.[100] With keen interest in all that exists around her, almost nothing is lost to her. It is Philip who is first impressed with her eyes which are "full of unsatisfied intelligence,"[101] and only he at this early stage of her life is capable of appreciating her interest in literature, music, and art.

Philip also notes in her "unsatisfied, beseeching affection" a motivating force which prompts many of her actions as well as, at moments, serves as a "wonderful subduer."[102] He is the first to remind Maggie of her duality and to warn her that she cannot hope always to restrict herself to that part of her nature that controls her desires. Disapproving of her renunciation, he tells her, "You will be thrown into the world some day, and then every rational satisfaction of your nature that you deny now will assault you like a savage appetite."[103] He senses that one side of her cries out for love, and another side tells her to subdue these feelings. It takes no very penetrating analysis of Maggie's character to perceive that she, like many other women, cannot integrate her desires with society's expectations regarding the preservation of virtue.

The following passage underscores the essential life-orientation of Maggie's nature: she "was a creature full of eager, passionate longings for all that was beautiful and glad; thirsty for all knowledge; with an ear straining after dreamy music that died away and would not come near to her; with a blind, unconscious yearning for something that would link together the wonderful impressions of this mysterious life and give her soul a sense of home in it."[104] At school she often "wished for books with *more* in them."[105] Her need beyond what she can find in these volumes is "of some tender demonstrative love" which appears to vanish forever from her life when her father dies, when Tom begins his inflexible regimen to pay off her father's debts, and when the family quarrel with Wakem cuts her off from Philip. Sometimes in the midst of these sorrows she fills her vacant hours "with Latin, geometry and the forms of the syllogism," and at moments she feels "a gleam of triumph" that her understanding is "quite equal to these peculiarly masculine studies."[106] But she also passes through long periods of self-denial and renunciation when she tries to stifle her longing "for a full life."[107] Sadness, pain, and attempts to understand her own nature drive her to these periods of denial, which Philip labels a kind of suicide; these periods are consistently alternated, however, with periods of desire and longing.

We partially judge Maggie by the opinions of people who are fond of her; besides her father, Philip, Bob Jakin, and her Aunt Gritty, there is Lucy who, when Maggie is visiting her between stints of teaching, introduces her to Stephen Guest who immediately "falls in love" with her. It is at this point that Maggie is first introduced to "the young lady's life" and learns what it is like "to get up in the morning without any imperative reason for doing one thing more than another."[108] Maggie is not typical, however, for she is "so entirely without those pretty airs of coquetry" which have "the traditional reputation of driving gentlemen to despair" that she wins "some feminine pity for being so ineffective in spite of her beauty." There is "no pretention about her; her abruptness and unevenness of manner" are plainly the result of "her secluded and lowly circumstances." It is "only a wonder" that there is "no tinge of vulgarity about her."[109]

What this all adds up to is a young woman possessing intelligence, compassion, beauty, and a strong need for affection as well as the capacity to make very favorable impressions. Her faults lie in impetuosity (we remember her cutting her hair on the spur of the moment, pushing Lucy in the mud, and later, of course, going away with Stephen) and believing it possible to crush out of her system her own longings for the attention of others. Even though the opposing sides of her nature war within her, her character is sufficiently universal to be widely recognized and given sympathy by a large audience. She has zest for life, candor, and loyalty—all qualities that have great appeal with a diversified audience even though, in Maggie's case, many do not appreciate them.

Eliot proves herself very aware of the female bias that exists in settings like the one in which she places Maggie. Her father not only flaunts his superiority over the wife he chose for her weakness and passivity, but also often repeats that Maggie is "too 'cute for a woman" and that "a woman's no business wi' being so clever."[110] He states that he would never quarrel with a woman who kept her place. He, however, never taunts Maggie as Tom does with "You're only a girl."[111] Unlike himself, Tom says, Maggie will never have much money. She, like all girls, is simply silly.[112] He would not, of course, want her to go without his care; he would "make her his housekeeper, and punish her when she did wrong."[113] Tom's notion of the deficiency of females is so deeply ingrained that he also uses this bias to put Philip in his place by telling him he is no better than a girl.[114] (This is not the only hint in the novel that Maggie is just as "deformed" in the eyes of her detractors as Philip, meaning that these two share talents and understanding but are at odds with many of the conventional inhabitants of St. Ogg's.)

Although a tomboy, Maggie can scarcely compete with her brother at fishing and managing rabbits, but she continually outshines him altogether in comprehending books, paintings, and musical compositions. This capacity becomes obvious after Tom is put in Mr. Stelling's school, despite his expressed belief that "Girls can't do Euclid"; Mr. Stelling verifies his statement with "They can pick up a little of everything, I dare say. . . . They've a great deal of superficial cleverness, but they couldn't go far into anything. They're quick and shallow."[115] Maggie is extremely "mortified" at this because she is led to believe that the "quickness" her father has always admired in her is a brand of inferior-

ity. By having the prattling Mr. Stelling make such pronounce-
ments, Eliot is, of course, criticizing Tom's education, which we
later see to be practically useless to him. When Maggie claims she
will be a clever woman when she grows up, Tom assures her that
everybody will hate her for it.[116]

During Maggie's early years, Mrs. Tulliver seems to have two
preoccupations: caring for household accoutrements (at least in large
part so that they will be in order should anyone die) and grooming Maggie. When bankruptcy takes most of their family possessions, she turns her whole attention to Maggie who now, because
of the saddened state of the household and her father's illness, gives
way to her mother's grooming. Mrs. Tulliver becomes prouder of
Maggie but with some regrets: "It's a pity she isn't made o' com-
moner stuff; she'll be thrown away, I doubt; there'll be nobody to
marry her as is fit for her."[117] The graces of Maggie's mind and
body now feed Mr. Tulliver's gloom, for he believes their de-
pressed state will deprive her of what she deserves.

The Mill on the Floss has little happiness in it; in fact, as Eliot
implies, "the happiest women, like the happiest nations, have no
history."[118] Women have to suffer, or whatever they do is not
worth recording. Eliot does not want the reader to escape the realization that women have a special kind of scourge that is kept in
existence by crippling attitudes.

Maggie is set apart from most of the people around her by being
intelligent, by being less interested in material things, by not
wanting to punish others, and by being deprived of the kind of
attention that her nature craves. Rebelling against making coun-
terpanes for Aunt Glegg, wearing frills, keeping her long black
mane in order, copying Lucy's perfection and fragility, condemning her father as the Dodsons do, being vindictive toward the
Wakems like Tom and her father are—all are signs of the disparity
between Maggie's outlook on life and the outlook of those around
her. From the point of view of most of the Dodson clan, she is a
malcontent who gets herself into difficulties that can only be cor-
rected by punishment. Actually, these "difficulties" arise to a considerable extent from her wish to be kind to those who merit
kindness, such as her father in his weakened state and Philip whose
deformity causes him to have a very lonely life not totally unlike
her own. It needs also to be noted that Maggie's impulsiveness is

often augmented (and thus cultivated) by the insipidness of her surroundings; this insipidity propels her into actions that she thinks will check the ongoing vacuity of existence she faces.

Generosity in this world is frowned upon, and certainly all people, including the poverty-stricken Moss family, must be made to pay every cent they owe. The Dodsons try very hard to pressure Mr. Tulliver into revoking his loans to Gritty who is much in need of his generosity, and Maggie shows "violent resentment" against them.[119] "Everybody in the world seemed so hard and unkind to Maggie; there was no indulgence, no fondness, such as she imagined when she fashioned the world afresh in her own thoughts. . . . The world . . . was not a happy one, Maggie felt: it seemed to be a world where people behaved the best to those they did not pretend to love and that did not belong to them."[120]

She is not even in concord with Stephen, with whom she steals away when most of St. Ogg's believes he is engaged to Lucy. He can claim that the past does not matter, that they should not deny their love; however, he speaks only for himself since his past was by no means as painful and fraught with imagined or real responsibilities as Maggie's. Although Maggie never blames another for what she calls her shortcomings, it is hard not to suspect Stephen of some unconscious trickery in prolonging the time they spend on the water until it is too late to return and prevent her disgrace. Although Maggie's sexual impulses have something to do with her going away with Stephen, a larger measure of her motivation springs from her yearning for a fuller life than St. Ogg's can offer her. It is especially distressing to discover that those who gossip about her can forgive Stephen but not Maggie. Tom claims she is ten times worse than Stephen.[121]

From all corners of St. Ogg's, pity goes out to Lucy who is engaged to Stephen, but there is hardly any for Maggie. Gossip has it that she doubtlessly led Stephen on and that she has come home in a "degraded and outcast condition to which error is well known to lead."[122] Indeed, Maggie's conduct is of the "most aggravated kind" and certain to taint dangerously other daughters of St. Ogg's. Even among those who do not believe all that has been said about Maggie, there is the feeling that since it "*had* been said about her, they had cast an odour round her which must cause her to be shrunk from by every woman who had to take care of her own reputation—and of society."[123] The crowning blow comes when Dr. Kenn, whom Maggie believes will help her, dismisses her from caring for his children because the risk of having his name linked with hers is too great.

Unlike Clarissa, Maggie shows little tendency to prefer death to life. On one occasion after realizing she is attracted to Stephen, she does tell her Aunt Gritty that she is so wretched that she wishes she could have died when she was fifteen because things were so easy to give up then, but she rarely voices this kind of attitude.[124] Rather, she yearns for a more complete existence, and it is the possibility of Maggie's life being taken rather than her wish to die that is kept before the reader by references to the flowing stream and possible floods. Save for a certain amount of masochism in punishing herself, she seems to be action- and life-oriented. What becomes obvious is that, had Maggie been able to pursue the ends she preferred and not been thwarted by forces beyond her, her existence would have been far more positively directed toward living a full life.

In looking at the river which early in the book is so often associated by others with death, Maggie searches for the life that exists in and around, if not beyond, it. It is her mother, someone with whom she is often in conflict, who says "You'll tumble in and be drowned some day."[125] Her mother and her aunts Glegg and Pullet are enormously interested in the state of their possessions to which the younger generation will fall heir when they are gone, and they are much addicted to notions about proper dress at funerals and attention paid to mourning. Aunt Pullet cries in public at the loss of persons who are of slight acquaintance. These matters are of little significance to Maggie whose primary interest is in things that are alive. While Maggie is dark and possessed of some of the characteristics of the *femme fatale*, these aspects are only a small part of her makeup. In fact they may simply be exterior dressing that Eliot sees fit to attach to her, or what we automatically, because of the persistent use of this theme in literature, attach to the dark woman who brings sorrow and despair to others.

Maggie is particularly drawn into the tragedy of her father and his death; because they resemble one another in some ways, his dying prefigures her own to a degree. His life and death, however, form a more integrated tragedy than do Maggie's involve-

ments with Philip and Stephen and her subsequent death by accidental means. Maggie is potentially a much stronger and more
remarkable person than her father, so much more capable of giving to life as well as reaping rewards from her experiences. Her
death seems tacked on as a measure to end a story that has reached
an impasse.

When we remember that even Eliot did not like her ending, that
she was hurried in its composition, we may conclude that she quite
probably also found Maggie's death devoid of reason. It is important to reemphasize that persons in Maggie's world assumed that
women of intelligence were destined to be eclipsed by hardships.
It is just as important to point out that this viewpoint is not Maggie's. Forces beyond her control not only follow her throughout
her life but also determine that she face a natural disaster that
without forewarning commits her to death. Regretfully, we therefore have another work in which a woman is unrealistically linked
with death.

ANNA

Leo Tolstoy's *Anna Karenina* (1873–1876) has been described as
a remarkable portrayal of the many-faceted nature of Russian society and, within that society, of individuals with a diversity of
views. However, it cannot be said to do more than discourage
women who want to participate fully in life. The female as depicted in this work is either primarily a follower, a shrewd and
malicious manipulator, a wife on the brink of exhaustion, or, in
the case of Anna, a suicide. Almost without exception, men exploit women. This is no isolated phenomenon, but, in view of
Tolstoy's reputation, one would hope for a more rounded picture
of woman and something beyond the usual list of clichés about
women that have existed throughout recorded history. After going
into the hollow areas of Anna's personality and obvious sexism in
Tolstoy's novel, it will be illuminating to point out how Tolstoy
turns the positive sides of the "new" woman into negative ones.
An aura that he creates by constantly alluding to death seems to
coexist with an antifeminism that includes little approval or understanding of women's search for greater freedom.

First, however, it needs to be emphasized that Tolstoy frequently presents extremely sexist scenes without comment as to

whether or not he applauds them. Those who seek to extract Tolstoy's own views from his varied and sometimes ambiguous picture of Russian society have, besides his fiction, access to his correspondence and a variety of other writings, as well as the story of his life. However, it is less important to our purpose here to pinpoint Tolstoy's views in any broad sense than to assess the capacity of his works to perpetuate a concept of women that relegates them to a life-denying or crippled existence.

Some writers, on the basis of their convincing presentations, may pull into their camp many readers who would not otherwise be persuaded of their outlook. It is also true that, even if a writer does not share the attitudes of those characters presented in his or her fiction, the picture painted may nevertheless solidify a reader's preconceived notions. Mind-bending can, for instance, even take place when an author has tongue in cheek or is writing satire. Writers may also present patterns of behavior that set in play imitative action and vicarious sympathy. Likewise, even if the writer calls attention to decay in his or her society, the value of this effort may accrue while stereotypes are being filtered into the reader's consciousness. It seems likely that Tolstoy did not approve of much that Anna represented, but whether or not he approved of her, by depicting her as beautiful, compelling, and flexible in her approach to moral issues, he leaves open the possibility of the reader imitating her actions, vicariously feeling her torment, and finally undergoing (or at least contemplating) death for the purpose of getting vengeance.

Tolstoy's Anna, like many women in literature, is created out of the belief that a woman's primary function is to satisfy sexual needs and to procreate. She has many sisters who find themselves criticized if they are not sexual enough and damned if they are noticeably passionate. Tolstoy makes Anna almost totally a creature of passion and then allows that passion to destroy her. After she meets Vronsky, all of her activities revolve around maintaining a loving relationship with him. For example, her studies assist him in his art and later his projects as a landowner, namely founding a hospital and running a stud farm. Still later when she adopts a family, all of her efforts are designed to give her something to do in order that she not be overcome with shame and torment resulting from her passion. Even maintaining her social position is important only as it relates to love.

People who through their carnal instincts work themselves into a permanently helpless state seem dangerously less than whole, or, to put it another way, much that makes up the totality of a human seems missing in such persons. With regard to Anna, D. S. Merezhkovsky says, "We scarcely know what she felt and thought, how she lived—it seems that she did not exist before love: one cannot imagine an Anna who does not love. She is entirely love, as if her whole being, body and soul, were fashioned out of love, like the body of Salamander out of fire, and Ondine out of water."[126] Merezhkovsky also indicates that she never speaks for herself, only for the one she loves, and that passion hides her "intelligence, consciousness, higher selflessness and the unsensual aspects of her soul."[127] We are not given her views on subjects as near to her as raising children, her husband's work, entertainment in aristocratic circles, or the natural setting. We know how she looks; we see her dark hair, her costumes of black, her small white hands, and the way she moves.

Questions about her parents, her past life, and why she married Karenin are not answered. Thus, she is a person without ancestry. She is also ready to throw away parts of her existence in order that she might love. Her attraction to Vronsky causes a split between herself and Kitty just as it seems their friendship might flower into a lasting one. In such instances, circumstances rather than a willed gesture of her own seem to diminish her existence. Filling a stereotypic role, she, as has been the case with women in much of literature, is less than she might be. Even as a mother Anna is that at the exclusion of much else, until she meets Vronsky. Then the experience of motherhood in the case of her son is soon denied her, and later she is not sufficiently attracted to her daughter to make a relationship with her an essential part of her existence. When she subsequently adopts a foster family and becomes especially interested in the young English girl, she seems to be, besides occupying herself to ward off a catastrophic end, trying to recapture a side of herself that is diminishing in the face of her all-consuming love for Vronsky.

Even her clothing limits her. Often dressed in black, she seems destined for death before she actually is. Ostracized by society, she is labeled evil, cruel, vengeful, immature, and unreasonably jealous. All of these adjectives force her into their limitations rather than build an image of a generous give-and-take manner that shows variety and depth of tolerance and understanding. She takes on more guilt and shame than it seems likely any one person could carry. She is said to possess within her the legacy of Eve, plus a portion of cruelty and vengefulness generally assigned to Satan. Early in the novel, before the reader has had time to fully assess the impact of her relationship with Vronsky, it is stated that "Every time the thought of what she had done, and of what was to become of her and of what she should do, came to her mind, she was seized with horror and drove these thoughts away."[128] Here is a woman, carved almost totally from passion and its consequences, thrusting thoughts even of these consequences away from her, leaving much less than a complete human being. Tolstoy likes to show emotion flowing out of Anna; she thus becomes empty of even this aspect of her makeup and is never rounded or total.

Deception, Tolstoy tells us, further multiplies her shame,[129] and it is with a "terrible" sense of guilt that she recognizes her "fault" toward Karenin.[130] No such language is used to indicate that Karenin or Vronsky is at fault in his treatment of her. As with Karenin, her shame is not absent in Vronsky's presence. When she finally tells Karenin of her love, another "terrible" sense of shame comes over her and she is unable to tell Vronsky what she has done. " 'Why did I not tell him?' And in answer to this question a hot blush of shame spread all over her face. She knew what had stopped her, knew she had been ashamed."[131] As her shame increases, she can take refuge only in love; when Vronsky's love dwindles, she is eclipsed.

We are asked to take so much for granted, both as to the stereotypic ways women act and to matters of character delineation, that we have little more than a fast-moving love story in the book that covers a relatively short period of time. Accomplishments or reactions to a variety of situations that would round out Anna's character into a more total human being are not given. It is thus through a narrow and traditional approach that Tolstoy shows Anna to be a victim of the limited artificial upper strata of society. In this society, she manages to move into a very limited relationship with Karenin and finally with Vronsky to a state where no hope is left. Pessimism and finally suicide are from the book's point of view the logical culmination to a life that can be reduced to zero by the removal of a lover.

A closer look at the narrow and traditional approach to women from which Anna develops will further illustrate why suicide would seem to Tolstoy, as well as to most of his contemporaries (and many of ours), the only appropriate conclusion to Anna's life. Although Tolstoy makes it very clear that Anna's brother Stiva is involved in passionate relationships beyond his marriage and seems to utilize his amorous encounters to create the kind of climate where Anna's affair is not unheard of, as well as perhaps to show that there is a generous strain of amorousness in their common blood, he nowhere indicates that Stiva will eventually face any of the hardships that Anna faces. Stiva has few regrets, little shame, not much responsibility, and is the last person in the novel one might expect to have tendencies toward suicide. These siblings are alike in possessing passion but quite opposite in their responses to it. The world they move in responds to them in an almost diametrically opposite manner. Stiva is on the road to a new appointment as the novel ends; Anna is dead. Women are playthings to Stiva, like the "little decanters that were really women."[132] Vronsky is the center of Anna's world.

"Unfaithful" is the word applied to Stiva; "adulterous," a stronger term found much more often in legal jargon, is applied to Anna. Stiva is regretful not for carrying on with the governess, but for having failed to conceal it from his wife Dolly.[133] His children are not very important to him; he never interferes with Dolly's mothering, allowing her to fuss over them as she pleases. He can be away from them for long periods of time, yet, we are told, he needs his home very much, as most men do, for "their home, their wives, are their holy places."[134] So little harm is done to anyone, Stiva says, in having an affair, and "one gets so much pleasure."[135] In order to buy gifts for a woman, Stiva may take all the money there is in the house away with him, leaving Dolly with nothing to pay bills or buy necessities: "Try as he would to be a considerate husband and father, Oblonsky [Stiva] never could remember that he had a wife and children."[136] Tolstoy seems to expect the reader to find Stiva amusing and to experience a bit of a

lark in following him to the end of the novel. Dolly is such a good-
natured soul, she will make out some way, growing less and less
desirable, and continuing to put up with him. We are led to believe that she should be flattered that her husband is found attractive and simply expect him to philander, while she has just about
no opportunities to do so herself.

In contrast to Stiva, Anna is loaded with guilt and shame, unreasonable jealousy, concern for her son, and, when pushed far
enough, tendencies toward melancholy and death. She is restricted
in her activities, and by finding devious ways to meet her lover,
she becomes much more of a deceiver than her brother. Greater
harm (though Tolstoy does not emphasize this fact) is done by Stiva
who neglects his family, which includes six children, for Anna's
son and husband never lack provisions or the security money brings.
Stiva finds easy outlets for sex, while Anna finds little that is easy
in her relationship with Vronsky. Tormented herself, she is taunted
by those around her who, like Tolstoy, cannot allow women the
private or public freedom men have. The message we get in Anna's story is that women simply suffer and their ultimate suffering
is an early death. Reason, which this novel so often advocates as
important, finds little place in the divergent way Anna and Stiva
are presented as spouses, lovers, and siblings. Stiva chuckles through
his encounters; Anna flounders and we are never given sufficient
explanation as to why this need be so, especially for a child born
of the same parents as Stiva. It is hard to think of a place in literature where a more radical difference between man and woman is
exhibited than in this case of Anna and Stiva. We pause over the
severity of the contrast.

Anna Karenina, as much as any work treated here, supports the
notion that women were traditionally viewed as death-oriented.
One avenue for playing down tendencies to see the death-producing or death itself as essential to all women, no matter what age,
might be to have all women marry as Dolly does and, even though
miserable, find one's whole excuse for existence in motherhood
and the home. Anna at first leans in this direction in her relationship with her son. But Tolstoy makes this avenue very unattractive and uninviting. Marriage is a deplorable state where women
who marry lose all their appeal, grow careless of themselves, and
are deceived by their husbands or ignored. Given the belief that

marriage is a sad predicament, it subsequently follows that women may very well be driven into a corner like Anna's and be drawn to kill themselves. Levin does tell Dolly that women who do not marry "can find woman's work in the family."[137] As most would now conclude, she can be reduced to servant status, "woman's work" being mostly waiting upon others. Since most women tend to want to leave the family and marry, or are urged to, they are pushed into either the kind of life Anna has or the one Betty Friedan describes as death-in-life and represented in Dolly. One side of Tolstoy seems to approve of Dolly's way of life,[138] and it needs to be mentioned that at moments he seems to have a macabre interest in or attachment to Anna, but here he vacillates sharply. Both women, however, have vengeful tendencies, and Tolstoy seems to accept the notion that God will repay Anna, at least, for taking vengeance in her own hands. God will bring Anna to destruction and allow Dolly to bear children, have stillbirths, watch her family come to less than they might had they a father to help them out—in other words, be dead to most of the world except that within the province of her own misery. It should be remembered that the book alludes to another woman being beaten nearly to death by her husband[139] and shows Nicholas, despite his interest in making a better life for the peasant, mouthing the threat of thrashing his wife.[140] Misery is even the lot of Kitty, who in many ways comes closer to Tolstoy's, or at least Levin's, concept of what a woman ought to be, because she is extremely capable at tending the dying[141] and goes through a particularly painful trauma of giving birth, an experience Dolly calls torture.[142]

Tolstoy cannot, of course, be said to agree with *all* the notions aired about women in his novel. His reiteration of these notions may help play them down; on the other hand, it may merely make them more firmly established as acceptable. The latter is likely the case when Serpukhovskoy tells Vronsky that women are the chief stumbling-blocks in man's career[143] and that they are always more materialistic than men.[144] We sense here, especially if we are already aware of Vronsky's later predicament when Anna grows extremely jealous and kills herself, that Vronsky is being wised up by someone with authority, someone with "undoubted capacity for reflection and comprehension."[145] Readers may be awed before such "truths" spoken by such an intelligent man. Women, on the other hand, possess no such wisdom. Of Anna it is said, "When she thought about her son and his future relations with the mother who had left his father, she was so terrified at what she had done that she did not reason, but *woman-like* [my italics] only tried to comfort herself with false arguments and words in order that everything should remain as before and that she might forget the dreadful question of what would happen to her son."[146] These and other instances of what we have come to label blatant examples of sexism are startling today. There is also the query, "Why did she have to die?" directed initially at Tolstoy and subsequently to the world she inhabited. We cannot get our imagination to leap from an extra-marital affair to death, but it was surely a much shorter leap for Tolstoy and his contemporaries, and they had less difficulty in seeing Anna's end as deserving. It was shorter for all those, too, who saw validity in the sharp distinctions between man and woman and could watch woman come to death without over-whelming concern.

Tolstoy was aware of women's oppression resulting from in-equality but in this work possessed no vision of what it would be like should this inequality be eradicated. He sees Anna's own de-sire to operate in a nontraditional way as the very essence of her downfall. At one point Pestov speaks to the inequality of husband and wife which allows the former to be punished less severely than the latter for infidelity.[147] The code that Vronsky lives by allows him to lie to a woman but not to a man; in fact deception is out except in the case of the husband deceiving the wife. This fact is not good or reasonable, but it is "absolute."[148] Dolly questions the whole practice of courtship and emphasizes how it works to the man's advantage.[149]

Karenin, who forces Anna to give him her private letters, be-lieves that higher education for women is injurious when it gets mixed with women's emancipation.[150] Obviously, a woman who is educated would stand a very good chance of wanting freedom to exercise what she learns, and it seems Karenin does not under-stand the double bind that women find themselves in: uneducated, they are cramped; educated, they are thought masculine and there-fore condemned. Dolly understands women's situation better when she complains of the education mothers give their daughters.[151]

Kitty loses all interest in women's rights when Levin is near,[152] thus suggesting that women's primary concern is love and making a good marriage. Therefore, by their own automatic inclinations, they thwart change, and if they break their marriage vows, they cannot be other than ruined.[153] We gather from all these remarks that women will have a tremendous battle with society if they step out of the traditional codes. As for suggestions on how women can get beyond these problems, Tolstoy offers none. Kitty is a good but quite conventional woman who is willing to be a slave to her family.

There seems, therefore, to be little evidence in *Anna Karenina* that Tolstoy is not a victim of the stereotyped notion that if a woman chooses to free herself from the codes of conduct established *for* her, she will meet disgrace and ruin. If she chooses to test the waters of freedom and knowledge, she will come either to suicide much as Edna, Emma, and Anna do or to an inner death as Sue Bridehead does in Hardy's *Jude the Obscure*. Certainly, if stepping out of the small circuit set up for them does not bring total ruin, as it does for Anna, it will turn the woman into a despicable imitator of men or somehow relegate her to the shadows. There seems to be a tremendous reticence, on the part of male writers especially, to allow women intelligence and to escape from limited spheres where they possess only sexual power. This fear, of course, helps establish the prison women find themselves in, keeps them from doing intellectual work, and makes them greatly more available for sex.

Much in Anna that we would consider life-oriented is in Tolstoy death-oriented. The very fact that she keeps herself attractive and is the mother of only two children bodes no good for her. She would do better to be like Dolly who becomes unattractive and bears a child almost as often as possible. Unlike Anna, Dolly is not described in images of death. She stays in marriage and can think of no remedy to her problems except the reestablishment of Stiva's attentiveness and love. Anna finds marriage to Karenin exceedingly boring, and, in keeping with her uninhibited way of approaching life, she does not see remaining married to him as a first priority. She does not consider it degrading to be friendly with other men. From our point of view, Anna is the more alive ("She wishes to live"[154]) while Dolly is much more "dead." But Tolstoy makes no such evaluation of the two women and finds that the only "reasonable" way out is to do away with one and allow the other a less than mediocre existence.

While living in Italy and on Vronsky's estate, Anna becomes knowledgeable about art, horticulture, and raising animals. Vronsky finds her a very apt learner and comes to trust her judgment. She writes a "remarkable"[155] book and takes philanthropy seriously. Levin sees her as a woman of "intelligence, grace, and beauty" and possessed of sincerity, simplicity, and cleverness.[156] Levin's estimate of her capacities is later undercut when he thinks of himself as being a bit tipsy when he was so overwhelmed by her talents. Vronsky also knifes her for her intelligence at a time when their quarreling prefigures a near-total break between them. He laughs at her wanting a high school for girls, and she takes his comment as a contemptuous allusion to her intelligence. Tolstoy will not let anyone give Anna unqualified applause. Being thrust into an isolated corner, she has that stripped from her which might have helped save her, that is, her intelligence. She herself, as we have indicated, undercuts her own efforts by acting solely for love of Vronsky or elimination of pain resulting therefrom.

Anna is something of a new woman for, besides her philanthropic efforts, she expresses her desire to divorce and not bear more than two children, even though Vronsky wants more. But Tolstoy obviously does not want to applaud her for these inclinations. Her feminism is used against her, and she and her theories have a reciprocal taint. Had Tolstoy seen worth in her inclinations, it seems he would not have associated them with Anna's decline. Actually, Tolstoy seems to paint as cruel a picture of his heroine as Flaubert does, especially in the later stages of her decline, when she proves cruel and vengeful in her desire to hurt Vronsky by her death. To us Anna had far too many potentially positive things going for her to be dispensed with. For Tolstoy death is the logical end for a woman who defied tradition and moved into what we would call a more positive arena. To reiterate, her positive sides help undermine her existence and thus are negated.

The predicament of women is thus clearly defined in *Anna Kar-*

enina: if she transgresses into the active and positive, she is less than if she remains in the trap from which she is trying to escape. Tolstoy exhibits in Anna none of the stamina found in women of our times who recover from a divorce or love affair by going to college, finding a new job, or moving to a different locality. These women would find nothing but discouragement in Tolstoy's Anna. Ample and evenly spaced allusions to Anna's propensity for death, the breaking of Frou-Frou's back, and Anna's affinity with Levin, who thinks much on death, are part of the programmed brainwashing exercise that *Anna Karenina* proves to be. Shrouding women in death, it supports the exaggerated connection between the two.

Anna with all her beauty moves through the book in black; a velvet evening dress, a riding habit, and dark hair and eyes all prefigure her end. When she is first seen, a watchman is run over by a train and killed; Stiva and Vronsky view the mangled corpse as they will view Anna's at the end of the book. Several times in the novel Anna has a terrible nightmare about the railway and an old peasant.[157] Owning to having a skeleton in her closet, we not only catch her implied meaning but realize her brittleness and fragility hidden under an exterior power that captivates. Closely aligning sexual love with death, Tolstoy likens Vronsky to a murderer when they first experience overwhelming passion. He says Vronsky feels as a murderer must feel when viewing his victim. The corpse is like their love as it first flowers. It revolts Vronsky to recall what once had been, and realize how that love must be paid for with shame. Despite Vronsky's horror, however, he is likened to a murderer who cuts the body in pieces, hides it away, and makes use of the gain achieved through murder for his own benefit. Then Tolstoy's metaphor becomes even more explicit: as a murderer might throw his efforts into hacking and dragging at the body, Vronsky covers with kisses Anna's face and shoulders.[158]

Answering those who accuse her, Anna argues that they do not know how Karenin smothered everything that was alive in her;[159] she suggests there are other ways of dying than the one she will later take. Well before the middle of the book, she threatens to take her own life,[160] and once back in the city after spending time on Vronsky's country estate, it occurs to her often that one door

out of her predicament would lead to death. It is with some feeling of satisfaction that she writes Karenin that she is dying at the
time of the birth of her female child; she expresses the wish later
that she had died at this time. After this episode, Tolstoy concentrates more sharply on her gradual drift toward suicide and her
disintegrating capacity to control her person. Disregard for this baby
girl serves to castigate the female sex and is fittingly tied to Anna's
decline.

The episode most often alluded to, however, which seals the association between Anna and death and involves Vronsky with both,
is the death of Frou-Frou which occurs early in the book and is
prophetic of Anna's end and Vronsky's response to it. Frou-Frou
is obviously run down in the race as Anna will be by the train.
Whether we are to assume that both horse and woman are just not
up to the paces they are put through or that Vronsky is totally
responsible for both deaths is not satisfactorily answered. Vronsky
assumes that he ruined the "unfortunate mare."[161] I do not believe
Tolstoy implies that Vronsky also kills Anna, but rather that she
is more responsible for her own death than he is. What is important here is that Frou-Frou's death helps to tell us Anna's will occur, and we thereafter sense its impending occurrence. Both Anna
and the horse are beautiful, take nothing lightly, and are very attractive to Vronsky. The reader's thoughts are on Anna when
Tolstoy writes of Frou-Frou before the race: "Vronsky . . . glanced
at the beautiful fascinating shape of the mare, whose whole body
was trembling."[162]

By dropping back in the saddle and pulling up her head at an
important point in the race, Vronsky breaks her back. Perhaps a
lighter rider or a tougher animal would have prevented this catastrophe, but Vronsky is not a cautious man. Tolstoy is using a
memorable event with some sexual overtones to prefigure Anna's
end, one he probably did not see as degrading to women as we
do. However, linking woman with the animal had been a practice
as far back as Aristotle, without a registered consciousness of the
degrading implications.

A significant link between Anna and Levin is their interest in
death. Allowing that he never stops thinking of death, Levin, while
searching for reasons for existence, finds that death helps make the
pessimistic approach the most viable one. The impending death of

his brother Nicholas is but one of the troublesome occurrences that cause Levin to be preoccupied with death. Anna is not basically pessimistic and would not dwell as persistently on death as Levin does were she not involved with the one major event of her life, her association with Vronsky. Although Anna is not as disposed toward joy as her brother Stiva, she more consistently thinks living to be more important than Levin does. It is especially obvious that Levin and Anna appreciate one another when Levin meets her for the first time and discovers her mental power and attractive aspects. She makes contact with Levin on a number of levels, and as a result, to the contemporary reader, both are bigger people. Later in the novel, we discover that Levin once considered suicide,[163] and he is many times without hope—never quite to the point Anna reaches before throwing herself under the train, but at moments without motivation to go on because what he is doing seems useless. Anna is made to appear less controlled than Levin and thus more prone to go through with suicide. As with Stiva, we see the person with whom she is pointedly contrasted to be more capable of avoiding a complete breakup. Again it needs to be stated, however, that Tolstoy does not show Anna's affinity with Levin to be a point in her favor; as noted earlier, we are left thinking that Levin believes his tipsiness has deceived him in thinking her worthy. Although Levin is considerably more distrustful of reason at the end of the novel than he was in the beginning, he has not developed a full-blown philosophy that will alter his pessimism. Neither is he unsympathetic to the staid morality which Anna has found so restricting and Tolstoy exemplifies in bringing about divine justic.

In summary, Tolstoy's sex bias stifles his capacity to create in Anna a full human being; her limited portrait is a result of this bias and one which, from Tolstoy's point of view, dictates suicide as the only appropriate conclusion. By remaining blind to the total nature of women, he has constructed a cage for them from which the only escape is an untimely death.

TESS

Virginia Woolf called Thomas Hardy "a gentle and humane soul,"[164] and it is difficult to read any insincerity into his concern for the difficulties humans face. Always, his object is to put before the reader individuals beset by inner conflicts, troublesome forces in their surroundings, and, beyond these, those controlling powers from on high which may dictate a not-very-savory destiny. His picture of humanity is most often a dark one, and he shows victims subjected to demoralization or death, thus making cruelty and suffering the substance of his study. He seems, however, to sympathize with his characters in an unstinting way, and women are not dismissed casually. His Tess is a memorable example of a woman whose difficulties arise when she is used by persons around her and when fate seems to deal her the least appealing hand. Although Tess is not flawless and possesses more than her share of guilt and self-loathing, one senses Hardy's sympathy and humaneness in treating her and is aware of his pleas for the reader's sympathy for her. Unlike Flaubert, his approach to women is basically kind.

In order to elevate his heroine to a level where we sympathize with her, Hardy in *Tess of the d'Urbervilles* (1891) positions people around her who, using her and failing to comprehend her pathos, come off as lesser beings than she. She towers above nearly everyone she meets by virtue of her compassion, her capacity to learn, and her appearance. Alec, who for reasons of prestige has adopted the name of d'Urberville, seduces her and proves himself a total scoundrel; Angel Clare has been pronounced by some as worse. Alec takes advantage of her at a particularly vulnerable age and when she is so driven by guilt feelings toward her family whose stress she believes she must alleviate that she will listen to anyone who might conceivably help her. Getting her with child, Alec "goes off to London" leaving her to handle pregnancy and their child's short life and death by herself. His sadistic cruelty is underscored when he whips his horse into a frightening gallop over treacherous roads while he is taking Tess to his dwelling to care for his mother's poultry. Forcing Tess to hang onto him, he proves his power over his horse as he will soon prove his power over her. She is afraid to do other than sit still as he gives her "the kiss of mastery."[165] When he later finds Tell in the vicinity of Flintcomb Ash, he uses his power to frighten her relentlessly in more subtle ways. By destroying her integrity with her employer and preying upon her inability to help her family, by offering her help which she does not want to take, or by preying on her guilt for not appreciating what he previously has given them, he undermines her will. His most unscrupulous taunts come near the end of the novel when he accuses her of causing him to backslide from his newly found religion, saying she owes him her person in recompense. Trickster and accomplice "of Satan," he at one point emits a "long low laugh," chilling Tess by the ghastly comicality of a disguise he wears in order to more easily intrude himself into her presence.[166] Although his laughter may show his uneasiness at what Tess can arouse in him, she is not the one who manipulates him, but he her. Shades of the monster Lovelace color his depiction.

Angel's priggishness is perhaps even harder to bear than Alec's cruder invasion of her person. Tess' hopes are allowed to grow in the possibility of happiness precisely because of Angel's differences from Alec. Angel appears to be refined and interested in helping Tess become more like himself. Her attractiveness and consideration for him, as well as her farm skills which he is attempting to gain himself, first gain his attention, and the knowledge of her reputable ancestry causes him to overcome any obstacles that he or his pious family might pose to thwart marriage. Discovering a short time after their marriage, however, that Tess is not the virgin dairy maid he had thought, he rejects her. Unable to mark Tess' misadventure with Alec up as the victimization of her as a child, he not only proves his morality spurious but also that of his family whose teachings still influence him (although he likes to think they do not). Angel will have to suffer immeasurably before he can recognize his mistake. Hardy perhaps sees Alec as the greater villain since he does not allow him to live, let alone change for the better as Angel is allowed to do. Beyond the span of the novel, Angel will presumably have a purposeful existence, if a greatly more saddened one, as a result of Tess' fate and his part in helping make her miserable.

Other characters in the novel who use Tess include her mother, Joan Durbeyfield, who constantly hopes for a marriage for Tess that will bring influence and material assistance to the family. Joan puts Tess forward in her best dress to attract Alec and condemns her sharply when she, out of conscience's sake, tells Angel of her seduction by Alec. Calling Tess a fool, Joan bemoans what will happen to the family since she has proved so unthoughtful as to reveal her past.[167] Tess' father is less outspoken, but his drinking and inability to work, plus his desire to have Tess reclaim their ancestry, spell a vulnerability that weighs heavily on Tess. The other children in this poor and unpredictable household look to Tess for leadership and support.

In search of new employment after Angel leaves her, Tess runs into a "well-to-do boor" who responds to her negatively because of a past experience with Angel,[168] and later she fears she will be fired from her job because Alec pesters her at work.[169] The dairy maids at the Talbothay farm who are also in love with Angel give Tess a good deal of concern since she in no way wants to hurt them. The preacher in Marlott, in refusing to help Tess give Alec's and her child a decent burial, is hostile and thus closes the door on any help from the Marlott church. Even those whom Tess meets casually, such as the text painter, cause her pain through moral condemnation.

Hardy thus makes individuals the tools of the gods who sport with Tess throughout her relatively short life. Meeting her in her early teens, we again, as in most novels about women, are asked to draw our concept of her from those years between puberty and the early twenties, a time traditionally thought to be woman's most attractive age sexually and one which ignores all the rest of her life. Typically, she goes to her death when she is only approaching the period of life's fullest experience.

Our sympathy for Tess results from her moving at a vulnerable age in circles where there is scarcely anyone to whom she can turn for advice or help. When such persons are available, chance or fate manages to make it impossible for her to call on their generosity. Dairyman Crick and his wife at the Talbothay farm might be disposed to help her, but she cannot turn to them for fear of hurting Angel or because distance separates her from them. One wonders if their practicality would allow for more than meeting the minimal material needs of anyone with Tess' difficulties. Understanding her situation or her scruples may be beyond them. All people in Hardy are tinged with trouble or somehow incapable of giving themselves fully to others; as Tess' younger brother Abraham emphasizes, they are on a blighted star[170] and they are basically alone: Tess was to most only a passing thought.[171]

Fate often plays a destructive role on such a planet as Abraham envisions, and Tess is not exempt from its power. First of all, a better fate than being conceived in the Durbeyfield household would have lifted a good deal of her pain. Second, the destruction of the Durbeyfield horse and cart, hit by a faster vehicle when it is dark and driver Tess has fallen asleep, owes a good deal to chance. The deprivation Tess felt she had brought on her family because of this incident prefigures numerous other incidents that are no less due to the particular moment when they occur. Alec seems to have a way of coming upon her when she is the most vulnerable and least resisting. Her letters do not reach Angel at a time when they will do the most good. Had she found Angel's parents at home rather than at church, she might have melted their scruples and found help there. Had Angel arrived a few days earlier, he might have prevented Tess' final association with Alec and her subsequent murder of him.

In order to implant Tess' character in our imaginations and implement his plot, Hardy chooses to make his heroine what he calls "passive" and possibly not as resistant to destruction as some, to have her undergo several experiences where death occurs, to cause her to reach such a state of self-loathing that she wants to end her life, and to make her finally take another's life. In thus depicting Tess, Hardy misses no chance to call attention to the amount of unhappiness leading to death that is allotted to women and calls on folk ballad, superstition, and myth to bolster his effort. Showing Tess' struggle with mortal and immortal forces, he spells out her defeat, leaving the reader overwhelmed with pity and with nothing to buoy the spirit.

Consequently, from a feminist point of view, this book must be faulted especially for setting up a very close association between its central female character and death. Although Hardy does not seem to be as obsessed with death as someone like Poe, his view of life is such that death must be the final victimization and threats of it constantly a barrier to living fully. Certainly, *Tess of the d'Urbervilles* is no less a conditioner that carves the association of woman and death into our outlook than numerous other works before us which make clandestine sex or adultery the motivation for death or death-dealing experiences. This book merits praise for its sympathy for women, but it cannot be applauded for lifting the prevailing shadow of death from their image.

Some readers find Tess so passive in her responses that she is unrealistic and thus not totally a character with whom they can sympathize. Although my sympathy for her never lags, it is not impossible to see why these readers view her as such, for I think Hardy conceived of her as passive, even if he did not always so convince his readers. Part of the reason some may view her as excessively passive may be that they have never found themselves in comparable situations to those Tess faces and mistake her inability to cope for nonaggressiveness. Problems of poverty, the importance of ancestry and of meeting an Alec d'Urberville may have never been theirs. Tess has had little experience or instruction to assist her in charting her actions; she is often groping her way *through* difficult experiences which sap her capacity to devise or pursue goals, up at least until her final act of aggression against Alec. It is easy to see how simple inability to act could be taken for passiveness. At other times, we find her acting with intelligence and nobility. She is moved by Izz, Retty, and Marian who also find Angel lovable, and she shows no sign of feeling she has conquered where they could not.[172] She does not agree with her mother when she constantly schools her in ways to get the most from situations involving men. She is praiseworthy in her concern for her and Alec's dying infant. She is a dependable worker and learns skills readily. She is capable of love.

It is true that we can find few girls of Tess' age who would so willingly let a parent doll them up for a prospective suitor, even though their interest in the suitor might exceed Tess'. Hardy writes: "And to please her parent the girl put herself quite in Joan's hands saying serenely—'Do what you like with me, mother.' "[173] Tess lives in an era when obedience to parents was much more a reality than we recognize, and, of course, she feels extremely obligated to her parents after having been involved in the death of their main means of livelihood, a horse. Even so, the fact that Hardy makes Tess passive in this instance does not seem totally consistent with her strength as a worker at a not-too-distant time. She also has the most responsible position among her siblings, that of the oldest, which often makes for a strong personality. Moreover, in view of her later job responsibilities and capacity to think and act, her allowing her mother to so adorn her seems inconsistent with her more positive and active sides.

Hardy's novel necessitates the depiction of a woman who can

be acted upon to an extreme degree, and he has written with an eye on working out a plot rather than a sufficiently consistent Tess. Other instances of her passivity from the modern viewpoint occur when, as she leaves Trantridge after being seduced by Alec, she allows him to kiss her. After saying in response to her seduction, "I didn't understand your meaning till it was too late," she allows him "though she were nearly unconscious of what he did" to kiss her on each cheek. After the first kiss, she "turned her head in the same passive way, as one might turn at the request of a sketcher or hairdresser" for the other one.[174] Later when about to be married to Angel, she overcomes her reticence at allowing her past to thwart her, drifts alone without will, and passively responds to "all things her lover suggested."[175]

Hardy seems very determined to make Tess passive, even using the word to describe her actions several times. He might have emphasized this quality in order to support the notion that a residue of passiveness is building up that will finally erupt like a volcano into an act over which she has little control, that of killing Alec. Hardy makes a mistake, however, in defining Tess as passive in such an unqualified manner. His plot demands are met at the expense of creating a totally realistic woman. *Numb* would be a better word to describe the state a woman finds herself in after experiences like the ones Tess has when she is recovering from the effects of the accident with the horse and from Alec's seduction. Hardy's use of the word *unconscious* in connection with the latter experience aligns it more with numbness than passivity. Love may also have its numbing effects as it overwhelms her for the first time when Angel grows attentive to her. Perhaps Hardy is not totally capable of understanding the kind of responses women make to seduction and desertion; he may mistake an incapacity to respond as passiveness when it may be a reaction made in shock, or a numbing one.

In Tess Hardy gives us yet another portrait, claimed by many to possess universality, in which woman is *defined* as passive. Thus, we have another stereotype that needs to be eradicated and made to be less of an inevitable destiny for women. In other works, we find passivity is often a preliminary to death, the most passive of all experiences; women who remain inactive are often referred to imagistically as dead. This does not, however, explain Tess. In one

of our first encounters with her, she is dancing. This action and
the life-orientation it suggests are severely numbed by the world
into which she soon moves. Passiveness seems to be a quality more
often emerging from within. Tess does not possess this inner quality
as Hardy has for the most part fashioned her. As is often the case,
a character may fluctuate between action and passivity, but Tess'
personality does not show this tendency to a marked degree. Dif-
ficult-to-alter manipulation by others seems to be a stronger factor
in her responses than emotions arising out of a passive nature. Tess
does talk back to Alec and strikes him on one occasion; these actions do not indicate passivity but growth for a normal woman
who is becoming wise or awakened to her torturers. Hardy needs
to exhibit passiveness consistently rather than use the word de-
scriptively if his intent is to develop a consistently passive Tess.
As is often the case, he may have concluded too quickly that most
women are passive and that he need not extend himself in depicting her.

In view of Hardy's concentration on the victim and the victimizers, one might conclude that his book is a study in cruelty, that
cruelty is his major theme. Subsidiary to this theme are problems
of economy, religion, and rural life, but death overtaking the living in the cruelest circumstances serves as an umbrella over all of
these concerns. The central character's gradual diminishment to
death not only prefigures other problems and cruelties, but also
sets up a pervasive symbol of the victim even as it gives substance
to the author's personal concern, that of the cruelty meted out to
women. By making his major theme hinge on the cruelty inflicted
upon Tess, he can speak broadly to a generally pessimistic attitude
toward life, as well as to specific issues. Using women as symbols
is one of the spurs to lumping them together into a stereotype
founded on tradition rather than on reason, and thus molding our
concepts in a disproportionate way.

Fulfilling this stereotypic role, Tess is Hardy's main vehicle for
developing his major theme. He offers us a dense concentrate of
cruelty by showing animals as well as people in extreme pain and
by making death and thoughts of suicide inevitable for certain of
his characters. Though Tess' frame of mind improves a great deal
at the Talbothay farm, she never experiences pure joy. The varying shades of pain she experiences provide the kind of underpin-

nings Hardy finds necessary for developing his major theme, but he is not content with depicting her pain only; her world mirrors her as she mirrors it. The horse's blood which Tess tries without success to stanch runs parallel to that shed in the extermination of the rabbits, hares, snakes, rats, and mice that are surrounded and beaten to death by the harvesters after the mowing machine has driven them into a circle where they are trapped;[176] to that of the pheasants which Tess finds struggling after having been mutilated, driven into a corner, and abandoned (she is prompted to put them gently out of their misery);[177] to that of the rat-catching experience she must undergo in her semi-exhausted state with Alec looking on;[178] to her slapping Alec with her field glove and making his lip bleed;[179] and even to her finding a bloodied butcher paper on the day she attempts to secure help from Angel's parents.[180] Blood is not a new sight when she opens Alec's veins with a knife at the end, causing his blood to soak through to a lower ceiling in the inn where she has stayed with him. The author has woven an elaborate texture which often makes specific the hurtful act, and his fabric includes and reflects Tess.

Death touches Tess' life numerous times before it becomes her own preoccupation. The early death of two of Tess' siblings, of her and Alec's child, of her father, and the threat of death for her mother give reality to this experience, as do the death of Alec's mother and Retty's attempt at suicide when she cannot bear Angel and Tess' marriage and departure from the Talbothay dairy. Tess is especially touched by Retty's act as she believes several of the dairy maids are more deserving of Angel than she is.

Early in Hardy's novel, the reader learns that Tess blames herself, as no one else does, for destroying the "breadwinner" of the family, the means by which her father can carry on his haggling business. As she stands by the horse's grave, she regards herself as a murderess.[181] Hardy proceeds to burden her with excessive guilt throughout the novel, especially in her association with Angel when she takes on guilt that ought to have been shared. Her belief that Angel's clandestine love affair prior to their meeting will make her affair with Alec more pardonable is short-lived. For almost all of Tess' life, with the possible exception of the few days before her death, she assumed that men felt no guilt at all, or at least little compared to women. Hating and loathing herself for what she calls

her weakness, she wishes she had never been born after Alec seduces her.[182] At this early point in the novel, there are hints that
nonexistence is a possible way out of overwhelming problems.

Hardy misses no opportunities to clarify his notion that happiness is not to be the lot of women and that death is a factor they
will have to contend with even when happiness may seem to be
nearly theirs. Tess and Angel's wedding, for example, is beset with
ominous signs, from the cock crowing in the afternoon to very
inclement weather. Their conversation wanders to a gloomy story
of a crime committed by a certain d'Urberville of the sixteenth
and seventeenth centuries, a story about a carriage seen by persons
when they are going to die or when they have committed a crime—
Tess can't remember which.[183] Retty's attempt to drown herself
at their marriage suggests that the orientation toward death in the
novel focuses outwardly toward other women and not specifically
on Tess alone. After Tess tells Angel about her past, their es-
trangement is noted: "It was said afterwards that a cottager . . .
met two lovers in the pastures, walking very slowly, without
converse, one behind the other, as in a funeral procession, and the
glimpse that he obtained of their faces seemed to denote that they
were anxious and sad."[184] Before Angel leaves Tess, she is again
preoccupied with putting an end to herself,[185] and Angel in his
distress has a nightmare in which he carries Tess to an empty stone
coffin by her ancestral Abbey and places her in it. The dream seems
to show Angel giving vent to a wish that his "new" Tess will die
and to prefigure the end of the story. Here Hardy allows Gothic
trappings to help him couple woman and death. Tess' search for
family "skeletons" which Parson Tringham and her father so en-
thusiastically supported previously reaches its ultimate pathos when
she is finally brought to the ancestral coffin herself as the most
notable and legitimate representative of the old family. Cautious
after Angel is gone about becoming involved with casual lovers,
Tess diminishes herself by putting on her oldest field gown, by
tying a handkerchief around her face under her bonnet, and clipping her eyebrows. Her desire to reduce herself to less than her
total power as a person is symptomatic of her desire for death on
other occasions.

After Tess' fruitless attempt to contact Angel's parents, she walks
back toward her work place, "her footsteps echoing against the

houses as though it were a place of the dead,"[186] and in one of her vulnerable moments, she hears Alec's voice preaching a sermon "of the extremest antinomian type."[187] It is Alec's corpse that hangs over the last few days that she and Angel have together before the police arrive to see that she eventually hangs for taking Alec's life by stabbing him. Her act was prefigured when she hit him on the mouth with her work glove and drew his blood. She tells Angel that she had feared long ago when she hit Alec that she would be capable of inflicting the deadly wound someday.[188] She is ready for her own death because she does not want to outlive the tender moments Angel has given her during the hours when they are hiding from the police. She is glad to clear away her presence from his life and offer to him "the best of herself" in the form of her sister Liza-Lu. Hardy wants us to recognize her innocence up to the very end, for he reminds us that she has never been cruel: "Yet formerly I never could bear to hurt a fly or a worm, and the sight of a bird in a cage used often to make me cry."[189]

As further support for his thesis regarding woman's fate and in order to broaden his field of vision to include women in the aggregate, Hardy parallels Tess' story with ballad, story, superstition, and myth which suggest the extent of the prevailing situation of which Tess is but a part. Not wanting her to be just an isolated example, he thus makes a statement about all women. In Marlott when she emerges after the birth of her baby, her friends, in singing together, cannot "refrain from mischievously throwing in a few verses of the ballad about the maid who went to the merry green wood and came back in a changed state."[190] When Tess first comes to the Talbothay farm, the cows won't let their milk down; superstition and tale dictate that this phenomenon reflect upon a newcomer's character. The story of Jack Dollop told by dairyman Crick hits close to Tess: Jack deceived a young woman ("as he had many afore") and was made by the girl's mother to promise to make it right with the victim.[191] The story of the d'Urberville coach about a man who "abducted a beautiful woman, who tried to escape from the coach in which he was carrying her off," and who then killed her, or she him, Alec can't remember which,[192] places Tess' story right in the family tradition. Milkmaids, especially in balladry, are always susceptible to seduction, and the rural setting is the most common scene for it. Alec as Satan and Tess as Eve[193] further establish an archetype of long standing and of sufficient universality to burden the many, not the few.

Hardy does not think Tess deserving of the death penalty, and he pities her to the very end, as is made obvious in his saying as she is hanged that the President of the Immortals has now ceased his sport with Tess. She has been played with as wanton boys play with flies, and finally there is no more sport in the game; she is dead. It is as if Hardy is saying, "And such is the lot of women like Tess. The gods control the pain-producing machine and now sadly they've finished off one more." Although Hardy's philosophy is not more unappealing than others which are much further from the truth, by throwing the blame for Tess' tragedy on a world beyond our own he lifts the onus of responsibility from those who brought Tess much of her pain. It drops the core of the argument that change needs to occur among the mortals. He takes us back to the old stance that tells us God simply created women to suffer by making them biologically different from men. That change has occurred in women's lives surely must cancel out Hardy's position and suggest more can be done to enlighten and make the Joan Durbeyfields, the Alec (alias) d'Ubervilles, and the Angel Clares less exploitative.

Hardy deserves honorable mention for his concern for women, even though in *Tess of the d'Urbervilles* he perpetuates some stereotypes about women, the one of most interest to this book being the link between women and death. Tess not only experienced death, but she also lived with thoughts of suicide and was driven to inflict death on another. What is noteworthy about Hardy's treatment is that he never allows the reader to lose sympathy for Tess. She holds his loyalty and ours throughout the book. It is, however, as if Hardy had diagnosed the case with attentive concern and then left us with a tremendous problem on our hands to find a remedy. In Tess' case, all remedies would be too late, and she is denied all but a fraction of her life to work out positive courses of action. Caught in isolation among the unconcerned, mortals and immortals alike, and inheriting a legacy of dread, guilt, and custom that stifle clarity of action and the capacity to find needed relationships, such women cannot expect much more, Hardy seems to say, than what is meted out to Tess. We can only compliment Hardy for handling this old story with gentleness, not for omitting a number of stereotypes or pointing to any realizable remedies or goals for action.

Real life does furnish portraits of women that are as grim as this one of Tess, and there is always a certain value in clearly outlining them. However, the brainwashing effect of having such portraits ground into us over and over in popular and more impressive literature cannot be other than destructive to developing the kind of stamina needed to avoid Tess' feelings of guilt and self-hatred, as well as the catastrophes that propelled her into extreme pain and finally an act of violence.

Tess pleads the case for women by showing what a precarious world they live in. Although Tess comes from the peasantry, she has risen above her beginnings and has claimed the recognition of a reformed Angel Clare who, through suffering, has acquired a stature no longer as hollow as it once was. If Alec had not continued to pursue Tess for his own pleasure and if Angel had not previously grounded his morality in custom and his own priggishness, but rather in his love, Tess might have been able to find a measure of joy and purpose in life. As Hardy says after Tess' seduction by Alec and before she meets Angel: "Let the truth be told—women do as a rule live through such humiliations and regain their spirits, and again look about them with an interested eye."[194] Hardy does realize Tess' potential here and begins to show how it might be realized at the Talbothay farm; Angel and her past with Alec, however, rise to crush her. Hardy knows the actuality of this, feels pity for her, and wants to show us the basis on which his pity rests. Virginia Woolf was correct not only when she said Hardy was humane but also when she claimed that he was our greatest tragic novelist. One needs to remember also that he is elevating Tess to a pitiable and tragic position, a position often reserved for men. All this is true despite the fact that he washes women in death and charges the President of the Immortals with crushing them when powers much closer to home need to accept his charge, recognize inequities, and correct them.

EDNA

Because Kate Chopin in *The Awakening* (1899) builds a narrative in which the death of the main female character at its end does not come unexpectedly, we might at first dismiss it as just another novel that carefully and persistently keeps women's association with death before the reader, at the exclusion of most aspects of life. It does have an emphasis, however, on the importance of women having a full life, an emphasis that causes the novel to look to the future and to push concentration on death aside from the central focus. If death could be extracted from this novel, there would be much, in the delineation of a woman's inner self and aspirations, for persons looking for positive elements in fiction about women to salvage. One wishes Chopin had been able to ignore the demands of an audience who thought Edna's "sins" made her deserving of death and who found compatible that sentimental and romantic tradition which sees marriage or death as the only excusable alternatives subsequent to heterosexual love. Her audience possessed the same outlook as had been in existence for centuries—and is still found in some quarters. As Leslie Fiedler indicates, this audience found suicide far more acceptable than sex: "Death even in a form as shocking to Christian orthodoxy as self-murder, offends the bourgeois mind less than sex."[195]

From the standpoint of modern thinking on women's predicament in the typical family, the problem area of the novel results from Edna Pontellier's growth during the course of the novel, by sorting out and putting behind much that interferes with her freedom, and becoming a many-sided and complete being capable of serious thought and maximum creativity—and all this being negated by her taking her own life in the end. Before *The Awakening* was published, Henrik Ibsen in *The Doll's House* (1879) allowed Nora to walk out of her home without feeling it necessary to cancel her for having done so with death. Although Edna is more complex than Nora, with greater tendencies toward introspection and coming to terms with life, this certainly does not seem a sufficient reason to have her commit suicide and thereby to suggest that living as an emancipated woman is impossible. One suspects Chopin of catering to an audience that frowned on unconventional women and demanded retribution for nontraditional acts associated with sex and marriage. That Chopin wrote a first-rate novel with an enviable style and structure[196] makes it all the more regrettable, from the viewpoint of those who would like to see the association between women and death played down in fiction.

Unfortunately, she did not use her talents to depict women who were able to live with their new freedoms.

Lewis Leary oversimplifies this matter, however, when he states that Edna, "a valiant woman" is "worthy of place beside other fictional heroines *who have tested emancipation and failed*"[197] (italics mine). Edna was definitely a multifaceted person, and a combination of factors motivated her actions. However, one cannot state categorically that she failed at emancipation. She is quite successful at freeing herself of a good many of her chains. In view of Chopin's desire not to be a typical[198] housewife and her own success as a writer and businesswoman, one does not imagine that she felt women of Edna's makeup failed because they had sought emancipation. Rather, Chopin envisions Edna as a complex being who, even with her impetuous nature and tendency to act without forethought,[199] could under different circumstances successfully achieve a freedom many would envy. Chopin attempts to carefully delineate Edna's mental processes and certainly sympathizes with her. Not surprisingly, Chopin's book was revived after being out of print fifty years, for female writers with Chopin's talents are not being ignored at this point in time. But it is the life-orientation of the book, and not the ending, that speaks to us today. Women can live with emancipation, and it need not be a death-producing yoke but rather the opposite. It should also be added here that those who argue that art must deal with death and that no one would wish to tamper with artistic freedom or the capacity of artists to analyze any subject may wish to rethink their arguments in the face of how depictions that limit women to a short life mold the outlook of susceptible readers.

Edna's life-oriented side deserves our attention because women of our time are making parallel efforts. Even though she is addicted to solitude and is concerned with her own self-development and preservation, things a mother traditionally was supposed to subdue or sacrifice, Edna is not without interest in people. Often visiting Adèle Ratignolle, she finds much to discuss, even though this companion is very unlike herself. Adèle is a typical "mother-woman," giving birth to a child every two years and very attentive to her brood, her husband, and the demands of a conventional household. Mademoiselle Reisz's music moves Edna to tears, and when in town she often goes to her quarters to listen to her play the piano as well as discuss openly with her the arts, Robert, and her own future. About Reisz, Chopin says "the woman, by her divine art, seemed to read Edna's spirit and set it free."[200] Raoul and Etienne, Edna's two sons, do not have to press too hard to get her attention. She is capable of telling them a story, and she sends them gifts and letters when she is separated from them. It is not because she is overtly cruel to them that they are not always in her company. They are used to doing without her and have an attractive kind of independence that some of their friends lack. They can pick themselves up when they fall down.

Edna has a hunger for male company that is not satisfied by her husband Léonce who is often away on business for several days or in the evenings is gambling with his friends. He hopes for a kind of security which property, including wife and children, brings to a man who needs a conventional home base to keep up respectability. It is not surprising that Edna welcomes male companionship apart from that of her husband. Edna's sociability includes going to the races and attending and giving dinner parties, although it becomes obvious when she terminates her At Homes on Tuesdays that she understands the shallowness and pretentiousness of much social life.

Edna's solitude is not empty. She admits to descending on the social scale as she has risen in the realm of the spiritual after she begins to spend more time alone.[201] Edna looks upon this spiritual development as one that helps her understand better herself, her relation to larger forces, and what her future is to hold. As Chopin says, it is while alone that she begins "to realize her position in the universe as a human being, and to recognize her relations as an individual to the world within and without her."[202] Alone with only the sound of the sea, she realizes the importance of "inward contemplation" as well as reaching out toward the great expanse before her. As she learns to swim, she feels she will be able to control the working of her soul as she has the working of her body. Clutching for more than surface meaning, Chopin says "she was like the little tottering, stumbling, clutching child, who of a sudden realizes its powers, and walks for the first time alone, boldly and with over-confidence. . . . She wanted to swim far out, where no woman had swum before."[203] The danger of the sea further enhances her self-awareness; being able to rally her "staggering faculties" and return to the land, she grows in the command of her own life.[204] Stripping bare of all clothing near the end of the novel, she gets in touch with her own body and thus another part of reality.

While still at Grand Isle, she begins "to feel like one who awakens gradually out of a dream,"[205] but it is after she returns to the town that she, without her husband even conceiving of such a possibility, feels she is "becoming herself and daily casting aside that fictitious self which we assume like a garment with which to appear before the world."[206] She resolves never to take a step backward. Seeking release from the strictures of husband and home, toward the end of the novel she is able to tell Dr. Mandelet, "I don't want anything but my own way."[207] She becomes much more interested in her art, works with considerable success at it, and finally moves into her own dwelling in order to feel in command of her own self and talent. Unlike Adèle who keeps up with her piano lessons in order to enhance the atmosphere of her home, Edna is a dedicated artist who endeavors to accomplish good work because she believes in its importance and because of its relation to her own personal development. When her portrait of Adèle does not turn out as she wanted it to, she destroys it. Her effort to paint her friend is no lark; she takes it seriously. Edna's interest in Mademoiselle Reisz is due primarily to this woman's dedication to music, but she also listens to her statements proclaiming that one must be strong to move above the level of tradition and prejudice[208] and that it takes courage to be an artist.[209]

Edna's awakening is many-sided and not just in the realm of sex, as many who rejected the novel upon publication thought. Her sexual longing is symptomatic of a much greater, more pervasive, and more generalized longing,[210] which includes becoming sharply aware of her own nature,[211] of her need for solitude and the opportunity to be an artist, and of the removal of the prison-like atmosphere of her own married life. Offshoots of this new awareness become reality in her swimming, walking through town and by the sea,[212] practicing in expressing herself,[213] and proposing a "course of improving studies."[214] She knows there is much in her old life she must give up; hence, she eliminates the Tuesday social hours, spending more time away from home and moving out to the "pigeon" house.

Unlike so many women, she does have the capacity to become awakened, which for her was the process of acquiring a new self, of arising out of a "life-long stupid dream."[215] Even though she realizes life is "that monster made up of beauty and brutality,"[216] she tells Dr. Mandelet that "perhaps it is better to wake up after all, even to suffer, rather than to remain a dupe to illusions all one's life."[217] Edna is not death masquerading as life. Everything about her is alive as she talks to Mademoiselle Reisz, arranges her furnishings in the new house, and paints. She is even alive to the world's needs very near the end when she rushes to help Madame Ratignolle in childbirth. She may lack forethought or be unable to fix strongly on one goal, but she is awake and alive to what goes on around her and, until the end, is interested in her capacity to reshape her life. For Edna being quite alive includes a realization that death follows life.

When Edna comes to the belief that death is the only means available to keep from being overwhelmed by life, she becomes destructive of the positive life-oriented force that has been driving her. She explains that to keep herself intact, she must lose herself.[218] Suzanne Wolkenfeld states that "The vision of life that emerges from the novel constitutes an affirmation of the multiple possibilities of fulfillment, an affirmation made with a clear and profound grasp of the problematic nature of reality."[219] One can agree with this statement even if one must qualify it, as does Wolkenfeld, by giving reasons for Chopin's need to show that Edna cannot rally the forces within or without herself sufficiently in the end to keep alive.

Chopin's attempt to give us a kind of totality that includes life and death, her adherence to novelistic structure and believability, her use of the traditional equating of women and death, and her catering to her reading public dictate the emphasis on death that is found in the novel. As is typical in the treatment of women in fiction, our acquaintance with Edna is limited primarily to the years when she is sexually active. Despite its importance as indicated above, her working life is very much bound up with an awakened sexuality and is not shown to consume as much of her time as reality might dictate. The leap from sexuality to death is obviously one that unreasonably excludes most of what makes up the productive and invigorating years of many women's lives. The book makes it obvious, as do most books dealing with women, that the world of women's work is not a subject that can be endured for long in fiction.

Despite the novel's life-orientation signified by a sexual awakening and the numerous other areas in which a new awareness occurs, Chopin's artistically written novel underscores and perpetuates the link between women and death. More than this, it puts this artistic rendering of Edna's life and her movement toward suicide beside some very important realizations that every woman needs to make. These realizations regarding her oppressed role, the need for self-expression, and her relationship to her surroundings are unfortunately undercut, canceled out, and made to seem unimportant by her death. It is very easy to quickly conclude that they are responsible for her death, although the reasons for her taking her life are obviously greatly more complex than this. Thus, the book is pessimistic and redeems itself only partially in the contemporary feminist's eyes by suggesting that Chopin could point the way to greater freedom and self-realization for women, even if she could not conceive of a woman in her time capable of living such a role and of using freedom once she gained it.

As we have noted in dealing with Clarissa, Emma, Maggie, Anna, Tess, and now Edna, novelists who insist on closing their works with death feel that, in order for this death to seem realistic and believable, they must plant imagery, symbols, and prophetic situations throughout to make the outcome tally with what has gone before. Endeavoring to mold a sound structure, they keep before the reader an aura of death that subtracts from the preoccupation with life and diminishes the reader's capacity to be involved vicariously in the lives of the characters in the work. Critics applaud the concentrated texture of writings like Chopin's that throw into focus an unreasonable emphasis on death, which would not be found in life except in extreme cases of necrophilia such as that, for example, found in Edgar Allan Poe. Both novelists and critics have thwarted the removal of images of death that motivate conditioned responses, responses which feminists would like to see eradicated.

In making the destructive aspects of the sea a major emphasis in the novel and aligning the sea's "embrace" with the soul, Chopin often thrusts death upon the reader before it finally occurs in actuality. On the night early in the book when Edna swims far out to sea, "A quick vision of death smote her soul, and for a second of time appalled and enfeebled her senses."[220] By linking the sea with the meadow of tall grass Edna ran through as a child, the image of death appears to pervade her life from childhood to the time of most of the events presented in the novel.[221] Appearing nearly always together throughout the time spent on Grand Isle are a lady in black and two young lovers; few works of fiction have a more clearly specified link conveyed by symbolic characters between women, sex, and death. At the dinner attended by Léonce, Dr. Mandelet, and Edna's father, Edna tells the story of "A woman who paddled away with her lover one night in a pirogue and never came back."[222] When Edna moves toward greater and greater solitude and those around her (Léonce, Robert, and her children) recede from her immediate surroundings, she gradually nears the greatest isolation of all, death. Her often falling asleep is another premonition of death, as is her interest in tragedians.[223] Like the shortlived sea bird with a broken wing, she is destined to succumb to the water.[224] Edna's moods cause her to be unhappy some days, and there are times when it does "not seem worthwhile to be glad or sorry, to be alive or dead; when life [appears] to her like a grotesque pandemonium and humanity like worms struggling blindly toward inevitable annihilation."[225] In these moments of morbidity, Chopin can fling death over us with consummate skill in passages that subtract from the novel's strong life-orientation. Our response is especially poignant because Edna shows such promise as a "new" woman who will conquer her reticence, oppression, and all that keeps her from being an enviable person. We look, however, for women of her stature who have exorcised death from their systems, become less impetuous, and in some ways more possessed of single and realizable aims. Having all these things, we anticipate that they will also, with the exercise of patience, align themselves with like-minded males and females who will buoy their existence from without. We would have Kate Chopin much less prone to rely on tradition, which seems greatly responsible for the negative sides of her book, and wring other emotions from us in place of those connected with death.

NOTES

1. Dorothy Van Ghent, "On Clarissa Harlow," in *Samuel Richardson: A Collection of Critical Essays*, ed. John Carroll (Englewood Cliffs, N.J.: Prentice-Hall, 1969), p. 57.
2. Samuel Richardson, *Clarissa* I (London: J. M. Dent, 1932), p. 287.
3. Ibid., I, p. 383.
4. Ibid., I, p. 483.
5. Ibid., IV, p. 496.
6. Ibid., I, p. 78.
7. Ibid., I, p. 87.
8. Ibid., I, p. 143.
9. Ibid., I, p. 196.
10. Ibid., I, p. 211.
11. Ibid., I, p. 433.
12. Ibid., I, pp. 438–39.
13. Ibid., I, p. 495.
14. Ibid., II, p. 504.
15. Ibid., IV, p. 386.
16. Ibid., III, pp. 450–51.
17. Ibid., I, p. 172.
18. Ibid., I, p. 150.
19. Ibid., III, p. 399.
20. Ibid., III, p. 206.
21. Ibid., IV, p. 501.
22. Ibid., I, p. 171.
23. Ibid., IV, p. 245.
24. Ibid., IV, p. 306.
25. Ibid., I, p. 205.
26. Ibid., I, p. 145.
27. Ibid., II, p. 53.
28. See Elizabeth Bergen Brophy, *Samuel Richardson: The Triumph of Craft* (Knoxville: University of Tennessee Press, 1974), p. 104 and Mark Kinkead-Weekes, *Samuel Richardson: Dramatic Novelist* (Ithaca, N.Y.: Cornell University Press, 1973), p. 212.
29. Richardson, *Clarissa*, IV, p. 454.
30. Ibid., I, p. 150.
31. Ibid., IV, p. 262.
32. Ibid., III, pp. 476–77.
33. Ibid., II, p. 337.
34. Ibid., I, pp. 151–52.
35. Ibid., I, p. 454.
36. Ibid., IV, p. 535.
37. Kinkead-Weekes, *Samuel Richardson: Dramatic Novelist*, p. 156.

38. Jean Rousset, "*Madame Bovary*: Flaubert's Anti-Novel," in *Madame Bovary: A Norton Critical Edition*, ed. and trans., Paul de Man (New York: 1965), p. 455. Reprinted by Norton from *Forme et Signification, essais sur les structures littéraires de Corneille à Claudel* (Paris: Librairie José Corti, 1962), pp. 109–33.

39. Jean Pierre Richard, "Love and Memory in *Madame Bovary*," Norton Critical Edition, pp. 435–36. Reprinted by Norton from "La Creation de la forme chez Flaubert" in *Littérature et sensation* (Paris: Editions du Seuil, 1954), no page given.

40. Henry James, "Style and Morality in *Madame Bovary*," Norton Critical Edition, p. 346. Reprinted by Norton from *Notes on Novelists with Some Other Notes* (New York: Scribners, 1914), pp. 59–66.

41. Charles Augustin Sainte-Beuve, "*Madame Bovary*, by Gustave Flaubert," Norton Critical Edition, p. 329. Reprinted by Norton from *Causeries du Lundi*, 13 (May 4, 1857).

42. Ibid., pp. 329–35.

43. Ibid., p. 336.

44. James, "Style and Morality in Madame Bovary," Norton Critical Edition, p. 349.

45. Percy Lubbock, "The Craft of Fiction in *Madame Bovary*," Norton Critical Edition, pp. 355–56. Reprinted by Norton from *The Craft of Fiction* (New York: Viking, 1921), pp. 77–87, 88–92.

46. Albert Thibaudet, "*Madame Bovary*," Norton Critical Edition, p. 377. Reprinted from *Gustave Flaubert* (Paris: Gallimard, 1935), chapter 5.

47. Gustave Flaubert, "Letters about *Madame Bovary*," Norton Critical Edition, p. 316. Reprinted by Norton from *The Selected Letters of Gustave Flaubert*, trans. and ed., Frances Steegmuller (New York: Farrar, Straus, and Giroux, 1953).

48. Charles Baudelaire, "*Madame Bovary*, by Gustave Flaubert," Norton Critical Edition, p. 340. Reprinted by Norton from *Oeuvres*, ed., Y. G. Le Dantec (Paris: Bibliothèque de la Plèiade, 1951), pp. 995–1005.

49. Baudelaire, Norton Critical Edition, Ibid.

50. Gustave Flaubert, *Madame Bovary: A Norton Critical Edition*, ed. and trans. Paul de Man (New York: 1965), text of novel, p. 90.

51. Ibid., p. 250.

52. Thibaudet, "*Madame Bovary*," p. 380.

53. Harry Levin, "*Madame Bovary*: The Cathedral and Hospital," Norton Critical Edition, p. 424. Reprinted by Norton from *Essays in Criticism* (January, 1952): 1–23.

54. Flaubert, *Madame Bovary*, pp. 77–78.

55. Levin, "*Madame Bovary*: The Cathedral and Hospital," p. 411.

56. Flaubert, *Madame Bovary*, p. 28.

57. Ibid., pp. 27–28.

58. Ibid., p. 24.
59. Ibid., p. 40.
60. Ibid., p. 43.
61. Ibid., p. 44.
62. Ibid., p. 47.
63. Ibid., pp. 77–78.
64. Ibid., p. 79.
65. Ibid., p. 118.
66. D. L. Demorest, "Structures of Imagery in *Madame Bovary*," Norton Critical Edition, p. 284. Reprinted by Norton from *L'expression figurée dans l'oeuvre de Flaubert* (Paris: Louis Conard, 1931), pp. 454–74.
67. Flaubert, *Madame Bovary*, p. 8.
68. Ibid., p. 23.
69. Ibid., pp. 27–28.
70. Ibid., p. 26.
71. Ibid., pp. 34–35.
72. Ibid., p. 43.
73. Ibid., p. 48.
74. Ibid., p. 59.
75. Ibid., p. 77.
76. Ibid., p. 78.
77. Ibid., p. 138.
78. Ibid., p. 89.
79. Ibid., p. 86.
80. Ibid., pp. 89–90.
81. Ibid., p. 108.
82. Ibid., p. 116.
83. Ibid., pp. 148–49.
84. Ibid., p. 169.
85. Ibid., p. 191.
86. Ibid., p. 210.
87. Ibid., p. 215.
88. Ibid., p. 193.
89. Ibid.
90. Ibid., p. 217.
91. Demorest, "Structures of Imagery in *Madame Bovary*," p. 288.
92. Flaubert, "Letters about *Madame Bovary*," p. 315.
93. Flaubert, *Madame Bovary*, p. 236.
94. Ibid., p. 238.
95. Albert Béguin, "On Reading *Madame Bovary*," Norton Critical Edition, p. 292. Reprinted by Norton from "En relisant *Madame Bovary*," *La Table Ronde* (March 27, 1950): 160–64.
96. Jean-Paul Sartre, "Flaubert and *Madame Bovary*: Outline of a New

Method," in Norton Critical Edition, p. 303. Reprinted by Norton from *Search for a Method*, trans. Hazel Barnes (New York: Knopf, 1963), pp. 140–50.

97. U. C. Knoepflmacher, *George Eliot's Early Novels: The Limits of Realism* (Berkeley: University of California Press, 1968), p. 219.

98. George Eliot, *The Mill on the Floss* (New York: Signet, 1965), p. 19. All references to the novel are to this edition.

99. Ibid., p. 25.

100. Ibid., p. 24.

101. Ibid., p. 192.

102. Ibid., p. 45.

103. Ibid., p. 345.

104. Ibid., p. 250.

105. Ibid., p. 301.

106. Ibid., p. 302.

107. Ibid., p. 321.

108. Ibid., p. 419.

109. Ibid., p. 418.

110. Ibid., pp. 17, 22.

111. Ibid., p. 42.

112. Ibid., p. 46.

113. Ibid., p. 47.

114. Ibid., p. 187.

115. Ibid., pp. 162–63.

116. Ibid., p. 159.

117. Ibid., p. 310.

118. Ibid., p. 401.

119. Ibid., p. 239.

120. Ibid., p. 249.

121. Ibid., p. 507.

122. Ibid., pp. 513–14.

123. Ibid., p. 529.

124. Ibid., p. 472.

125. Ibid., p. 18.

126. D. S. Merezhkovsky, "Tolstoy's Physical Descriptions," in *Anna Karenina: A Norton Critical Edition*, trans. Maude Gibian, ed. George Gibian (New York, 1970), p. 805. Reprinted by Norton from Merezhkovsky's *Collected Works*, M. O. Volf Edition (St. Petersburg-Moscow, 1912), VII: 154–57, 193–201.

127. Merezhkovsky, "Tolstoy's Physical Descriptions," Norton Critical Edition, p. 806.

128. Leo Tolstoy, *Anna Karenina: A Norton Critical Edition*, trans. Maude

Gibian, ed. George Gibian (New York, 1970), p. 136. All references are to the Norton Critical Edition.

129. Ibid., p. 168.
130. Ibid., p. 173.
131. Ibid., p. 262.
132. Ibid., p. 1.
133. Ibid., p. 3.
134. Ibid., p. 64.
135. Ibid., p. 148.
136. Ibid., p. 236.
137. Ibid., p. 361.
138. Ibid., p. 242.
139. Ibid., p. 87.
140. Ibid., p. 83.
141. Ibid., pp. 448–49.
142. Ibid., p. 550.
143. Ibid., p. 284.
144. Ibid., p. 285.
145. Ibid., p. 283.
146. Ibid., p. 173.
147. Ibid., p. 356.
148. Ibid., p. 278.
149. Ibid., p. 246.
150. Ibid., p. 353.
151. Ibid., p. 62.
152. Ibid., p. 355.
153. Ibid., p. 359.
154. Ibid., p. 551.
155. Ibid., p. 629.
156. Ibid., p. 634.
157. Ibid., p. 680.
158. Ibid., pp. 135–36.
159. Ibid., p. 266.
160. Ibid., p. 325.
161. Ibid., pp. 182–83.
162. Ibid., p. 176.
163. Ibid., p. 714.
164. Virginia Woolf, "The Novels of Thomas Hardy," in *Collected Essays I* (London: Hogarth Press, 1968), p. 266.
165. Thomas Hardy, *Tess of the d'Urbervilles: A Norton Critical Edition*, ed. Scott Elledge (New York, 1965), p. 45. All references to the novel are to this edition.

166. Ibid., p. 289.
167. Ibid., p. 214.
168. Ibid., p. 231.
169. Ibid., p. 277.
170. Ibid., p. 27.
171. Ibid., p. 77.
172. Ibid., p. 181.
173. Ibid., p. 40.
174. Ibid., p. 66.
175. Ibid., p. 171.
176. Ibid., pp. 73–74.
177. Ibid., pp. 232–33.
178. Ibid., pp. 277–78.
179. Ibid., p. 275.
180. Ibid., p. 248.
181. Ibid., p. 28.
182. Ibid., p. 64.
183. Ibid., p. 180.
184. Ibid., p. 195.
185. Ibid., p. 200.
186. Ibid., p. 251.
187. Ibid., pp. 251–52.
188. Ibid., p. 318.
189. Ibid., p. 323.
190. Ibid., p. 78.
191. Ibid., pp. 113–14.
192. Ibid., p. 293.
193. Ibid., p. 289.
194. Ibid., p. 88.
195. Leslie Fiedler, *Love and Death in the American Novel* (New York: Criterion, 1960), p. 91.
196. Kate Chopin, *The Awakening: A Norton Critical Edition*, ed. Margaret Culley (New York, 1976), pp. 165, 186. All references that follow are to this edition.
197. Lewis Leary, "Kate Chopin and Walt Whitman," in *The Awakening: A Norton Critical Edition*, p. 199. Reprinted by Norton from *Southern Excursions: Essays on Mark Twain and Others* (Baton Rouge: Louisiana State University Press, 1971), pp. 169–74.
198. Margaret Culley, "The Context of *The Awakening*," in *The Awakening: A Norton Critical Edition*, p. 117.
199. Chopin, *The Awakening*, p. 33.
200. Ibid., p. 78.

201. Ibid., p. 93.
202. Ibid., pp. 14–15.
203. Ibid., p. 28.
204. Ibid., p. 29.
205. Ibid., p. 32.
206. Ibid., p. 57.
207. Ibid., p. 110.
208. Ibid., p. 82.
209. Ibid., p. 63.
210. Ibid., p. 88.
211. Ibid., p. 82.
212. Ibid., p. 105.
213. Ibid., p. 104.
214. Ibid., p. 73.
215. Ibid., p. 107.
216. Ibid., p. 83.
217. Ibid., p. 110.
218. Ibid., pp. 113–14.
219. Suzanne Wolkenfeld, "Edna's Suicide: The Problem of the One and the Many," in *The Awakening: A Norton Critical Edition*, p. 220.
220. Chopin, *The Awakening*, p. 29.
221. To document the notion that the sea symbolizes both life and death, Suzanne Wolkenfeld quotes Kenneth M. Rosen, "Kate Chopin's *The Awakening*: Ambiguity as Art," *Journal of American Studies* 5 (August 1971): 197–200, in her article, "Edna's Suicide: The Problem of the One and the Many," p. 219.
222. Chopin, *The Awakening*, p. 70.
223. Ibid., p. 19.
224. Ibid., p. 113.
225. Ibid., p. 58.

VI

THE DEATH AURA PERPETUATED IN MODERN POETRY

Turning from fiction to relatively recent poetry, we find, among other twentieth-century poets, Wallace Stevens (b. 1879) who speaks with enviable clarity in his "Peter Quince at the Clavier" to the tradition that yoked women to death as a consequence of "slips of virtue." Stevens elevates his catalyst Susanna to the compelling world of the universal, where derivativeness that calls up numerous antecedents is deemed essential. Scarcely becoming a thinking/feeling individual in her allegiance to this universality, she is seen as susceptible to those persons whose company dooms her to shame and death.

Susanna's elders are attracted to her music which plaintively speaks to her spent emotions, bringing on the "noise" of those who recognize her predicament; her actions among the "leaves" are magnified to giant proportions. A few moments in her lover's arms wither her beauty, a thing that is "momentary in the mind." Countering any reader who may puzzle over how anything so beautiful could be so transitory, Stevens assures us that beauty lives even though the body dies. Susanna, however, is in life nothing but beauty; like evenings and gardens, she passes and her music leaves "only Death's ironic scraping."[1]

Elsewhere, Stevens tells us he is dealing with an "ancient aspect touching a new mind/it comes, it blooms, it bears its fruit and dies."[2] In "Sunday Morning," the less erotic prelude to "Peter Quince at the Clavier," Stevens repeatedly underscores woman's giving "her bounty" to the dead. Her beauty is but the child of death.[3] His "Girl in a Nightgown" paints a scene which has "a revolution of things colliding" that finally "burst into flames," again placing woman in the path of death.[4] His theorizing in "Connoisseur of Chaos" that "the pretty contrast of life and death" proves "these opposite things partake of one" does not alleviate the marked stress he places on woman as the symbolic embodiment of what takes place on a vast scale in the world about him.[5] In "Burghers of Petty Death," Stevens broadens his symbol to man and woman who also become part of a greater death, one that is total and devastating. In "Madame La Fleurie," he is back with another lone female, now a cruel queen whom the male knows is "wicked in her dead light" and will feed on him. Here the "black fugatos are strumming the blacknesses of black."[6] Again indicating the ease with which Stevens couples women with things/objects that quickly die is the following: "Violets, doves, girls, bees and hyacinths/Are inconstant objects of inconstant cause/In a universe of inconstancy"—(from "Notes Toward a Supreme Fiction").[7]

Numerous other modern poets closely associate women with death through excessive imagery, narrative, and emotional outpouring. Often love or sex and death are intimately associated in their writings, with direct statement, metaphor or simile, and symbol performing the link. Some poets exhibit a fascination with women from myth, history, or contemporary experience who have died, and their writings are not always tribute. Poets frequently reveal their awareness of the female as killer but less frequently, it seems their desires to kill her. At still other times, some poets picture lovemaking tied closely to war or the extremely violent, and others see women as quite susceptible to death, violent or otherwise. For the most part, female poets do not parrot the old association, but examples can be found of where they do. This chapter shows how the women/sex and love/death linkage penetrates poetry and discusses one poet's suggestion for moving beyond it. The discussion first underscores the poets' prevalent tendency to equate sex or love and death by means of direct statement.

Theodore Weiss (b. 1916) puts it simply in "A Sow's Ear": just call love killing.[8] Ezra Pound (b. 1885) tells of being fourteen and writing the river-merchant's wife to say he has desired that his dust be mingled forever with hers.[9] In Canto VII, Pound, like scores of other poets, sees Eros mingled with Death.[10] Alan Dugan (b. 1923) is as explicit in "Love Song: I and Thou" where, in images of coffin-making, he defines marriage as hell, but a hell he planned and one he will live with until it kills him.[11] Louis Simpson (b. 1923) writes of another male who finds himself in the predicament of marriage, here coupled with the adulteress Magdalene with whom he quarrels much. Finally, however, Magdalene nakedly leaps upon "that narrow horse," exhaustion comes, to be followed by sleep, and "Death" grants a divorce.[12] W. D. Snodgrass (b. 1926) begins metaphorically but jumps quickly to the concrete: blown flowers are as wide as women's faces that will open as casually as stars "or cancer cells."[13] Explicit reference to disease-shrouding women jumps at the reader here, just as caskets and nails do in Dugan's poem and the penis and/or the flying horseman with its death associations do in the passage from Simpson.

William Everson (b. 1912) also uses direct language in "The Narrows of Birth" where he couples the twin compulsions desire and death. He leaves out the father, mentions castrated sons, himself escapes the catastrophic experience he is delineating, and emphasizes only semen and dung as male products, as he throws his focus predominately toward the female. Women prepare rites for killing. They make their victims senseless before the sacrifice, and their deadly ingredients of childbirth include milk, dung, blood, semen, menses, and afterbirth. In their activities, Everson sees passion and death as forces which religion seeks to overcome; the vow of the monk is aimed at delivering him from women's work.[14] Their work, more than that of men, becomes a part of the inexorable force that drives humanity. Everson's graphic description explicitly links women's productive aspects to death.

LeRoi Jones (b. 1934) is likewise matter-of-fact in "Crow Jane" where he speaks of Mama Death and the dead virgin, presumably meaning by the latter the nonvirgin recently deflowered.[15] Robert Graves (b. 1895) in "Sick Love" and "The Blue Fly" also explicitly links seduction and death; in "Sick Love," he appears to allude to Eve's association with the tainted, dark, and easeless. The blue fly's debauchery of the peach in the other poem likewise parallels Eve's "crime."[16]

Other modern poets besides Snodgrass mentioned above, as well as a long line of older ones, make repeated use of metaphors linking women to wilting plants. In "These," William Carlos Williams (b. 1883) tells us that love is a flower rooted in dry ground, and in "The Young Housewife," he compares his subject to a dropped leaf. In writing a tribute to D. H. Lawrence, he speaks of flood waters rising and ripping through a quiet valley trapping a gypsy and a girl who clings to a flowering bush as she drowns. Even when speaking of handling Queen Anne's lace, Williams says that whatever his hand touches makes a small purple blemish; the purity of a flower that has been blighted presents images suggestive of the virgin sullied which is repeatedly found in literature,[17] but should the reader feel that the suggestiveness of the flower imagery used in connection with women is beyond impairing anyone's consciousness, he or she needs only to turn to Vernon Watkins (b. 1906) for a sharper statement.

Working with the old metaphor that parallels people with coins, Watkins manages a precise statement on the death-dealing sides of women and his speaker's way of handling them. He "catches" death from a woman and makes his frustration more obvious than imagist Williams does in his commentary on women who are not as fresh as they have been previously. His speaker in the "Ballad of the Three Coins" gets in exchange a pain in the head, back, and groins. The three women are likened to the Furies, and his state to that of a corpse on midnight escapades and in the pangs of fire. The coins are actually no more like women than Williams' flowers, but they share with them the fact that they can be eliminated, signifying the end to what they represent. Allusions to cuckoldry, crones, and curses are sprinkled throughout Watkins' stanzas which tell of further experiences with the three bad coins. He carries the first, buries the second, and throws the last into the sea. At the end, he questions what he has come to win from death; girding his loins, he can only answer with reference to his swollen feet, his pack on a pole, and his lack of any coins whatsoever.[18]

Theodore Roethke (b. 1908) speaks of woman waking both ends of life in what he has called his favorite poem, "Words for the Wind," and in "I Knew a Woman," the female is the sickle and he the rake.[19] Austin Clarke (b. 1896), like numerous other poets, writes of the dark side of woman in "The Young Woman of Beare."[20] Both of these poets, along with Langston Hughes (b. 1902) in "Sylvester's Dying Bed" where we find a cry for love when the "Lawd" puts out the light,[21] spread the aura of death around love and woman in a direct way by first seeing birth and death as somehow parallel, by connecting woman with the dark and the night, and finally by seeing her as an embodiment of sin, if not a destroyer.

Seeming to echo Wallace Stevens, Stanley Kunitz (b. 1905), in his "A Spark of Laurel," emphasizes that woman strikes a mortal blow; the evidence in support of this accusation includes allusions to Ulysses' experience with the sirens and Agamemnon's murder by Clytemnestra.[22] The past directly underscores the present, and woman becomes the carrier of a club or some death-dealing instrument. Gregory Corso (b. 1930) is bereft of "the bath of life," calling up baptismal and sexual connotations, and he thinks on the heroine of H. Rider Haggard's *She* who was without her lover for thousands of years, much as Corso thinks he will be.[23] Michale McClure (b. 1932) chants about the darker side of women, as did Clarke, with a cry that bursts out with "THE PLUMES OF LOVE ARE BLACK!"[24]

In addition to all these direct statements about women and death or love and death and the many images that show these associations, some poets personify death and time as female. Here the images move closer to an established symbol and take on meaning in an even more generalized way. In some cases, woman is welcomed, but in others, she is a deliberate destroyer. It has been noted in this book that the male is also used as a symbol of death, but that woman is often caught in her prime, whereas the male in at least one symbolic guise, that of Father Time, is at an advanced age.

Walt Whitman (b. 1819) does not see woman as devouring or destructive. In fact, he sometimes has his own mother in mind when he mentions death, or possibly even when he addresses Death as a personified form. Not reluctant to use erotic language, he depicts Death as female and a welcome force. Speaking to a "love, sweet love" who has "sure-enwinding arms" in "When Lilacs Last in the Dooryard Bloom'd," he becomes especially effusive when describing her gentle approach and when asking that she be given signs of sympathy.[25] D. H. Lawrence (b. 1885) in "The Ship of Death" repeats this feminization: Death is gone, gone, he says, but somewhere she is present.[26]

Wallace Stevens personifies the "ever-hooded, tragic-gestured sea" as female in "The Idea of Order in Key West,"[27] and Ezra Pound speaks in the same breath of both a botched civilization and "an old bitch gone in the teeth," offering an exception to the general statement made here that women in their prime are the major target for this kind of personification.[28] In the poetic tradition, old women become crones and are looked upon with more dread than are old men who become comic.

In a memorial poem for Dylan Thomas, George Barker (b. 1913) sees Time or death's essence as female: he mourns "the maternal future tense, Time's mother," and Time whose face is scar-ridden.[29] James Merrill (b. 1926) in "A Timepiece" carries the time symbol into the concrete when he speaks of a woman giving birth as a clock. Taking on the Earth Mother tradition with all its associations with birth and death, his pregnant sister is in pain and enfeebled but will push life out as in death.[30] Gregory Corso in "You, Whose Mother's Lover Was Grass" speaks similarly of the Earth Mother in language of fecundity and death[31] as does James Tate (b. 1943).[32] Robinson Jeffers (b. 1887) in "Shiva" writes of a goddess of destruction who sweeps away everything in her wake.[33] Finally, Roger Bly (b. 1926) in "Romans Angry About the Inner World" very pointedly shows woman as a personification of the affairs troubling Rome. She is destroyed by executioners.[34] This symbolic use of woman traps her within the generalized and stereotypic, just as Wallace Stevens' story of Susanna does, although the fact that Stevens gives his heroine a name, a great deal of beauty, the capacity to be musical, and something of a localized setting puts her in a different category from these abstractions.

Nineteenth-century poets such as Dante Gabriel Rossetti (b. 1828) and Edgar Allan Poe (b. 1809) were especially fascinated with dead women; other poets treat the subject more casually or simply pay tribute to the dead, particularly those who die in connection with startling events, while others dip into myth, where women are killed or do the killing, for their inspiration and/or to exercise their obsession. Still others pick their women out of personal experience, the daily news, or from the billboard.

Even Robert Frost (b. 1874) in "The Witch of Coös," "The Black Cottage," and "The Subverted Flower" shows considerable interest in females responding to death or the death-producing as he writes on subjects that seemingly spring out of his experience or the broader setting where he is. The aura of death and danger where women are involved seems to spur him into some intensely emotional writing. In "The Subverted Flower," the reader awaits impending entrapment and bombardment from the tiger-like male only to be spared both in the end. The beast lopes off without his prey. In "The Witch of Coös," a mother cares for the bones of an old suitor, and in "The Black Cottage," an old woman has died leaving behind many traces of her life but long after the men in her family meet their demise.

John Crowe Ransom (b. 1888) plays the woman/death theme in a more varied way than Frost, ranging from the sincere to the flippant but nearly always with one foot in the traditional. Evidently he is sincerely elegiac in "Bells for John Whiteside's Daughter." In "Here Lies a Lady," however, he speaks lightly of one who died of a fever and chills, doing so with suddenness and therefore luck, that is, a fine funeral. "Blue Girls" has some of the same quality and warns women to "practice" their beauty before it fails. It should be noted here that the *carpe diem* theme that he repeats finds much of its argument in the threat of decay or death. In view of the age at which thousands of women were presented with the argument, it would appear that the threat was quite hollow, since death, even in less healthy times, was often not immediate enough to spook, in a genuine way, the recipient. "Judith of Bethulia" and "Philomela" also reveal Ransom's interest in women of the past who have been involved in violence and death. Judith cuts off Holofernes' head, and Philomela is raped, has her tongue cut out, and finally is turned into a nightingale.[35] The Philomela story, of course, is not lost on T. S. Eliot (b. 1888), who uses it in "Sweeny Among the Nightingales," joining numerous other poets preoccupied with the myth.

Joseph Bennet (b. 1922) is drawn to dead women, and his "To Eliza, Duchess of Dorset" is noticeably necrophilic, macabre, and vindictive. Torture seems appetizing to him, for he pictures her having blood drawn by a spike, her neck punctured by marble claws, her mouth and splintered teeth feeling the black soil as she lies dead. Bennet catches for posterity the screech of agony of the strangling Eliza on the lawn at Knole.[36]

Hart Crane (b. 1899) calls up his grandmother's love letters,[37] and Robert Duncan (b. 1919) speaks of Virginia Woolf's suicide, Desdemona's murder, and Orpheus' claiming his wife from the

dead, all in "An African Elegy."[38] Philip Larkin (b. 1922) draws
on actual happenings, as conveyed by a billboard, rather than dip
back into myth for his horror related to women. "Sunny Prestatyn" is about a poster of a laughing girl dressed in white and
kneeling on the sand. Palms from behind seem to expand from
her legs and branch out to support her breasts. But the winds slap
her until she is snaggle-toothed and boss-eyed; huge tits and a fis-
sured crotch are drawn upon her and between her legs is scrawled
a "tuberous cock and balls." Autographed *Titch Thomas*, her smil-
ing moustached lips are knifed. Soon, however, she is all gone except for a transverse tear, leaving only a hand and some blue. Then
the spot where she was is pasted over with a new poster called
Fight Cancer.[39]

In an account that is almost as graphic, a young girl runs mad
when her pet is killed in "Goose" by Richard Emil Braun (b.
1934).[40] Ian Hamilton (b. 1938) shows a mother exhausted, out of
use, almost loving the grave, and with her husband dead and her
family having deserted her, in a poem called "Complaint."[41]

Interestingly, men seem to write more about women killing
them, at times speaking figuratively but not primarily so, than of
their killing women. In view of statistics showing that men murder their mates more than the opposite, we may question how much
literature reflects real life. Does all this talk of women's murderous intent slip off the tongue as easily as the description by James
Stephens (b. 1880) of a lanky woman in an inn who "nearly killed"
him for asking a free beer of her.[42] Pound is equally ready to use
death-dealing terms when he writes of a woman not true but more
likely to knife or poison him.[43]

Robinson Jeffers (b. 1887) also sees a pale-eyed woman con-
cealing a knife; in his poem "Shiva," mentioned earlier, the female
is killer of everything from good sense to the wild swan.[44] James
Merrill's "Laboratory Poem" shows sadistic cruelty in a woman's
being able to kill turtles for scientific use.[45] William Plomer (b.
1903) writes of a widow whose proximity could kill, and his snakes
in "In the Snake Park," which leave a man in total nightmare with
loss of hope and extreme distress, appear suspiciously like women.[46]
In Stanley Kunitz's "A Spark of Laurel," a woman strikes a mortal blow; Kunitz also alludes to the sirens who brought shipwreck
to Ulysses and his sailors, and to Clytemnestra who murdered

Agamemnon, ending on the union of the mother and mistress motif.[47] Kenneth Rexroth (b. 1905) tells us in "Proust's Madeleine" that his father died of various things like crooked cards, straight whiskey, slow horses, and fast women.[48] Randall Jarrell (b. 1914) in "Women" adds blindness to the list of injuries done men by the sight of female breasts and belly: how can a man go into their fire and "come out living"? In "Thinking of the Lost World," he adds still another tactic: women cause automobile accidents.[49] Delmore Schwartz (b. 1913) in "For the One Who Would Take Man's Life in His Hands" adds Samson's problem to those of Othello and Troy—all these atrocities lie at women's feet.[50]

"Suicide" by John Berryman (b. 1914) seems to contain strong suggestions of impotency for which the wife may be held partially to blame; she finds the male speaker in the poem not adequate and fails to "nurse" him, thereby sometimes making life not worth hanging on to.[51] Robert Creely (b. 1926) in "Naughty Boy" has another wife talking like she could kill her husband,[52] and Jon Silkin (b. 1930) in "The Shirt" speaks of a woman, presumably a wife, whose eye cauterizes and calcifies, here calling up Hercules' being devoured by a shirt given him by his jealous wife Dejanira.[53] Desmond O'Grady (b. 1935) is very direct: his "masculine" woman swears she will kill her husband, plots to do so, and does.[54]

But it takes the horror films to rub in woman's murderous tendencies so that no question of intent is left unanswered. In the poem "Curse of the Cat Woman," Edward Field (b. 1924) has done a good job of bringing together aspects of the perversion of enjoying pain and death inflicted by women. It should be noted, however, that the poem seems to lift its subject matter out of the horror film medium into actual life, for it is prefaced with a stanza stating that the woman *you* fall in love with may be of Transylvanian background and have an affinity with cats. She may turn into a "black panther" and bite *you* to death. She has compulsive needs to claw people, but desiring her gets one in her danger zone so there is no escape. Finally, of course, one night she must be stabbed to death, and she dies with an angelic smile on her face.[55]

Beyond all this talk about literal knifing and contriving ways to get rid of the male, there is woman's capacity to drive man into sin which, of course, brings his ultimate destruction in the hereafter. Woman's vanity destroys men, says Peter Kane Dufault (b.

1923), who then laments God's dooming men from the first moment they lay eyes on women.[56] Dunstan Thompson (b. 1918) likewise thinks a female will not sign off the pangs of conscience: his snake-like woman persistently spells his "failure."[57] He would like to drop his head on a "beatific virgin's breast," though probably there is little chance. George Barker is also troubled with the "double damnation" of love,[58] as is Dylan Thomas (b. 1914),[59] although the reader can never be sure if these statements come from a heart-felt response or are simply the mouthing of the traditional. Sincere or not, the number of such poems is endless and to be expected inasmuch as sex is so persistently equated with sin.

Let us turn now to male expressions of the desire to kill women. In addition to the destructive intent of the speaker in Vernon Watkins' "Ballad of the Three Coins," we have Robert Lowell (b. 1917) allowing a woman to speak of her hopped-up husband, who comes home intermittently from cruising for prostitutes, as a man who might kill her and then pledge never to indulge again. While he is whiskey-blind and swaggers home at five, her only thought is how to keep alive.[60] Robert Duncan writes of a love like a "knife between us," giving mutuality to the image tied exclusively to males in many poems.[61] Dannie Abse (b. 1923) writes in "The Victim of Aulis" of a father who must kill his daughter; the poem is based on the sacrifice of Iphigenia, daughter of Agamemnon and Clytemnestra.[62]

Arthur Pfister in "To a Black Woman, From a Knee-Grow Man"[63] asks a "black bitch" to scream fifteen times in the course of a relatively short but very violent poem. His demands build to an excruciating shout as he bullets statements about the black man's power and the woman being just a good shack. He asks that she give piercing sharp cries, hold her breath, open her frightened eyes, and feel his lance. He will deceive her, he taunts, make her back bloody and sore, and demolish her treasure. It would appear she would scarcely be alive at the end of the poem.

There are probably numerous other instances in which sex seems to be inflicted upon the female in such a way that she appears near death. William Butler Yeats (b. 1865) in "Leda and the Swan" speaks of blows that stagger Leda. She is terrified as she is "mastered" by the brute blood of the swan.[64] Violence in sex where death is actually mentioned or alluded to is best illustrated, how-

ever, by looking at "Tortoise Gallantry" and "Tortoise Shout" by
D. H. Lawrence and "Imperial Adam" by A. D. Hope (b. 1907).
Lawrence's poem is not about people per se, but it does seem that
the implications throughout his works treating animals nearly always underscore the human. In the two poems to be discussed, he
adds passages obviously to pin his thoughts to human sexuality.

The tortoise's gallantry includes dragging at his mate like a dog
would in an "awful persistency." Self-exposure and "hard" hu-
miliation are his lot. He must "crash against her." Calling him a
small gentleman, Lawrence moves into his second poem to delineate the rape but not without asking why one is crucified into sex.
The tortoise's scream in sex is a death agony and a cry of war.
Screams come on in spasm after spasm, and Lawrence thinks of a
frog being caught and swallowed by a snake. He remembers other
creatures from nightingales to cats going through the same agony
and recalls how he ran away from a woman in labor. The poem
seems long on male response but very short on how the female is
responding. After thinking on the agonies of other creatures, he
turns back to the tortoise and dwells on Christ and Osiris whose
death agonies were similar to that of the animal he watches.[65]

Death is clearly associated with sex in A. D. Hope's poem in
which Adam mounts Eve like the beasts do; when impregnated,
she cries in a terrible triumph much like a crack of lightning.
Leaping over nine months quickly, Hope finishes by saying our
number one murderer then begins to inhabit the earth.[66]

From violence in connection with sex, let us turn to associations
between women and the ravages of war, as presented by male poets.
As noted by Dunstan Thompson in "Largo: For William Andrews," women are the practice field for developing the kind of
stamina and daring it takes to be a "good" soldier.[67] Although
Wilfred Owen(b. 1893) believes that a woman's love cannot approach the love of those who die on the battlefield, in "Greater
Love" he paints the soldier's death in terms of the female love crisis.[68] Charles Causley (b. 1917) writes that on recruitment day
soldiers are told they will storm passes and come upon farms where
"bonny lasses" can be ravished. A few lines further he speaks of
death, the bleeding air, and a butcher-bird singing.[69]

Lawrence Durrell (b. 1912) moves into the upper echelons of

the military: in "A Ballad of the Good Lord Nelson" he applauds Nelson for avoiding "self abuse," by having a woman in the bush who is worth two in hand and for now standing phallically stiff in Trafalgar Square to inspire men to treat their women as he did— so not to be frigid and definitely more heroic at the Bay of Biscay. Nelson had practiced his art with Emma[70] making her his slave; his virility, of course, has made for good wars.[71]

W. H. Auden (b. 1907) in "The Shield of Achilles" shows an urchin boy exposed to this same military mentality: he cannot escape knowing about raping girls, knifing others, not keeping promises, or showing compassion.[72] In this poem Auden may have deplored the pervasive corruption, but Thompson is seemingly ready to excuse the warring "hunter": soldiers must seize the moment to make love and not blame their "nameless Eros" for it. It is simply a novelty to surprise the "fawn at end of day."[73] Frederick Mortimer Clapp (b. 1879) goes even further, attributing licentiousness to just being himself. Moreover, mirth is not uncalled for in the soldier's grief; in the face of such "comic" death it is acceptable to make obscene and amusing gestures, as one would, according to Clapp, in connection with birth.[74] In the almost exclusively male world of the military of the past, these allusions to things female again focus on the pervasive triad: women, sex, death.

Stephen Spender (b. 1909) in "The Coward" ties his male experiencing death to an eventuality that started with his mother's nurturing and his lover's embrace.[75] But according to Delmore Schwartz, the soldier often turns to liquor and girls to bolster his courage.[76] Love and war are so commonly linked, Jon Stallworthy (b. 1935) reminds us, that former poets like Wilfred Owen and John Donne knew quite well that in both love and war front dispatches are all important.[77]

Before discussing how a group of women poets deal with love and death, it is important to mention that several poets see women as weak and particularly susceptible to death. J. V. Cunningham (b. 1911) writes of a doe that moved slowly to be trapped.[78] Randall Jarrell points out suggestively that the female pig always returns to her muddy slime.[79] And James Tate seems to be saying something about females who cause their own problems when he mentions girls being inclined to "fall off their porches." But he presents an opposite notion in "Little Yellow Leaf": there a female is "a deathless dream."[80]

In *A Room of One's Own*, Virginia Woolf states that women writers do not dwell on men as males do on women.[81] Among those who might agree with her is Esther Mathews who in one poem divulges that she cannot speak of love.[82] Edna St. Vincent Millay (b. 1892) may also echo Woolf when she says that love is not nourishment, adding that she will withstand death while treasuring life. At another point, she rejects the death orientation when she admits that the beautiful, tender, and kind as well as the intelligent, witty, and brave go to death, but that she is not resigned. In another poem, she forcefully reveals how she will close the door on death as long as possible.[83]

Even Christina Rossetti (b. 1830), whose kinship with her brother Dante Gabriel might lead us to expect her to treat the subject of women and death excessively, asks that no sad songs be sung for her when she is dead.[84] However, Ruth Herschberger (b. 1917), in her love poem called "The Lumberyard," writes of bones on fire that are fed by warmer flames that approach death, and obviously there are many women who have written love poetry of one form or another. The question that needs further study is whether the poetry written by women about men is as tainted with negativism as that which we find men writing about women. We do not sense that Herschberger's speaker will die of her embrace, but rather that the fire will simply diminish, having caused no permanent destruction.[85] There is a strong positive tone here which can also be found in Rita Mae Brown's notion that women lessen death,[86] in Sonia Sanchez's not fearing the night,[87] in Denise Levertov's finding nourishment as she lives and works,[88] in Ruth Stone's wanting to help those in need,[89] and in Susan Sutheim's statements about first finding herself and then those within her private life.[90]

Muriel Rukeyser (b. 1913) in "Ajanta" describes a "real" world to be filled with creation; in this place, only good arises as life emerges silently in the throes of love. The emphasis on the body is without limit, and people enjoy one another. They are told to try to live like there was a God. In this world where everything is whole, everything is what it itself dictates. The speaker, when in this world, can proudly claim completion, but when thrown back into the every day will not be so alive and searching for fulfillment. The reader is made aware of what the poet would like to see evolve.

Some kinds of wealthy women do perfume the air with death, according to Rukeyser, but they must undergo change, for women have to start a new race. In fact, women have to move into the present where there is Sacco, not Sappho. Youth are trapped in a dead vocabulary and need to breathe in experience and breathe out poetry. Women need something to do, something to be. As she is growing up where there is talk of war and atrocities such as the Loeb and Leopold murder, she does not ignore death but rather than intimately tie it to sexuality, she sees it as a reality in day-to-day living. She wants strong peace, delight, and a good that is not simply harness. She does not wish to instigate violence.[91]

Even H. D. (b. 1886), writing earlier in *The Walls Do Not Fall*, can join these women to speak optimistically about her situation: she applauds escape, exploration, and not being intimidated, and she claims that she profits by calamity and can eat her way out finding nourishment while spinning her own shroud—just as the worm does.[92]

Gwendolyn Brooks in "Gang Girls" states that love is a departure,[93] but her emphasis does not reach the love/death equation. Speaking sometimes in the language of destruction, Denise Levertov observes that love cracked her open but that she is still alive to tell of it and capable of breathing and changing pace. In *To Stay Alive*, she speaks to those who go on schedule to kill and inquires if they realize they are being watched by those they destroy. These watchers, who may, for example, have seen their five children die, Levertov explains, will continue and outlive their victimizers, forever keeping eyes upon them.[94]

Another aspect of the woman-death preoccupation that would bear exploration involves Emily Dickinson (b. 1820), Sylvia Plath (b. 1932), and Anne Sexton (b. 1928) who wrote a great deal about death. Plath and Sexton eventually committed suicide. With all three poets, the emphasis on death seems to go deeper, to be extremely more personal, and to extend in more directions than does a flourish linking death to sex or love. Florence Howe states that Plath found being a woman unbearable.[95] Howe's statement quite likely

arises from the belief that the male response to women is not easy
to live with, or useful and applicable in our times, even to the male
poet. Emilie Glen suggests that the woman whom men seek *is*
death. Possibly she is implying that they are on the wrong track
and that there is something off center about their efforts to deal
with reality where women are concerned.[96]

Adrienne Rich (b. 1929) perhaps feels as deeply as most writ-
ers/critics that the male poet has reached an impasse because the
old way of depicting women is crumbling in his hands. Until he
can get beyond his unrealistic and damaging depictions, he will
remain stymied. In answering Galway Kinnell's article, "Poetry,
Personality and Death," she sees in Kinnell's concern for getting
at the essential and therefore universal self, in order *to live* in the
fullest sense, evidence of the need for the male writer "to break
through the veils that his language, his reading of the handed-down
myths . . . have cast over his sight." Rich thinks that he will have
to confront his "closed ego . . . in its most private and political
mode, his confused relationship to his own femininity, and his fear
and guilt toward women." She hopes that we are "on the brink
of a new bisexuality in poetry written by men, which in claiming
its own wholeness" will be able to "greet wholeness in women
with joy instead of dread." In answering Kinnell's pleas for a re-
birth after which poets will become *"more giving, more alive, more
open, more related to the natural life,"*[97] she offers a means for men,
having come to an end of an old way of perceiving women, to
possess a new awareness which will deal not only with traditional
blindness and rejection of women but also with their totality. This
will be part of men's new sensitivity which she thinks will take
them out of their incapacity to transcend self and into a new period of growth.

In "When We Dead Awaken: Writing as Re-Vision," Rich herself proves to be part of an awakening consciousness that is breaking the hold tradition has on women. The sleepwalkers, she says,
are awakening and she finds she is not alone in her efforts to work
back through our past in order to come to a new identity and
knowledge of ourselves. She feels poetry by men reveals pessimism and fatalism which can be erased if they will develop their
own subjectivity and not depend on women for inspiration or assistance. "Where woman has been a luxury for man, and has served
as the painter's model and poet's muse, but also as comforter, nurse,

cook, bearer of his seed, secretarial assistant and copyist of manuscripts, man has played a quite different role for the female artist."[98] Women are shedding the hold men have on them in their
art, and men must seek out a subject matter that will allow women
a voice not only equal to theirs but also as unique as each female
poet is unique in her efforts to define reality.

Before turning to a closer examination of Rich's poetry, which
will reveal her capacity to move beyond an absorption in death
and its connection with sex, it will be well to consider some examples of twentieth-century fiction that underscore points made
thus far in this work.

NOTES

1. Wallace Stevens, "Peter Quince at the Clavier," in *The Collected
Poems of Wallace Stevens* (New York: Alfred A. Knopf, 1961), p. 92.

2. Stevens, "Le Monocle de Mon Oncle," in ibid., p. 16.

3. Stevens, "Sunday Morning," in ibid., pp. 66–70.

4. Stevens, "Girl in a Nightgown," in ibid., pp. 214–15.

5. Stevens, "Connoisseur of Chaos," in ibid., p. 362.

6. Stevens, "Madame La Fleurie," in ibid., p. 507.

7. Stevens, "Notes Toward a Supreme Fiction," in ibid., p. 389.

8. Theodore Weiss, "A Sow's Ear," in *The Last Day and the First* (New
York: Macmillan, 1968), pp. 52–54.

9. Ezra Pound, "The River Merchant's Wife: A Letter (1915)," in
American Literature, ed. Cleanth Brooks et al. (New York: St. Martin's,
1974), p. 1294.

10. *The Cantos of Ezra Pound* (New York: New Directions, 1956), p.
27.

11. Alan Dugan, "Love Song: I and Thou," in *Contemporary American
Poetry*, ed. A. Poulin (Boston: Houghton Mifflin, 1975), p. 97.

12. Louis Simpson, "The Man Who Married Magdalene," in *Poems of
Our Moment*, ed. John Hollander (New York: Pegasus, 1968), p. 261.

13. W. D. Snodgrass, "Planting a Magnolia," in *After Experience* (New
York: Harper and Row, 1968), pp. 53–54.

14. William Everson, "The Narrows of Birth," in *The Postmoderns: New
American Poetry Revised*, ed. Donald Allen and George F. Buttrick (New
York: Grove, 1982), p. 43.

15. LeRoi Jones, "Crow Jane," in ibid., p. 311.

16. Robert Graves, "Sick Love" and "The Blue Fly," in *Collected Poems*
(Garden City, N.Y.: Doubleday, 1958), pp. 84, 285.

17. William Carlos Williams, "These" and "The Young Housewife," in *The Collected Poems of William Carlos Williams* (New York: New Directions, 1938), pp. 136, 361–64.

18. Vernon Watkins, "Ballad of the Three Coins," in *The Death Bell* (London: Faber and Faber, n.d.), pp. 79–83.

19. Jay Parini, *Theodore Roethke: An American Romantic* (Amherst: University of Massachusetts, 1979), p. 145; Theodore Roethke, "I Knew a Woman," in *Today's Poets*, ed. Chad Walsh (New York: Charles Scribner's, 1964), pp. 70–71; Theodore Roethke, "Words for the Wind," in *Verse of Theodore Roethke: Words for the Wind* (Garden City, N.Y.: Doubleday, 1958), pp. 147–50.

20. Austin Clarke, "The Young Women of Beare," in *Selected Poems* (Winston-Salem, N.C.: Dolmen Press, 1976), pp. 6–12.

21. Langston Hughes, "Sylvester's Dying Bed," in *American Literature*, ed. Brooks et al., p. 1641.

22. Stanley Kunitz, "A Spark of Laurel," in *The Poems of Stanley Kunitz 1928–1978* (Boston: Little, Brown, 1979), pp. 146–47.

23. Gregory Corso, "Marriage," in *Poems of Our Moment*, pp. 38–41.

24. Michael McClure, "Mad Sonnet I," in *The Postmoderns*, p. 295.

25. Walt Whitman, "When Lilacs Last in the Dooryard Bloom'd," in *Collected Poetry and Selected Prose and Letters*, ed. Emory Holloway (London: Nonesuch, 1964), p. 306.

26. D. H. Lawrence, "The Ship of Death," in *The Faber Book of Twentieth Century Verse*, ed. John Heath-Stubbs and David Wright (London: Faber and Faber, n.d.), pp. 199–203.

27. Stevens, "The Idea of Order in Key West," in *Collected Poems*, p. 129.

28. Pound, "Hugh Selwyn Mauberley," in *American Literature*, ed. Brooks et al., pp. 1294–96.

29. George Barker, "Epistle I," in *Collected Poems: 1930–1965* (New York: October House, 1965), p. 63.

30. James Merrill, "A Timepiece," in *The Norton Anthology of Modern Poetry*, ed. Richard Ellmann and Robert O'Clair (New York: Norton, 1973), p. 1102.

31. Corso, "You, Whose Mother's Lover was Grass," in ibid., pp. 1253–54.

32. James Tate, "Pity Ascending with the Fog," in *The Oblivion Ha-Ha* (Boston: Little, Brown, 1970), p. 21.

33. Robinson Jeffers, "Shiva," in *The Selected Poetry of Robinson Jeffers* (New York: Random House, 1959), p. 61.

34. Roger Bly, "Romans Angry About the Inner World," in *The Light Around the Body* (New York: Harper and Row, 1967), pp. 9–10.

35. John Crowe Ransom, "Bells for John Whiteside's Daughter," "Here

Lies a Lady," "Blue Girls," "Judith of Bethulia," and "Philomela," in *Selected Poems* (New York: Alfred A. Knopf, 1978), pp. 7, 140–41, 11, 30–31, 63–64.

36. Joseph Bennett, "To Eliza, Duchess of Dorset," in *A Pocket Book of Modern Verse,* ed. Oscar Williams (New York: Washington Square, 1967), pp. 605–6.

37. Hart Crane, "My Grandmother's Love Letters," in *The Collected Poems of Hart Crane,* ed. Waldo Frank (New York: Liveright, 1946), pp. 65–66.

38. Robert Duncan, "An African Elegy," in *The Years as Catches* (Berkeley, Calif.: Oyez, 1966), pp. 33–35.

39. Philip Larkin, "Sunny Prestatyn," in *The Whitsun Weddings* (New York: Random House, 1964), p. 35.

40. Richard Emil Braun, "Goose," in *Children Passing* (Austin: University of Texas, 1962), pp. 14–15.

41. Ian Hamilton, "Complaint," in *The Visit* (London: Faber and Faber, 1970), p. 26.

42. James Stephens, "A Glass of Beer," in *Collected Poems* (New York: Macmillan, 1926), p. 185.

43. Pound, "Homage to Sextus Propertius," in *The Oxford Book of American Verse,* ed. F. O. Matthiessen (New York: Oxford University, 1950), pp. 722–29.

44. Jeffers, "A Little Scraping" and "Shiva," in *The Selected Poetry of Robinson Jeffers,* pp. 457, 61.

45. Merrill, "Laboratory Poem," in *Twentieth Century Poetry,* ed. Malcolm Brinnin and Bill Read (New York: McGraw-Hill, 1970), p. 286.

46. William Plomer, "In the Snake Park," in *The Oxford Book of Twentieth Century English Verse,* ed. Philip Larkin (Oxford: Clarendon, 1973), pp. 347–48. See also "The Widow's Plot: or, She Got What Was Coming to Her."

47. Kunitz, "A Spark of Laurel," in *The Poems of Stanley Kunitz,* pp. 146–47.

48. Kenneth Rexroth, "Proust's Madeleine," in *The Collected Shorter Poems of Kenneth Rexroth* (New York: New Directions, 1966), pp. 320–21.

49. Randall Jarrell, "Women" and "Thinking of the Lost World," in *Randall Jarrell: The Complete Poems* (New York: Farrar, Straus and Giroux, 1969), pp. 327, 336–38.

50. Delmore Schwartz, "For the One Who Would Take Man's Life in His Hands," in *Modern Verse in English 1900–1950,* ed. David Cecil and Allen Tate (New York: Macmillan, 1962), pp. 566–67.

51. John Berryman, "Suicide," in *Love and Fame* (New York: Farrar, Straus and Giroux, 1970), pp. 69–70.

52. Robert Creeley, "Naughty Boy," in *For Love: Poems 1950–1960* (New York: Charles Scribner, 1962), p. 49.

53. Jon Silkin, "The Shirt," in *The Norton Anthology of Modern Poetry*, p. 1281.

54. Desmond O'Grady, "A mad male-hearted woman in a prouder age," in *The Dying Gaul* (London: MacGibbon and Kee, 1968), p. 24.

55. Edward Field, "Curse of the Cat Women," in *Writing Poems*, ed. Robert Wallace (Boston: Little, Brown, 1982), pp. 168–69.

56. Peter Kane Dufault, "Notes on a Girl," in *A Pocket Book of Modern Verse*, p. 612.

57. Dunstan Thompson, "Largo: For William Abrahams," in *Modern Poetry*, ed. Kimon Friar and John Malcolm Brinnin (New York: Appleton-Century-Crofts, 1951), pp. 405–8.

58. Barker, "Secular Elegy III," in *Today's Poets*, pp. 136–37.

59. Dylan Thomas, "Lament," in *The Collected Poems of Dylan Thomas* (New York: New Directions, 1957), pp. 194–96.

60. Robert Lowell, "To Speak of Woe That Is in Marriage," in *Contemporary American Poetry*, p. 229.

61. Duncan, "Passage Over Water," in *The Years as Catches*, p. 5.

62. Dannie Abse, "The Victim of Aulis," in *Selected Poems* (New York: Oxford University Press, 1970), pp. 21–23.

63. Arthur Pfister, "To a Black Woman, From a Knee-Grow Man," in *Human Voice* 30–31 (Homestead, Fla.: Olivant, 1971), pp. 32–34.

64. William Butler Yeats, "Leda and the Swan," in *Selected Poems and Two Plays of William Butler Yeats*, ed. M. L. Rosenthal (New York: Macmillan, 1962), pp. 114–15.

65. Lawrence, "Tortoise Gallantry" and "Tortoise Shout," in *The Complete Poems of D. H. Lawrence* I, ed. Vivian de Sola Pinto and Warren Roberts (New York: Viking, 1964), pp. 362–63, 363–67.

66. A. D. Hope, "Imperial Adam," in *Poems of Our Moment*, pp. 153–54.

67. Thompson, "Largo: For William Andrews," in *Modern Poetry*, pp. 405–8.

68. Wilfred Owen, "Greater Love," in *The Collected Poems of Wilfred Owen* (New York: New Directions, 1963), p. 41.

69. Charles Causley, "Recruiting Drive," in *The Oxford Book of Twentieth Century English Verse*, pp. 492–93.

70. Lady Emma Hamilton, wife of the English ambassador, who according to the *Columbia Encyclopedia* "became his mistress." He may have refused an order to go to Minorca, and he did separate from his wife, Frances Nisbet, on Emma's account. Emma bore him a daughter, Horatia. During an interlude of peace (1802–1803), he lived in the country with the Hamiltons, evidently on friendly terms with the ambassador.

71. Lawrence Durrell, "A Ballad of the Good Lord Nelson," in *Collected Poems of Lawrence Durrell* (New York: E. P. Dutton, 1960), pp. 273–74.

72. W. H. Auden, "The Shield of Achilles," in *Collected Shorter Poems: 1927–1957* (New York: Random House, 1966), pp. 294–95.

73. Thompson, "Largo: For William Abrahams," in *Modern Poetry*, pp. 405–8.

74. Frederick Mortimer Clapp, "Pushed Nude into This Assignment," in *A Pocket Book of Modern Verse*, p. 402.

75. Stephen Spender, "The Coward," in *Collected Poems: 1928–1953* (New York: Random House, 1955), pp. 89–90.

76. Schwartz, "For the One Who Would Take Man's Life in His Hands," in *Modern Verse in English: 1900–1950*, pp. 566–67.

77. Jon Stallworthy, "A Poem About Poems About Vietnam," in *Root and Branch* (New York: Oxford University Press, 1969), p. 50.

78. J. V. Cunningham, "The Chase," in *The Collected Poems and Epigrams of J. V. Cunningham* (Chicago: Swallow, 1971), p. 33.

79. Jarrell, "Woman," in *Randall Jarrell: The Complete Poems*, p. 327.

80. Tate, "Little Yellowleaf," in *The Oblivion Ha-Ha*, p. 24.

81. Virginia Woolf, *A Room of One's Own* (New York: Harcourt Brace, 1957), p. 27.

82. Esther Mathews, "Song," in *A Pocket Book of Modern Verse*, p. 620.

83. Edna St. Vincent Millay, "Love is Not All: It is Not Meat nor Drink," "Dirge Without Music," and an untitled sonnet, in *Collected Poems* (New York: Harper and Row, 1956), pp. 659, 240–41, 206–7.

84. Christina Rossetti, "When I am dead, my dearest," in *A Pocket Book of Modern Verse*, p. 75.

85. Ruth Herschberger, "The Lumberyard," in ibid., p. 598.

86. Rita Mae Brown, "Dancing the Shout," in *No More Masks!*, ed. Florence Howe and Ellen Bass (Garden City, N.Y.: Anchor, 1973), p. 318.

87. Sonia Sanchez, "poem at thirty," in ibid., p. 259.

88. Denise Levertov, "Stepping Westward," in ibid., p. 153.

89. Ruth Stone, "Advice," in ibid., p. 106.

90. Susan Sutheim, "For Witches," in ibid., p. 297.

91. Muriel Rukeyser, "Ajanta," "More of a Corpse Than a Woman," "Poem Out of Childhood," and "Waking This Morning," in *The Collected Poems of Muriel Rukeyser* (New York: McGraw-Hill, 1978), pp. 207–11, 115, 3–5, 491.

92. H. D., *The Walls Do Not Fall*, in *Norton Anthology*, pp. 374–79.

93. Gwendolyn Brooks, "Gang Girls," in *In the Mecca* (New York: Harper and Row, 1968), pp. 47–48.

94. Levertov, "The Third Dimension," in *Norton Anthology*, pp. 1058–

59; Levertov, "Enquiry," in *To Stay Alive* (New York: New Directions, 1971), p. 18.

95. Howe and Bass, eds., *No More Masks!*, intro., p. 9.

96. Emilie Glen, "Woman," in *Human Voice*, p. 98.

97. Adrienne Rich, "Poetry, Personality and Wholeness: A Response to Galway Kinnell," in *A Field Guide to Contemporary Poetry and Poetics*, ed. Stuart Friebert and David Young (New York: Longman, 1980), pp. 230–31.

98. Rich, *On Lies, Secrets and Silence* (New York: Norton, 1979), pp. 36, 113.

VII

TWENTIETH-CENTURY FICTION

Women have gradually shaken off some aspects of the aura of death that surrounds them. The twentieth century has witnessed great advancements in political and social rights for women and has provided the advantages of better health, contraception, education, and time-saving devices. Women can now walk away from some of the things that both literally and figuratively diminished them to nonexistence in the past. They have shown themselves capable in nearly every area of life, from handling sophisticated equipment to being a college president. Society continues to be exceedingly backward, however, in accepting them as equal in every way to men. Even as women have been advancing, a persistent antagonism toward them has persisted and in this century has risen to a loud crescendo of outspoken and misogynistic protests as well as violent and destructive acts.

The means of degrading women have not changed; in fact, these means are straight out of early history: women are still degraded because of and through their sexuality. As Kate Millett and others so ably tell us, some of the most misogynistic fiction writers (and to many, our "greats"), such as D. H. Lawrence, Henry Miller, and Norman Mailer, portray women solely as sexual beings and for the titillation or ego reinforcement of seeing them suffer and die.

The greater sexual freedom acquired during this century has not always been to women's advantage, for it has focused on their sexuality at the expense of their other sides. A feminist is believed to be sexually peculiar, and the antifeminists would have women stay at home and be what they have always been, the bearers of the male seed. If women seek more from life than they have, to antifeminists they are always where they do not belong; where they belong is at home where sex and the results of sex are entirely visible. There, of course, women can easily dwindle into extinction. Without sex, they are told, they cannot be total human beings.

Of all the forces working against women at the present, those involved with sex and its resultant violence remain the most devastating.

History seems to indicate that power is destructive and that the main reason for acquiring it is to keep from being overrun by another stronger power. Yet we go on in an unreasonable way to acquire more and more power; we stair-step up someone else's back, and our opposition stair-steps up ours, each carrying at every step increasingly more devastating and destructive ammunition. There is one area in human life where two opposing forces have met but without this extreme and simultaneous grasp for greater power by both forces, and this area is in the female and male relationship. Rather, with only minor exceptions, the consistent trend has been to keep women subservient to men, with men apparently needing subordinate persons near them to maintain their supremacy. Women have not yet worked a major overthrow in this pattern and various forces continue to move against such a prospect.

The thinking behind the search for power on a global scale is as unreasonable as that which goes on between women and men; it also helps breed an individual frenzy in our complex urban environments in which communication is often limited to a hit, take, and run mentality and insecurity is ever present. All is speeded up to greatly multiply the hits and thus sacrifice more victims. Elucidating this aspect of society in *The Wanderground*, Sally Miller Gearhart indicates that "The City is a specter of violence and necrophilia" which projects the "misogynistic element" of our culture into the future. "The City symbolizes the future of patriarchy, a place where women's lives are subject not only to violence, but also to trial and death at the hands of hunters who track and kill those 'witches' insubordinate to their rule."[1]

The impetus toward violence as a means to power is strong with those who enslave people for private gain, manipulate populations by manipulating the sale of contraceptives, or furnish arms to

countries that condone torture. In other words, the impetus is strong
not only on a private level but also within global politics, to say
nothing of all-out war which has great appeal to many people:
"Many men only feel they are men when they are in uniform, and
the susceptibility of many women to men so dressed 'to kill' is
notorious."[2]

Within this global or national world of unreason are diverse
subgroups that do not look critically upon violence. One such group
that gives support to the creative artist is that of the intellectuals,
particularly those involved with students and/or teaching "the best"
literature and other forms of art. Many creative artists associated
with universities get their financial support and often subject matter from academia, and can scarcely dismiss the university as a
valuable audience. Both professor and student may be ambivalent
about violence because it is fashionable in the arts, and the artists
feed reciprocally off those who appreciate, teach, or support their
works. Liberal in their thinking, the artist, teacher, and student
are against censorship. Their stance, even if formed with the best
intentions to promote the arts, thus helps escalate the inclusion of
pornography and its basics of violence and death in the arts and
media. All this is done with no thought given to the far-reaching
power structure that feeds on linking feelings of cruelty with sexuality as a means of control.[3] It is even done with laughter and
often a certain element of identification with sadistic wife beaters
or criminals such as Richard Speck who "greeted at one level with
a certain scandalized, possibly hypocritical, indignation, is capable
of eliciting a mass response of titillation at another level."[4]

No great efforts are made in academia to protect the rights of
women or to free them from the intellectual emasculation that exploitation of their bodies via pornography causes. Whatever reading is popular is what is consumed, sometimes only for enjoyable
conversation. Romanticizing the killer, making interracial brutality legitimate because of persisting oppression, and applauding the
latest thriller with a coldly unemotional and unthoughtful perspective are just some of the ways that intellectuals support the
demand for more violence and cushion the artist in their midst.
What is regrettable is that even in levels of society where one would
expect greater sensitivity to social issues, such as women's oppression, it does not exist to any degree.

Some critics have enhanced the connection between sex and death. For example, a seemingly well-done scholarly treatment of modern erotic literature, *The Secret Record* by Michael Perkins, reads in its second sentence: "Like death, sex obsesses us all in ways we often cannot define or admit."[5] Sex is really not like death at all but rather is exceedingly pleasurable for many people. Yet, it suffers by being associated with something that is far more traumatic. It seems odd that scholars go on writing about sex as if it were an act of finality. Even when it is sought and not realized, it is a hunger that gnaws, not kills. The paucity of our language is not the sole factor that keeps the two subjects closely allied, for, later, Perkins discusses a work called *Death and Sensuality* by Georges Bataille with the same illogic: "The relationship between sensuality and death is religious, for, although they are superficially opposed to each other, they are the only means we possess of approaching unity with existence."[6] Whose religion? With so few people in the world Christian, and so few people seriously believing in sin or the origins of Christianity, how can we go on talking about a parallel between sex and death that is religious? If we have no religion, what happens to the parallel? Can the *connection*, not the lack of such, be the only thing that is superficial? It would seem so, in view of the life-oriented and pleasure-producing aspects of sex. If one were to ask anyone with even moderately pleasurable sexual experiences if death hovers over her or him while engaged in sex, I am rather sure the answer would be negative, accompanied by a laugh. To base the parallel on the notion that sex and death are the only means we have of finding unity presupposes that death is not dying, not finishing life, not deteriorating in the grave or smoke. Unity? We go back to the soil but so do the leaves. Unity as part of religion is also an unrealized notion. Unity in sex is a possibility if by this is meant coming to a point of experiencing pleasure together. But as far as transcendence is concerned, this may be in the realm of fantasy. An acceptance of sex and death as being similar, no matter how scholarly the elucidation, seems built on thin air and does little more than perpetuate a notion that distorts life. Moreover, as noted earlier, it hinders women from becoming separate from the sexual and death-producing.

Escalation of violence among artists is further influenced by the efforts of competing male artists to convince themselves that their masculinity is not subverted to a profession that might just as well be oriented toward the female as the male. Female artists have much less need to be troubled about virility and so do not, to any great extent, strive to maintain their position by diminishing or writing about killing the male. Virginia Woolf may be less right today than she was in 1929 when she wrote that women do not write as much about men as men write about women,[7] but it is true that women writers who concentrate on sexuality to the exclusion of all else often fail to depict strong women capable of going their own way and at ease with men's hold on them. Books like Erica Jong's *Fear of Flying* or Judith Rossner's *Looking for Mr. Goodbar* say very little to the woman who sees more to life than sex. The first gives far too much attention to women's sexuality, and the second presents proof of my thesis that women, sex, and death are so inextricably and unreasonably bound together in literature that not even in the area of sexuality can they be allowed an equitable portion of existence. Writers such as Marge Piercy, Joanna Russ, and Ursula LeGuin go beyond Jong and Rossner, seeing the possibility of a kind of shared sexuality, with both participants finding equal pleasures and benefits.

To argue that there would be no art if sexuality were not treated, and if treated there must be violence connected with it, is to argue in such a way as to omit much literature and support violence. First, there exists a goodly number of books that are not overtly sexual, certainly not heterosexual, and not necessarily violent because of the sexuality treated. In *Moby Dick* and *Huckleberry Finn*, for example, heterosexuality plays a very small part. The homosexuality found there is subdued and often not violent. The work of Conrad, to name another, does not pivot on sexuality. Virginia Woolf is also capable of focusing on people who are not embedded in sexuality in such works as *Mrs. Dalloway* and *To the Lighthouse*. Rather than look at our literature which does not treat women, and deplore its lacks, perhaps our more severe judgments should be reserved for those works that do treat women but distort their reality or use a nonhumanitarian approach.

Writers who rely on violence outdo one another in their attempts to interpret their milieu or to satisfy those who will buy their books. These works help increase our tolerance level for violence and in so doing increase our tolerance level for making women the victims. Even when they are critical of violence, the writers raise the tolerance level of victimization. With no end in sight to this kind of escalation, some women writers have chosen to step off the bandwagon and to look within themselves for subject matter, or into their immediate group which may often be made up of females only. They are asking for an end to violence and death and are proposing to write about their own experience which they think they understand well enough to treat realistically. They do not think they are sacrificing valuable aspects of art to do this but rather are pushing into a much more humane and honest way to deal with their lives and/or other subject matter.

In *Sexual Politics* Kate Millett invited us to take a good look at our "greats," and other feminists have been working at the same task since. She makes it clear that D. H. Lawrence could not tolerate equality among classes, races, or sexes, that he grew to use the word *power* for love (though he had interchanged them mentally throughout his writing career), and that finally he equated coitus with killing in such works as "The Woman Who Rode Away." Henry Miller, she says, reduces woman to her sexual organs, uses her like a toilet, uses fuck to mean kill,[8] and tells us that "in the experience of the American manchild sex and violence, exploitation and sentimentality, are strangely, even wonderfully, intermingled."[9] To indicate the way in which Miller linked the "loss of sexual polarity, e.g., the feminist movement" with broader issues, Millett quotes him as saying this loss is part and parcel of the "larger disintegration, the reflex of the soul's death," and is "coincident with the disappearance of great men, great causes, great wars."[10] Norman Mailer, Millett emphasizes, sees murder as so very sexual that it is not only an act that is the final pleasure in sexual experience but, according to *An American Dream*, something that must be done again and again after it is done once. Once having killed her, he shudders from desire to kick the woman and kill her again making sure it is done rightly.[11] Implying that rape is good for people (men, he surely means), he seems to speak from a totally irrational basis. Ingesting the power of women, raped and killed, Mailer indicates that his characters thwart the womanization of America and take on their strength. Mailer suggests that violence is a result of repressed homosexuality. In this respect, he is unlike Jean Genet who, though as violent in his parodies of heterosexuality as the other writers discussed, hopes for a world where homosexuality will not be taboo.

Add the names of Ernest Hemingway, Wright Morris, and Nathaniel West and a host of lesser known writers, who cannot boast of their stylistic niceties, and the thesis that hatred and violence toward women are standard fare in twentieth-century fiction begins to take plausible shape. Of course, it is sometimes impossible to tell if these writers endorse the life they parody; the point is, however, that they contribute to the residue of violence in literature.

The remainder of this chapter is not an attempt to illustrate the kinds of violence that one can easily find in literature and film, and that Kate Millett dealt with in connection with Mailer, Miller, and others. Rather it will illustrate tentative efforts in Doris Lessing, Margaret Drabble, and E. L. Doctorow that emphasize women's coping with death or a preoccupation with it; in Lessing and Doctorow, female characters break away from the typical stereotyping while in Drabble, the main female character exhibits a crippling death orientation that arises from a more deep-seated tendency to vocalize about death than any other female character dealt with in this book. The discussion of D. H. Lawrence will illustrate his tendency to emphasize the connection between sex and death, while the discussion of Heller's *Good as Gold* will reveal a writer with almost no interest in either violence or sex as it is related to death. Gold is a writer who shows tendencies to perpetuate a stereotyped view of women that has been, and continues to be, at the basis of the whole trend to link women excessively with death. Although Gold does not dwell on death, there is little that is innovative in his depiction of women that would suggest their capacity to move out of the stereotypes.

D. H. LAWRENCE

A well-known phenomenon repeated in literature as if it were something of an absolute to sex is that men often feel like killing the woman with whom they seek a relationship or have sex. The manner in which Lawrence and Doris Lessing treat this phenomenon is strikingly different. An examination of Lawrence's "The White Stocking" and Lessing's "One Off the Short List" will elucidate how we may alter the recurrent preoccupation with death which has been so conducive to creating a fatalistic aura around women's lives. Both stories center on a man's effort to bend a woman to his will. Lawrence's Ted succeeds while Lessing's Graham does not. Lawrence attempts to enter the mind of both his characters, while Lessing seems purposely to tell the story from the male point of view, though only as the third-person narrator in order to indicate how man's thinking appears to the reasonable female outsider. Lawrence sets up a typical female/male marriage where the male is physically much stronger than the female. His Ted is possessive but at first indulgent with his minx-like partner who has become bored with her gloomy house and finds some relief from this boredom by going about town during the day while her husband is away at work, and by treasuring a number of small gifts sent her by an admirer whom she had known before marriage. Although Lawrence states that Ted has Elsie "utterly in his power,"[12] it seems that Ted is in her power also, because she is able to make him do things for which he feels some shame,[13] and she at times hurts him "deeply."[14] When brought to tears by his jealousy, it is only Ted who can "restore" her—evidence of a pervasive Lawrentian belief that the female must be made whole and kept intact by the male. Marriage, according to Lawrence, brings Elsie a kind of "liberty" because she is then "rid of the responsibility of herself. Her husband must take care of that."[15] She tests her husband to limits beyond which he can control himself and plays with Sam Adams, her admirer, though "she cared not a jot for the man himself," according to Lawrence. Elsie's jeering scorn of her husband and flaunting of her gifts at one point leave him "white-hot, molten," and he is moved "to kill her." "Have anything to do with Sam Adams, and I'll break your neck," Ted tells Elsie who becomes "transfixed in terror" and attempts to scream.[16]

Ted in an instant strikes her such a forceful blow across the mouth that she is flung blindly against the wall. His brutality evokes a startled sound from her, and he advances slowly toward her, seemingly arrested by her sight and desirous of seeing more clearly her bleeding mouth. Lawrence says Ted lusts to see her bleed, to break and destroy her. Like a duelist, he wants "satisfaction," but when comprehending her pitiable and horrified state, he turns aside with nausea and shame. Instead of further molesting her, Ted throws himself in a chair where an ease, such as one has with sleep, comes over him.[17] She sobs. His desire "to destroy" returns. She admits more trifling with his affections by not acknowledging having received other gifts by mail from Adams. Elsie then feels that nothing can prevent him from killing her, should he want to, and does nothing to protect herself, finally yielding to him. Both tremble "in the balance, unconscious."[18] Her rage remains, but within moments they are in each other's arms, she sobbing, he still in anguish, but one senses he has conquered and that Elsie will be more cautious next time.

Lawrence has pictured this male as a machine-like monster (white-hot, molten) of power who advances on the enemy like a beast stalking prey and who wants the enemy's blood. He wants to destroy and is on the brink of doing so. His crash against her mouth is very like penetrating with the penis. Both are done under male control, and Ted here feels that "curious ease, almost like sleep" after his blows that more often is the result of intercourse for men than for women, or so it is thought. The experience is also tinged with nausea, another common response by males to sex which they consider debilitating or disgusting.[19] Judging from Lawrence's other fiction and comments in essays and letters, Ted has performed as he naturally should; he has righted an unbalanced situation. Now Elsie will be back in the position women ought to be in. Elsie is a woman who can be pitied for her lack of opportunity and freedom and her desire for it; Lawrence has no pity for her.

DORIS LESSING

In "One Off the Short List" Doris Lessing throws a penetrating searchlight on the nature of man's attempt to seduce a woman. The female character, Barbara Coles, is successful in the theatre, well-liked by her associates, a wife and mother, poised, and impersonal. Her poise may unbalance the reader who is unready for a picture of a woman who is other than passive. As Lessing's title indicates, she is presenting a woman who is one on a short list.

Graham, who has a "stable" marriage, sees her and decides he must have her. Sex is not the central issue; he just feels he must add her to his list of conquered females. He comes as a journalist to interview Barbara, but she does not at first remember him and she keeps him waiting, thereby beginning her emasculating process without being conscious of it. He later maneuvers her into "his" pub to find her tired, unresponsive to his manipulation, and eager to finish without any personal involvement. His "manhood" has little or no attraction for her. Her success, which he envies, and her attention to business, rather than to him, disarm him, even though she is not abrupt or discourteous. He is persistent and forces her down, as Lessing says, onto a personal level which she despises.[20] Troubled because "he couldn't remember not being in control of a situation with a woman for years," he is thrown into a quandary by her half-humorous, half-annoyed treatment of him. The scene that follows "when he looked back on it afterwards, was the most embarrassing experience of his life."[21] She, being much shorter than he, cannot control him physically, but she remains poised and in control of the situation, as well as her sense of humor. She calls him crazy as he goes on "squeezing, grinding, kissing," and thinking: "It's only a really masculine woman who wouldn't have given in by now out of sheer decency of the flesh."[22] Here he voices the typical reduction of woman to sex; obviously, he is finding out that there is more to her than sex. Graham realizes that there is only a contest of wills with her as she finally asks him to go ahead and get it over with; because she is fed up with his preliminaries, he becomes so angered, so absorbed with hate for her, "That wanting her was like needing to kill something or someone."[23] Making it seem that she will allow him to go ahead if he must, he is put "in the position of raping a woman"[24] and given added assurance that he simply bores her. Gritting her teeth at his touch, she finally makes him come "by using a cold skill that was the result of her contempt for him."[25] He hates her consolation; he hates her intelligence and that he had not been able to get away with anything, that she had been watching every move he made.[26]

In both Lawrence's and Lessing's works, the male protagonists imply they are ready to kill. Thus, the man of older times remains with us in the twentieth century when few people still forage for food; and the hunt persists in fiction about sex in terms of language and emotional response. Barbara, however, is a woman who has moved beyond her sexuality, who is much more than her sex (and who is consequently not regarded as a "normal" woman by Graham). Lawrence seems to feel that the male in his story is acting out of a perfectly normal drive to conquer, by killing if necessary, and is not ridiculing this "natural" bent. Lessing finds the whole process of seduction to be ridiculous. She shows a woman of strength capable of keeping her conqueror at bay so that his fixed drive is thwarted. Barbara makes choices; Elsie is denied the possibility. Lessing does not forget imminent danger, however, and gives passing comment to "kill or conquer," the two alternatives which in the case of "kill" is nearly below the surface and in the case of "conquer" uppermost in Graham's mind.

It might be argued that Barbara has emasculated Graham and therefore done him injury, just as men have done women injury throughout history. Is she just reversing the old process? We remember, however, that it is Graham who is using up her valuable time and that she has not, of course, brutalized him physically by drawing blood. Barbara does not appear to gain any ease from what she has done; she has no sense of conquering, and she is not nauseated. She is merely glad to get his urges out of his system.

These two stories may be dated now. For most of the first half of the century, Lawrence was thought to have an open approach to sex. Few of his readers realized, however, that he held marriage sacred and thought that women should always follow, never lead. His prudishness coupled with his misogyny would date him even if other aspects of his cramped approach do not. Doris Lessing's story is on the forefront of new approaches born out of the current women's movement where attitudes toward marriage are not so limited and women are exercising choice. Even though she eschews the label "feminist," she speaks to issues to which women seeking to reshape consciousness are drawn. Her story is dated in the sense of being a "first" by playing down violence and showing that the emphasis on brutality can also become outdated.

MARGARET DRABBLE

A 1969 novel written by a woman reveals a strong death-orientation suggesting that some women as well as men associate death with sexuality. One notable difference between this work and those that Millett discusses in *Sexual Politics*, however, is that it does not equate sex with conquering, and it has almost nothing to do with ego-building. In Margaret Drabble's *The Waterfall*, Jane's excessive preoccupation with death seems to rise out of a pessimistic approach to life. Her approach is at least partially explained by her inability to reconcile her parents' hypocrisy and dishonest social attitudes[27] with her own thinking. Drabble, however, seems to employ death imagery to describe the effect of excessive emotions rather than to suggest the possibility of the actual experience of death. Her work shows woman as victim to brutality only insofar as she inflicts it on herself.

Jane has as strong a death-orientation as the poet Keats who knew he would die of tuberculosis. Jane, however, has no clear-cut cause for her preoccupation with death. Neither is she persistently in the grips of thoughts on death, nor is she without ambivalence in her attitude toward her state. It is not certain whether or not Drabble sees Jane as a victim of a culture which rubs her nose in death. While such thoughts may sometimes surface, there is a greater concern for love dictating a life of misery (and a modicum of pleasure *at moments*) for this one special person whose peculiarities stem from overwhelming feelings of inadequacy, guilt, and inertia.

The novel seems to exhibit some awareness of the trap marriage and sex can be for women, and its abundant death imagery underscores aspects of this trap. Its protagonist is not strong enough, however, either to surmount her difficulties in the entrapment or shake off her death-orientation or feelings of guilt to make for a productive life. Jane has far too many shades of Sylvia Plath and Anne Sexton,[28] suicides whose creativity was not a sufficient outlet for their sensitivity, vulnerability, or defiance. The book is *almost* a study in the suicidal, but Drabble holds off from the extreme that the two poets found their only recourse, and even suggests some slight possibilities of growth on Jane's part. Drabble's Jane, however, is not strong enough to escape extreme pathological suffering. If Jane is Ms. Everywoman, she has more than her share of desperation; men of very ordinary and nonviolent natures, such as those with whom she is associated, do not to a great degree prompt her suffering.

While Drabble has utilized the traditional link between sex and death, at the same time she gets inside the victimized woman who has enough insight to understand her own isolation and ambivalence in many areas of thought and action. Nonetheless, Jane has to exorcise a great deal of guilt and suffering in order to get on to more positive approaches to life. It is possible that love and suffering could make for good poetry, but one suspects her dedica-

tion to this art is not strong enough to be utilized to any degree.
Still *The Waterfall* seems to be on the brink of the approach which
fiction about women should take in order to get at the reality of
those who do suffer rather than merely exploit that suffering. We
learn a good deal about women from a woman's point of view.
We learn how she is a victim of her own self and her upbringing,
and we see how love can trouble her existence or approach even
causing her doom.[29] Drabble's outlook is not very bright, but those
looking for a way out of brutalization, victimization, suffering, and
death for women could do so much worse by turning to Lawrence, Miller, and Mailer, where brutality is inflicted upon heroines from without, that *The Waterfall* might be recommended as a
starting point for analysis and clarification of self prior to moving
into something more positive. Perhaps this work indicates that life
furnishes more examples of strong women than fiction was able
to exhibit in 1969.

Drabble uses so many negatives to describe Jane, or has Jane use
so many negatives about herself, that one imagines her to be the
epitome of defeatism and insecurity. She is flawed,[30] treacherous,[31] a failure,[32] inadequate and possessed of faults,[33] not a good
mother,[34] not in tune with her body,[35] a destroyer and murderess
masquerading as victim,[36] something of a *femme fatale*,[37] deformed,[38] exhausted,[39] and agoraphobic.[40] Put all of these self-defeating labels beside Jane's fear of being, and desire to be, consumed by love, and one has a person inordinately preoccupied with
her faults and possessed of an irrationality concerning her love for
James which she defines in terms of death: "I lay there, drowned
was it, drowned or stranded, waiting for him, waiting to die and
drown there, in the oceans of our flowing bodies."[41] James notices
she is crying and reaches "across and took her hand, and she said,
'There's something wrong with me, I'm going to die, I'm going
to die,' though that was not at all the reason for her tears. 'Then
let me kill you,' he said, holding her hand in his."[42] "They later
talked constantly of death. It seemed a way of preventing it."[43]
On another occasion,

> when she turned to him after the long delays of the day, she
> heard her own voice cry out to him, inarticulate, compelled,
> from such depths of need that it frightened her. . . . It was

like death, like birth: an event of the same order. Her cry was the cry of a woman in labor: it broke from her and her body gathered around it with the violence of a final pang. She had known it would be like this: dreadful, insatiable, addictive, black. How wisely she had avoided this destruction, with what self-preserving foreknowledge had she avoided it: and now it was too late, she had let herself be led here tenderly by the hand, garlanded with kisses, a sacrifice. And he would never be able to kill her, she would thrash on there alone forever, and he would hate her for it, he would hate her for having shown herself willing to die, for the ugliness of the near lethal wound.[44]

Many, many pages in *The Waterfall* read like this; even Keats' sonnets are not this death-filled.

These responses are symptomatic of inner emotions rather than descriptive of actual events, for Jane toys only briefly and halfheartedly with suicide.[45] One cannot help but think that if our language had words capable of expressing such extreme emotions which are not associated with death, Drabble would use them. She needs the extremes that the language of death can offer because, except for when Malcolm hits Jane once and when James becomes unconscious in the car wreck, there are no death-dealing experiences which would give occasion for Jane's outpourings on her case. Even love in *The Waterfall* is overwhelming, consuming, dangerous—all words that are suggestive of death but not concerned with ceasing to breathe.

Drabble spends some time telling us about Jane's upbringing and her failure to find a satisfactory sexual relationship with Malcolm, both of which magnify her reticence about sex until she meets James. One wishes Jane had had a freer and more knowledgeable approach to sex all along so that it could be faced more realistically when it finally does come. It is in keeping with Jane's sensitivity, imagination, and desire for solitude that her feelings are magnified into nearly the whole of her existence. Her activities, like doing the laundry and ironing, are of a masochistic sort, much like those performed by Alison Porter in John Osborne's *Look Back in Anger*.

Drabble shows Jane taking on far more than her share of guilt.

About Malcolm, she says "I did in a sense murder him, and I murdered him in the true lyrical sense, by rejection, by the breaking of vows, by the lending and withdrawal of my beauty."[46] This kind of murder, she says, is "hideously ugly, unspeakably shamefully ugly."[47] "If I hadn't tortured him, another would have done so: but perhaps less cruelly, with less finesse."[48] She rarely allows the two men in her life to share the guilt-ridden situation that surrounds her. She treats them both as innocent victims and her victims to boot. With Jane it goes much beyond evading certain responsibilities toward her husband and her children; she invents and multiplies her deceits much beyond the average and has a "terror of contraceptives"[49] which amounts to a perverse playing with fate in order to have something about which to be guilty. She is not the first to love in desperation, but she acts as if she must take upon herself all the guilt for everyone who ever loved as she does. The giant legacy of death discussed throughout this book seems concentrated in Jane, and her guilt is exemplary of all that which Christianity and our culture have assigned to woman. Drabble does not speak to this assumption; her efforts to make Jane unique may even counter the reader's coming to this conclusion.

Love for Jane is a bondage, a malady, a pain, a death, a danger, a jealousy, and a possession. She becomes inert to any other stimulus after she falls in love with James and he starts visiting her regularly. She does very little and gives up writing. After his accident, she resumes writing and is able to smile at some of her previous expectations. She crosses her fingers lest she be struck down, but nevertheless she likes "ripping along fast roads" in a car in true Sylvia Plath fashion.[50] She takes her feelings toward Malcolm more calmly and feels less guilty.[51] She wonders, in her old way, whether her amusement is a "sign of maturity, or a sign of the total depravation" of her character,[52] and at the end she still acknowledges an addiction to suffering.[53]

It is instructive to hold Jane beside Clarissa, Emma, Anna, Maggie, Tess, and Edna. None of these six women has Jane's obsession with death. They all find themselves caught in a web that arises much more out of the social fabric; they are manipulated far more from without while Jane's struggle is more self-centered and inner. Had any of the six heroines from the earlier novels found a life that was attractive to her, and in which a good relationship might have evolved, she would have clutched at it and not possessed thoughts on death to the extreme Jane does. Even Edna's inner self is not searched in the way Jane's is. Jane's love is analyzed for what it is, her sexual nature is delved into, and her masochism and excessive guilt are duly illustrated. These are not the kinds of subjects the older authors seem as capable of handling as Drabble is. It is also interesting that Clarissa, Anna, Maggie, Edna, and Tess clearly are portrayed at moments to have nobility, talent, or compassion, while Jane is often the embodiment of inadequacy. The heroines from the older novels are in a position where "falling" is inevitable, while Jane often can scarcely go any lower and a slight rise is her only inevitability. Clearly there is an evolving capacity here on Drabble's part to study the female personality in light of psychological discoveries not present for the older writers or taken into account by those who now merely exploit women for sexual and entertainment purposes.

Only by a few degrees can Jane shake loose, however, from the grip of death and progress beyond the state where sexuality is the whole of life. Jane's mind may tell her that sex is not all a woman needs, but her body is not yet convinced. Because of her sexuality, she is still isolated and caught in a world not adequate for a total experience. One cannot be sure whether Jane could function any differently even with altered circumstances; only an inner change could remove her more serious problems. Drabble's picture, while dark, is a fully realized one; nevertheless, it is long on diagnosis and short on positive cure. Admittedly, it is hard to find realistic female characters with the capacity for growth and change in twentieth-century fiction.

E. L. DOCTOROW

E. L. Doctorow's *The Book of Daniel* (1971) and *Ragtime* (1975) both treat women without negative bias and in general reveal a humanitarianism that condemns violence and the exploitation of one group by another. While some might argue that Doctorow's use of history places some restrictions on his depiction of women, it also is noted that he plays down or omits the kind of hatred of women found in those writers whom Kate Millett discusses at length in *Sexual Politics*. Both of Doctorow's books dwell on the nurturing sides of both sexes but do not exclude other aspects of human behavior. Doctorow seems to have freed himself from the traditional ways of handling women that make it acceptable to castigate, brutalize, or kill at will.

The Book of Daniel, Doctorow's version of the Ethel and Julius Rosenberg trial and execution for conspiracy to commit espionage, makes Rochelle Isaacson (Ethel) a stronger character than she may have been in actual life.[54] Doctorow shows her while in prison to be generally calm, hopeful, realistic, and much respected by the women in her cell block. These women speak to one another on a first-name basis, ask advice of her, and give her clothes for her trial. Here, as in *Ragtime*, women do not exhibit the hatred for one another that is often attributed to them. Rochelle endures great hardship being separated from her husband and children but reserves her tears for the privacy of her bed. When she goes to the death chamber, Daniel, her son, says: "She knew that my father [Paul] was dead. On her face was a carefully composed ironic smile. She calmly gazed at each of the witnesses until he turned away." She then sends the rabbi away, hugs the matron who has been with her two years, and keeps her eyes open until the hood goes over her head. The executioner said pointedly that it took more than one application of the current to extinguish her life.[55] Rochelle is so brave that some might call her cold, but Doctorow leaves that for the reader to decide. Had he been more prejudiced against Ethel than Julius Rosenberg, more prejudiced against women than men, or had he simply wanted to twist history more severely than he did, he could have made Paul the more courageous. He treats Rochelle as he does, not because of her sex, but rather because she is brave and consumed with the desire to prove their innocence to the world. If she has any weaknesses, so does her husband.

Doctorow invents a sister named Sarah for Daniel (both Rosenberg children were boys). Although Sarah is sometimes a burden, Daniel never rejects her. Doctorow seems to be caught up in capturing the reader's social consciousness when, in a manner almost equal to Dickens, he shows Daniel and Sarah running away from the shelter where they are supposed to be staying while their parents are in prison. Because they have no money, Daniel wants to steal, especially since Sarah is so hungry, but he is afraid to do so. The reader's emotional response is extremely high when, after they have walked great distances across the "wilderness" of New York

City, Sarah's socks disappear into her shoes, she cannot keep them pulled up, and blisters come to the backs of her heels. Doctorow makes us very sympathetic toward both children in scenes like these where Daniel's concern for Sarah is always apparent. Later he says of her voice:

> it is so familiar to me that I cannot perceive the world except with your voice framing the edges of my vision. It is on the horizon and under my feet. The world has always been washed in Sarah's voice. It breaks where her voice breaks, under declaration, or late toward sleep, or at moments of love—only to more fully characterize itself. It is the feminine voice that passes solidly through ontological mirrors. It lies at the heart of the matter, the nub of the thing . . . smack in the middle.[56]

At the funeral of their parents, he is proud of her and says he wants to love her the rest of their lives.[57] Doctorow calls attention to Daniel's being a willing nurturer toward Sarah and at the same time to the heart-rending sides of losing parents who are deprived of the chance to nurture.

Both children suffer greatly from the loss of their very attentive parents, even though the lawyer Ascher treats them kindly as eventually do Robert and Lise Lewin who adopt them. Sarah, although disturbed mentally, wants to establish an Isaacson Foundation and is less ambivalent in attitude than Daniel whose rage emerges in brutal treatment of his child-wife Phyllis and to a certain extent his son. Doctorow's social message is strong in these signs of the effect the treatment of the parents has on the children; a society which can so thwart the nurturing qualities of parents cannot do more than produce children like these two. Daniel's brutality seems to run parallel to what he has known, and he has a strong compulsion to make sure Phyllis suffers too, feeling that somehow this suffering will bring her closer to him. Although this brutality surfaces enough to be memorable, and from a feminist standpoint is disturbing, it is mild compared to the brutality in Lawrence, Miller, or Mailer where motivation is much less apparent. Doctorow seems to be saying that Daniel's treatment of his wife is symptomatic of a deeply repressed sadness which he cannot control.

Their foster mother, like their mother who died in the electric chair, has considerable fortitude. When a minor female character such as the mad grandmother or Linda Mindish is negatively depicted, circumstances demand this depiction, and being female does not seem to be the reason for the negativism. Linda, whose father testified against Sarah and Daniel's parents, suffers for having been drawn into the nastier part of the case. All three live with the desire for destruction,[58] and each has a different way of handling her or his problem. Linda moves with her father to California, Sarah commits suicide, and Daniel finds ways to cope, some of them bizarre like burning his wife's buttocks with a cigarette lighter while speeding down the highway fast enough to cause their death as well as that of their small infant.

Ragtime, a much more playful book than *The Book of Daniel*, captures the era of the early 1900s and depicts women sympathetically or with a refreshing noncommittal attitude. Often focusing on the hard lot of women, Doctorow gets the feminist ear: "Across America sex and death were barely distinguishable. Runaway women died in the rigors of ecstasy."[59] Women go to trial to save murderers: the first sex goddess of American history, Evelyn Nesbit, who is said to have caused the death of Stanford White, must testify to save Harry K. Thaw's hide. Freud comes to America: "his ideas begin to destroy sex in America forever."[60] Women also go to hospitals "to die of burst bladders, collapsed lungs, overtaxed hearts and meningitis of the spine."[61] Daughters of the working class are used for the pleasure of the wealthy. The laborer's wife is an "exhausted workhorse with the veins standing out in her legs."[62]

All this is true, yet there is the famous revolutionary Emma Goldman, the feminist-anarchist-socialist, who is allowed to deliver in the "bracing linguistics of radical idealism" a lecture advocating freeing women from sexual and marital bondage:

> Do you think the society that plunders your labor has no interest in the way you are asked to live with women? Not through freedom but through bondage? All the reformers talk today of the white slavery problem. But if white slavery is a problem, why is marriage not a problem? Is there no connection between the institution of marriage and the institution of the brothel? . . . Is our genius only in our wombs?[63]

There is also Emma's remarkable disrobing of Evelyn Nesbit to get her out of her corsetted bondage and addiction to adornment to attract men:

> "Are you wearing a corset? . . . You ought to be ashamed of yourself. Look at me, even with my figure I have not one foundation garment, I wear everything loose and free-flowing, I give my body the freedom to breathe and to be. . . . Your waist is pinched tighter than a purse string." . . . She unclasped Evelyn's skirt and had her step out of it.

Removing Evelyn's clothing piece by piece and allowing it to drop around her, Emma commands her to "Step out." When finished, she finds it amazing that Evelyn has "any circulation at all." Using her nursing skills, she gives her a generous rubdown to restore circulation.[64] "Gradually Evelyn relaxed and her flesh shook and quivered under the emphatic skill of Goldman's hands."[65] The bond Emma feels with Evelyn results from Emma's understanding of the need some women have to be prostitutes. Emma had only briefly experimented with this life, but she is touched by Evelyn's bondage to sex and the attentions of men. It is interesting that Emma, a woman who is pictured here as gentle and caring, can also lay on a horsewhip when she is denounced publicly.[66] Doctorow pokes fun at these people but allows them to remain intact as credible human beings with ambivalent but generally human and reputable sides to their natures. He does not reveal he thinks less of these women than he does of several of the men in the novel.

Emma is only one of the nurturers in the novel. Evelyn finds a child among the poor to nurture in Tateh's small daughter[67] and gives of her time and money in an effort to restore the child to health and to provide her with a better life. Climbing to their attic room, Evelyn disrobes and bathes the little girl in a parallel ritual to the one she has experienced with Emma. She hopes to hide her generosity under anonymity; only when Tateh discovers she is a prostitute does she lose the opportunity to care for the child.[68] Tateh himself is likewise a nurturer and is always attentive to his beautiful daughter. Mother (so-called throughout the book), aside from caring for her own child, takes in the black girl Sarah and eventually takes over the care of Sarah's boy who is the son of

Coalhouse Walker, the jazz musician. "At night in bed Mother held him and tried to warm the small of his back, curled him into her as she lay against his back cradling his strange coldness."[69] Sarah after a time is also an attentive mother until she dies trying to help her husband. Coalhouse himself spends numerous hours beside his son's cradle. Tateh's first wife Mameh, before she falls into the hands of a male buyer of her homemade garments and Tateh subsequently tells her to leave, is capable of mothering. Houdini's mother may be almost more loved than loving, but she is also an attentive parent.[70] If we can accept the interpretation of Houdini's career as bondage to her womb, she received his homage every time he entrapped himself and ingeniously broke out.

Doctorow seems interested not only in selecting striking women from history such as Emma Goldman but also in inventing them, as in the case of Mother, in order to show the multidimensional sides of women of the times. From the feminist's standpoint, all this mothering might be a bit much if we were not made aware that Mother does her nurturing when attending a good deal of the time to the family business; she has "executive responsibilities."[71] Father, incidentally, is a weak man, often away on expeditions, and sometimes not a good father.[72] Emma Goldman has a very busy life and Evelyn Nesbit is certainly no homebody. Mameh works hard as a seamstress. Any fun Doctorow pokes at nurturers is gentle.

Doctorow throws his spotlight on sufferers in such a way as to reveal the negative sides of those who victimize or torture. Ambivalence in a character, whom we might quickly dismiss, also attracts his interest throughout. Evelyn Nesbit, who seems to be involved in some shady testifying,[73] captures the reader's sympathy, as noted, by her care of Tateh's small daughter. Her brutalization in Europe by Harry K. Thaw, who habitually whipped her,[74] makes us sympathetic to her and, of course, antagonistic toward Thaw who, "because of her," murders Stanford White. In still another disrobing scene (but with remarkable and obviously pointed differences to other disrobing scenes in the novel), Thaw "threw her across the bed and applied a dog whip to her buttocks and the back of her thighs . . . shocking red welts disfigured Evelyn's flesh. . . . In the morning Harry returned with a razor strop."[75] Doctorow indicates that Thaw was "imperious, possessive and insanely jealous"; the reader, of course, has little sympathy for him. The comment on violence here is not left ambivalent as it was in some respects in *The Book of Daniel*. However, Doctorow does not exploit violence for its own sake in either book. Later, when Coalhouse and his friends turn violent as a result of racism, circumstances are very different, and the violence follows upon deep pain at being used and at the death of Coalhouse's wife. Again Doctorow leads our responses along the path to sympathy for a woman.

The female bonding in the book is noticeable enough to require further comment. Emma immediately wants to help Evelyn, the creature of capitalism; Evelyn helps Tateh's daughter partially because she feels close to her mother whom Tateh's had turned out when she innocently became involved with the buyer of her sewing. Mother takes in Coalhouse's fiancée with no qualms. If Doctorow had wanted to undercut the nurturing qualities in women, he could have shown these women fighting with one another, but he does not.

Mother's first marriage was never ideal partly because of her husband's absence from home; in her second marriage to Tateh, she finds her match in capacity to nurture. "She adored him, she loved to be with him. They each relished the traits of character in the other."[76] Together they care for Tateh's dark-haired, beautiful daughter, Mother's tow-headed child, and their adopted son, the black child of Coalhouse and Sarah. After the marriage, Tateh conceives of a brilliant film about a group of mischievous little children of all races, sizes, and economic levels having amusing adventures.

Doctorow not only captures the varied texture of early twentieth-century life but also seems to side with the gentler people, even as he raps America, the land where marriage is sacred and Mom is queen. Satire picks up at Niagara Falls when Freud witnesses "Thousands of newly married couples standing in pairs" watching the great cascades and pronounces America a gigantic mistake.[77] A much less appealing side of the American scene is represented by J. P. Morgan, with his diseased and bulbous nose, who controls 741 directorships and 112 corporations and has Madison Avenue dinner parties attended by hags who never laugh, sit on "large draped behinds, breasts drooping under their décolletage" and have not an ounce of wit among them or any light in their eyes.[78] Henry Ford, who cannot get his eyes off the gold, at first seems to be set up as a parallel character to Tateh who started out clipping likenesses from paper on the streets for pennies and ended in the moving-picture business and finally happily married to Mother. Unlike Ford, Tateh emerges with at least his nurturing side untarnished. He is undercut by his hard-nosed attitude toward his first wife, who, in trying to help the family, fell into an illicit arrangement; toward Emma for her liberal notions on marriage; and toward Evelyn for her prostitution. He also seems to be engaged in making "preparedness serials" at the end and so may be susceptible to supporting the unsavory, but he is still "good with kids" and has that in common with Mother.

The top moneyed class does not come off very well in *Ragtime*. The radicals, however sympathetic, get in deep trouble (example: Coalhouse) or have to be deported (example: Emma). The relatively plain folk who love one another, and above all chidren, get treated gently. Although usually close to actual events in history, this narrative is a little like melodrama, but through Doctorow's understated treatment it becomes penetrating commentary on the times. As in *The Book of Daniel*, violence is usually attributed to forces beyond the control of the individuals with whom we sympathize. We find energetic women capable of undertaking serious enterprises, and even those whom the self-righteous might condemn, such as Evelyn Nesbit, have winning aspects. If Doctorow has given his own coloring to events, it is not apparently done in order to degrade women but to point up their diversity and capacity to give of themselves. Part of his method is to pick from history remarkable women, something historians have, generally speaking, failed to do, and to give their lives some significance. His effort buoys the confidence of women rather than deflates it. Although women die in his novels, they are not victims of sexual assault; both Rochelle in *The Book of Daniel* and Sarah in *Ragtime* go to their deaths honorably.

JOSEPH HELLER

Joseph Heller's *Good as Gold* (1979) presents a considerably less sympathetic picture of women than Doctorow's two books. Heller's work is unique neither in content nor in style. He treats the subjects of power, waste, politics, education, writing, neglect, sadism, "Jewishness," and female and male interaction no differently than numerous other twentieth-century writers do. As Pomoroy, one of the characters, says, the Jewish experience has "been done hundreds of times."[79] The Jewish professor Dr. Bruce Gold does have numerous predecessors, although I know of no others who aspire to become Secretary of State. Striving to capture the ordinariness of life, Heller depicts women as they have been depicted before: the aging stepmother knitting, Ida and Linda teaching school, Rose as secretary, Andrea previously in home economics, and numerous wives in the shadow of their husbands. They also have the usual traits attributed to women; there are the aggressive nurse (Lucille), gossips (Belle, Andrea, Linda), a castrator (Andrea), the long-suffering seamstress (Gold's mother), the doting older sisters (Esther, Rose), and the passive and obedient wife (Belle—she "brought his [Gold's] dinner on a tray a minute before he was going to yell for it."[80]) The men in the novel have conventional jobs: doctor, professor, politician, writer, publisher. Represented are the typical tyrannical father (Julius Gold), the boaster (Lieberman), the not-very-attentive father (Gold), and fornicators or would-be fornicators (Gold, Sid, Lieberman). Working with a fairly large chunk of life, Heller seems to be attempting to make his audience laugh at or feel the emptiness of the predicaments the characters find themselves in. That most of these predicaments are familiar to the reader would not necessarily make for a bad novel, but here the reader gets a generous serving of the kind of conditioning that stabilizes the stereotypic. It should be pointed out, however, that violence, muted in this novel, only surfaces in our fright at what could take place if those who manage the arms race or pull the levers in time of attack are no more talented than those Heller depicts. In this respect, Heller is numerous cuts above the sheer pornography of Mailer and others, and this aspect of his book is applaudable.

Like so many books of its kind, *Good as Gold* shows no strong commitment to changing the way literature stereotypes women. Its central focus is on males who have no inhibitions about using women for pleasure or as stepping-stones to power. Generally, Heller seeks to capture actuality, although, as in most fiction, the heaviness of his concentrate is exaggerated at times, and it is difficult to tell whether he condemns or condones the world he depicts. Apparently, he wants to put Gold (that is, Kissinger) in a bad light by juxtaposing his background with the means he uses (or dreams of using) to attain power. One would also be shocked to discover that Heller has much sympathy for female Ph.D.s. Had he not wanted to lump all of them under the canopy of Andrea, he would not have needed to mention she had such a degree. It is less obvious whether he condemns several of the other women in the novel or just reacts indifferently to them. It would not be uncommon for readers looking only for a few laughs and unconcerned about sexism to find Gold quite interestingly absurd and the female characters closer to normal. One wonders how Heller felt about the absurdity he presents. Because the book focuses on the aspiring male diplomat and because men are often unaccompanied by women, it would seem that Heller thinks women play a secondary role to men (except on days when they bring their favorite dish to family potlucks). There are some hints that Heller might not consider this lesser role to be totally inevitable, but he does not make any kind of commitment to altering lifestyles for women. Even though Heller is no doubt familiar with enough feminists to realize they do exist, he does not risk depicting one even as a caricature. Whether consciously or unconsciously, he does make some faint stabs at examining the source of some of the problems women face, but since we focus most intensely on Gold in the novel and since he is blind to the full nature of women, being a typical male-oriented writer, anything substantive in Heller's dealing with women's problems is lost in the vague sympathy or identity the reader may have for Gold. The reader feels an element of concern for Gold because he is pathetic in having no sympathy from his family, his vulnerability and aggressiveness in sex, his expectations that Andrea will be a good servant and cook, and his failure to settle for what little good exists in his life as a professor, father, and husband. We tend to watch for any signs that he will learn from experience. Interestingly, we are never induced to concern ourselves in these ways with the women.

Heller espouses the notion that power is an aphrodisiac,[81] and if he had pursued this idea, he might have reached some conclusions about how societies use women as the training ground for getting men into positions of power. He spends no time discussing how women are greater losers than men in the kind of games Gold plays. Failing to do so, he violates reality. Of course, Heller should be praised for his definition of power, even if his depictions of women are not always realistic. If his definition did not, however, subvert the interests of women, he would make a more significant statement. Heller does not tell us explicitly that sexual excitement, as a byproduct of power, is as empty as the power itself. When we consider that the novel strongly condemns power chasers, it seems that sexual prowess is symptomatic of weakness rather than strength. Although Gold is not necessarily stronger at the end, he is perhaps in a better position not to be diminished by his actions as he has been throughout most of the novel. He returns to safer ground, to where he was before he started listening to Ralph's advice to hang in for the position of Secretary of State. However, he may just be in a momentary lull with regard to sexuality. Heller does not clarify this question.

Gold is more conventional and traditional than several women in the novel. In showing him to be less than flexible in some matters, Heller seems to be toying with the notion that women can get down to basics and the truth whereas Gold cannot. Andrea shocks Gold by talking about trimming a callus[82] and by saying she and her sorority sisters took each other's fathers to bed.[83] Joannie, his youngest sister, explains the Jewish experience as follows: "It's trying not to be. We play golf now, get drunk, take tennis lessons, and have divorce, just like normal Christian Americans. We talk dirty. We screw around, commit adultery, and talk out loud a lot about fucking." Gold draws back "in horror."[84] He is astounded when Linda reveals what her family knows and thinks about their going to bed together. In his exasperation he questions, "What is this horrifying obsession with the truth that all you women seem to be in the grip of these days?"[85] Surely, Gold's responses to all these women suggest disapproval, but Heller does not help us decide if by these responses he is making Gold into a dunce or if he himself agrees with him. Can Heller think of women in any other way than as "uncouth" (trimming calluses) or being outspoken about sex? Much of Heller's treatment of women in the novel focuses on sex, and he seems to insult women's intelligence giving Andrea only a home economics degree[86] as well as assigning a weak mind to at least two of his female relatives.[87] He therefore does not present a very exalted picture of female capability and exposes the reader to little that might (even in a negative way) suggest that women are finding new and worthwhile things to do.

Gold momentarily seems to recognize something about the woman's perspective in the above question concerning women seeking the truth. However, if the truth is limited to sex alone, then much else remains to be discovered. Basically, Gold is what Andrea calls him a number of times, silly,[88] or according to several of his relatives, a jerk.[89] He does not have Joannie's power to leave the torturous family nest, Andrea's power to be herself, or Linda's freedom to speak out on "delicate" issues. His stepmother knows how to get his goat and is not as insane as he thinks.[90] He appears slow in his adjustment to gains women are making (independent women frighten him), and it is hoped that Heller sees this as a deficiency on his part, but we are left in the dark here also.

Even though Gold's family members apparently assume that he is the most intelligent of any of them, he lives basically in a world of fantasy.[91] He may show a glimmering of understanding of his wife when he says, "I'm glad to see you're not perfect,"[92] as she refuses to agree to having Julius Gold live with them. Perhaps they are a little better suited to each other than Gold thinks, but Heller has not let us know that he thinks Gold has discovered this to be true. Gold, who falls in love at the drop of a hat, may be on his way out the door after another woman at the novel's end and thus on his way to another series of ridiculous experiences.

Books like Heller's are acclaimed to be "good" or even "excellent." We now need to readjust our critical comments to include the author's sensitivity toward much-exploited people. Just as we seek to alter patterns of behavior in life, we ought to reflect both efforts to change behavior and the resulting changed behavior in literature. A superficial treatment that entices traditional readers surely will not continue to suffice. When a book's message is revealed through negative images, the reader needs to know the author's stance on the issues discussed. This is more than obviously true when the negative images are of women because traditionally there have been almost no positive ones. Only some alteration in this pattern will show that change is possible and occurring. Heller has apparently not made the kind of change it takes to see women with objectivity and as full human beings. Doctorow comes closer to this possibility. As the next chapter indicates, Adrienne Rich commands the kind of vision and vocabulary necessary to effect the desired change.

NOTES

1. Summarized in a book review by Lou Roberts, *Frontiers: A Journal of Women's Studies* 5, no. 1 (Spring 1980): 74.

2. Roger Manvell, "Violence: Pornography or Art?"*New Humanist* 90, no. 4 (August 1974): 130.

3. Kate Millett, *Sexual Politics* (New York: Ballantine, 1969), pp. 61–62.

4. Ibid., p. 62.

5. Michael Perkins, *The Secret Record* (New York: William Morrow, 1976), p. 9.

6. Ibid., p. 55.

7. Virginia Woolf, *A Room of One's Own* (New York: Harcourt Brace and World, 1929), p. 27.

8. Millett, *Sexual Politics*, p. 419.

9. Ibid., p. 435.

10. Ibid., p. 437.

11. Ibid., p. 446.

12. William Smart, ed., *Women, Men, Men, Women: An Anthology of Short Stories* (New York: St. Martin's, 1975), p. 103. Both "The White Stocking" and "One Off a Short List" are anthologized here.

13. Ibid., p. 116.

14. Ibid., p. 103.

15. Ibid., p. 112.

16. Ibid., p. 115.

17. Ibid.

18. Ibid.

19. Phyllis Chesler, *About Men* (New York: Simon and Schuster, 1978), p. 227.

20. Smart, ed., *Women, Men, Men, Women*, p. 184.

21. Ibid., p. 185.

22. Ibid., p. 186.

23. Ibid., p. 187.

24. Ibid.

25. Ibid., p. 188.

26. Ibid., p. 189.

27. Margaret Drabble, *The Waterfall* (New York: Alfred A. Knopf, 1969), p. 63.

28. Ibid., pp. 283 ff.
29. Ibid., p. 184.
30. Ibid., p. 13.
31. Ibid., p. 70.
32. Ibid., p. 119.
33. Ibid., p. 123.
34. Ibid.
35. Ibid., p. 131.
36. Ibid., p. 150.
37. Ibid., p. 143. She tries to match Lucy in a number of ways.
38. Ibid., p. 217.
39. Ibid., p. 162.
40. Ibid., pp. 191 ff.
41. Ibid., p. 77.
42. Ibid., p. 85.
43. Ibid., pp. 96–97.
44. Ibid., pp. 179–80.
45. Ibid., pp. 127 ff.
46. Ibid., p. 103.
47. Ibid.
48. Ibid., p. 105.
49. Ibid., p. 118.
50. A. Alvarez, *The Savage God: A Study in Suicide* (New York: Bantam, 1972), pp. 13, 17.
51. Drabble, *The Waterfall*, p. 285.
52. Ibid.
53. Ibid., p. 290.
54. Robert Meeropol and Michael Meeropol, *We Are Your Sons* (New York: Ballantine, 1975), p. 267. See second note. Walter Schneir and Miriam Schneir, *Invitation to an Inquest* (Garden City, N.Y.: Doubleday, 1965), pp. 236, 249, 252, 253.
55. E. L. Doctorow, *The Book of Daniel* (New York: New American Library, 1971), pp. 314–15.
56. Ibid., pp. 224–25.
57. Ibid., p. 316.
58. Ibid., p. 301.
59. E. L. Doctorow, *Ragtime* (New York: Random House, 1975), p. 4.
60. Ibid., p. 30.
61. Ibid., p. 69.
62. Ibid., p. 71.
63. Ibid., p. 46.

64. Ibid., pp. 52–54.
65. Ibid., p. 53.
66. Ibid., p. 40.
67. Ibid., p. 51.
68. Ibid., p. 42.
69. Ibid., pp. 91–92.
70. Ibid., p. 83.
71. Ibid., p. 93.
72. Ibid., p. 189.
73. Ibid., p. 23.
74. Ibid., p. 5.
75. Ibid., pp. 20–21.
76. Ibid., p. 269.
77. Ibid., p. 33.
78. Ibid., pp. 115–17.
79. Joseph Heller, *Good as Gold* (New York: Simon and Schuster, 1979), p. 7.
80. Ibid., p. 319.
81. Ibid., pp. 174, 302.
82. Ibid., p. 112.
83. Ibid., p. 347.
84. Ibid., p. 73.
85. Ibid., p. 384.
86. Ibid., p. 358.
87. Ibid., pp. 18, 84, 361.
88. Ibid., p. 126.
89. Ibid., p. 137.
90. Ibid., p. 383.
91. Ibid., p. 43.
92. Ibid., p. 400.

VIII

TOPOGRAPHICAL AND ASTRONOMICAL IMAGES IN ADRIENNE RICH'S POETRY

Adrienne Rich challenges others to give full support to change that will better conditions for women, and her writings reveal a break from those traditions that have linked women solely with sex and death. The life-orientation of her work is remarkable, and her hopes for changing patterns of behavior and opening up the arts to the full participation of women are consistently apparent. As a feminist and a writer, she attempts not only to shake free from a history that limits woman to a procreative function and unreasonably aligns her with destructiveness and death, but also to find new ways of showing woman as a many-sided aspirant to a full life instead of a scapegoat, *memento mori*, virgin denying life, or victim to be mutilated, beaten, and murdered for sexual pleasure. She has brought feminism in poetry out of the closet and in so doing has helped strip away the unreason that has hovered over the image of woman in literature and life. Her success is a landmark in the long process of helping free the language so that it can register women's lives and achievements on a scale not realized before.

Poetry has also been greatly strengthened by the wealth of imagery Rich uses to suggest expanding vistas for women. Of all the areas she draws on for this imagery, two of the most effective for showing newer and broader horizons for women are topography and astronomy. Using metaphors from these areas, which have

This chapter was originally a paper delivered at the Colorado Women's Studies Association Annual Conference, May 1980, and at the South Central Women's Studies Association Conference, October 1980.

primarily been associated with men, she enhances the capacity of the language to record aspirations and intellectual capabilities that women possess. Even as early as *A Change of World* (1951), she is out in the open and preoccupied with light which she associates with intelligence. Some part of her mind works like that of the medieval man who watched the stars at night.[1]

In *The Diamond Cutters* (1955), landscape blooms "in monstrous cubes and coils,"[2] and Africa affords much raw material, for example, diamonds to be mined. Already her store of imagery includes worlds apart from the one her body occupies as she writes. As if to get beyond where she is in order to gain new perspectives, she tells us that she writes out of another "province" whose topography is changeable and showing signs of man and nature's effect on it.[3] Always speaking from a broader standpoint than that of the lover of nature, she sees all recorded history in the landscape, and as for the clouds, they "can be whatever you intend."[4] That the "crime" of women may be "to cast too bold a shadow or smash the mold straight off"[5] is a recognition she announces in "Snapshots of a Daughter-in-Law," a poem that traces her study of the history of women. Often she shows women in expanded and bold relief against the earth or sky rather than less than life-size as history has depicted them.

Growing toward self-knowledge and greater intellectuality and developing the capacity to tell others about it, in 1961 she is already asking that her readers be shocked into broader illumination: "Let me take you by the hair and drag you backward to the light."[6] This will not be easy, for "A geographical misery composed of oceans" lies around us and "we stalk in the raging desert of our thought." But "some mote of history has flown into"[7] certain eyes; when this happens, what is needed to depict experience is new metaphors.[8] At this point, she senses the world breathing beneath her bed and the evolution of a new planet arising out of chaos where two beings will exist in harmony as twins.[9] Here is an early vision of what *The Dream of a Common Language* (1978) will make explicit and concrete.

From a "larger than life"[10] perspective and often by comparing herself and other women to a vast terrain or a heavenly body, she feeds into a growing depository of topographical and astronomical images that contrast sharply with, for example, John Donne's very differently focused new land where woman is "manned."

Often comparing her to recently discovered territory, Donne says woman is like America; there all is free and readily available for handling, receiving his "seal" and generally becoming safely owned and exploited by him, as any acreage would be.[11]

Eroding and reshaping such reductive, body-oriented, and manipulative content and language with metaphors that identify woman with mind, strength, and the self-propelled, Rich parallels woman's productivity with that of the earth and creates other female images that connote a feminine consciousness and intellectuality expanding simultaneously with growth in social freedom. As a poet moving much beyond the cries of a newly awakened awareness, she allows her metaphoric language to suggest a widened scope, greater possibility for action, and movement directed outwardly toward nurturing and change. Woman likened to the sky, the earth, and the rivers can better be visualized as potentially more capable than if she is identified with the familiar fruits and flowers, caged birds, enclosed spaces, and sewing, all of which have much more limited scope.

Rich magnifies woman with a powerful lens; poets, speaking as Donne does above, narrowly funnel a vision of her down into a thick concentrate of sex and are seemingly unaware of any further implications that landscape ("America") might suggest. Conquered and explored by the male, she is made no more vital by this imagery than if she were likened to the proverbial rose, plucked and wilted. Rich takes her into the light of the out-of-doors; Donne does not.

Interestingly, in "The Days: Spring," Rich is reminded of one who asks, "Who will survive Amerika?" and ponders the "chance of beginning again" by working her way through the facts of her time and history. A whole "constellation" of these facts streams in her head, and she visualizes woman's body "nailed with stars."[12] Crucified though she may be, the picture of her crucifixion is pervasive and may be useful to point out the necessity of change. To show further breadth and depth, she says in "Planetarium" that the skies are filled with women and that she, the speaker, is "a galactic cloud so deep so involuted that a light wave could take 15 years"[13] to travel through her. Nothing second rate, she wants to be a part of "a conspiracy to coexist with the Crab Nebula, the exploding universe, the Mind."[14] Not concerned here as others have been with the negative aspects of woman's fragmentation, she is

struck by the intricate and multiple sides of her personality: "You
are split here like mercury on a marble counter, liquefying into
many globes, each silvered like a planet caught in a lens."[15]

Coming to earth, woman is likened to the "mind" of the river;
upstream, recognized as the river's historical past, she has lost her
"purity" to pleasure seekers who "witlessly" "careened" her and
took away her powers (which many females, Rich indicates, to this
day cannot even realize exist).[16] Rich's lioness has eyes which
"mirror rivers, seacoasts, volcanos, the warmth of moon-bathed
promontories."[17] In denial of the body-orientation, she as architect of the natural setting explains: "I am not a body, I am no
body." Rather, as writer she can "irrigate gardens," "dissolve and
project horizons," when her mind stirs the "inkpot" into an erupting
"volcano."[18] Contrary to the history found in manuscripts, Rich
insists again that her landscape shows the imprint of women as
they have existed through history.[19]

Acknowledging the power of the female as transformer,[20] Rich
fulfills the role herself by projecting woman on larger and more
diverse canvasses than she has been projected on before. Not only
is the landscape blown up for Rich's minute analysis and discovery, but it is made more perceivable by Rich, the medium,[21] for
her readers. Growing in knowledge of her own identity which includes identifying with other women, she makes the road easier
for others to follow, whether they be writers in need of a new
imagery or those in need of renewed self-esteem. As poet and architect, she makes blueprints for a city that waits at the back of
her mind; she would fashion it for all women, eliminating such
things as purdah and the sweatshop.[22]

In order to reshape history and myth, to "dive into the wreck"[23]
and work her way through it, she would begin with an unme-
chanized earth, a primitive landscape. Speaking of the man's world
which is finished because "They themselves have sold it to the
machines," she says, "I walk the unconscious forest."[24] By working her way backward into the unconscious and by starting from
the primitive forest, she will be able to begin anew the reshaping
process. The antiquated elemental settings have escaped much and
will make relationships simpler and provide the right kind of climate for her mind to work successfully, regardless of how pain-
fully, through to the present once again. She will gain by being

able to work as in former states of consciousness without loneliness, and she will be a central figure in the newly created consciousness.[25]

Rich calls for the earth-identity of woman wherein she can learn of her power; moving beyond this recognition, she will be "more than stone" when she can live freely. Bathed in the light of her own intelligence, woman, she hopes, will not be earthbound but interplanetary. It would be a mistake to see Rich as simply identifying woman with nature if such an identification meant accepting certain stereotyped roles as her natural (and thus unalterable) birthright. Such a birthright, Rich thinks, is not woman's true birthright, but one created for her by those more powerful than she is. Rich seems rather to be underscoring through her expanded imagery the breadth and depth of the possibilities for enrichment, mental growth, and directive power that can be woman's.

In saying that her body is political,[26] Rich again gives this body metaphorical proportions much larger than the actual. When war defoliates the fields, they are raped. Whether it be "The lovely landscape of southern Ohio betrayed by strip mining"[27] or the dog-eared earth and worm-eaten moon,[28] we think of both the earth and other planets and of woman being molested or ravaged. In further larger-than-life imagery, she connects the predicament of war and social unrest with the predicament of woman, as well as ultimately the history of both. As she indicates in *Of Woman Born*, the patriarchical system is nurtured on a terrain made of women's bodies.[29] It is not surprising that she would look back to pre-patriarchy and the worship of goddesses[30] for a starting point to reshape our consciousness.

For Rich and those who share her vision, history is already undergoing some alteration. With woman viewed in a broader perspective than that espoused by writers with whom Donne has much in common, "the house of childhood seems absurd, its secrets a fallen hair, a grain of dust." With woman "eternally exposing to the universe"[31] her situation, the images of the past come to fall on deaf ears. Calling again from another planet "to tell a dream light-years away,[32] she recognizes her own change and the possibility of its repetition in others. Giving credit to the early feminists whom she identifies as miners, she indicates that much of the earth still needs pickaxes and that she hopes to help with the important rehabilitation process.[33]

Women, she says, must be of a stature great enough "to close the gap in the Great Nebula, to help the earth deliver."[34] Rich is simply tired "of women stooping to half" their height.[35] Woman is sometimes solitary, disengaged, and rootless like a distant constellation in her study of her own life, but she begins to change in simple exercises which she practices until "strength and accuracy" become one.[36] Then she can leap into transcendence. This is Rich's projected dream, even though she knows that she leaped into an overwhelmingly difficult task when she was born into a world already cut out to thwart. The world into which she was born took her birthright away, told her nothing of her origin, and gave her nothing to help her regain wholeness.[37]

The Dream of a Common Language ends on a somewhat subdued note, but with no lessening of Rich's desire to create a new world where a new kind of language and thus a new poetry will exist. Having explored herself and the history of women, she thinks "a whole new poetry"[38] can be written out of her findings. Obviously, she objectifies her own notion as she shows the strength and power that women give one another, the closing of the gap between mind and body, and the nurturing that woman furnishes as that "stone foundation, [and] rockshelf further forming underneath everything that grows."[39]

When Rich ended "From an Old House in America" with the line "Any woman's death diminishes me," she was doubtlessly echoing and countering Donne's well-known "Any man's death diminishes me" of his Meditation XVII.[40] By the time *The Dream of a Common Language* is completed, she has asked for a language reshaped to eliminate bifurcation. This language universally spoken will move from the private to the political sector where nations will speak to one another in terms of true understanding. Rich herself has advanced the development of such a language by projecting women metaphorically onto larger and more meaningful topographical and astronomical canvasses than those on which they have heretofore been projected. By so doing she has helped to close the gap that has long separated and thus dwarfed people. Moreover, by seeing women in a much broader perspective than the one which has so pervasively limited them to the sexual and linked their sexuality with death, Rich has helped shatter the woman-sex-death triad that has been such a strong contributing factor to keeping women subservient and with little incentive to move away from traditional limitations. She has also shown us how women can have varied and nearly limitless experiences that span an entire lifetime.

A Wild Patience Has Taken Me This Far (1981), as one might expect, shows no tendency on Rich's part to surround women with death images. It does show the speaker in the first poem to be "starving for images,"[41] and suggests that she is involved in a war of images, with those she wants for rendering her experience pitted against those which show women "dismembered on the cinema screens" or in other media.[42] Neither does this latest work show Rich losing her dream of a common language,[43] even though, metaphorically, she is moving beyond the broad vistas she associated in earlier works with an awakening sense of possibility. She has not lost her radical/political approach[44] but rather is reassessing her position and moving on from an earlier awakening as she shifts her focus to vistas within herself and to woman-to-woman relationships or interests in women in the community or the past, all of which are vital to political change.

A look at the way she underscores the personal, and now uses the astronomical and topographical image, will indicate the nature of the tilt her focus is taking. In "Integrity," Rich writes: "I have nothing but myself to go by; nothing stands in the realm of pure necessity except what my hands can hold."[45] Calling attention to an early feminist's emphasis on grasping "solitude and personal responsibility" in our lives, she applauds early women for giving her back her dream of a common language and the "solitude of self."[46] In "A Vision," Rich wonders why we must test ourselves against God rather than throwing emphasis back to ourselves.[47] She is troubled by the lesbian archaeologist who sifts "her own life out from the shards she's piecing, asking the clay all questions but her own."[48] Rich ends *A Wild Patience Has Taken Me This Far* with a poem that closes on a purposeful note as the speaker puts aside seeing the expanse of the Grand Canyon for communion with another person.[49] In this poem which ends the section called "Turning the Wheel," she is beginning to turn the wheel now created by women's efforts both for herself and others. The wheel now invented and ready for turning is the conviction that association and work for and through women will reap the greatest personal and public harvest.

Rich's use of astronomical images seems more restrained in this work. One almost senses a greater down-to-earth at-homeness within the borders of the United States: Willa Cather and Julia in Nebraska, the "Coast to Coast" poem, the poems on the Southwest Indians, Mary Jane Colter who found challenge as an architect in the Southwest, the university scene in "Frame," the remarks about the Hudson River. When looking at the constellations, she says: "All the figures up there look violent to me . . . I want our own earth not the satellites, our world as it is if not as it might be then as it is."[50] The planets "out there" are the "piece of us" that is always out beyond ourselves,[51] but that part has diminished perhaps as Rich finds more within herself and within relationships on a personal level that have their own kind of broad expanse.

However important it has been "to walk out under the Milky Way, feeling the rivers of light, the fields of dark,"[52] this is not enough; freedom, she says, is "daily, prose-bound, routine remembering. Putting together, inch by inch the starry worlds. From all the lost collections."[53] Here as elsewhere in her latest volume, she obviously has not abandoned history: "it is the pictograph from which the young must learn";[54] she is riveted to it and its shock value, oppression, and nightmares, for it must be our "steadying and corrective lens."[55]

As with the sky, Rich's use of the landscape as metaphor is apparent when she is putting aside (rejecting is too strong a term) the distant vista for something closer to home, more inner, or more involved with another person. The Grand Canyon, the "female core of a continent" which is "stained in the colors of a woman's genitals," is a place she has decided not to see on the day she "turns the wheel," a day she will spend "talking to you."[56]

The paucity of expansive topographical and astronomical metaphors in *A Wild Patience Has Taken Me This Far* does not mean a rejection of the broad vistas she has opened for women and linguistically for poetry; rather, she is attempting to refine her own language, "never to romanticize" it again.[57] It is a drawing out and analysis of the fruits of the "earth" before her, earth meaning in her case, and at this point, the self, her many selves, or those of other persons near her or out of history. She visualizes slicing "the beetroots to the core," each one an "undiscovered planet."[58] One can sense here her commitment to search for diversity and peculiarity and variety in women as well as herself. It is in the small beet that she can turn in her hands that she now finds her landscapes.

That Rich is involved in a new, deeper, and more carefully searched investigation is amply illustrated. With Ethel Rosenberg and Emily Dickinson, she is retracing her steps in light of her current thinking. In several of the poems in the section called "Turning the Wheel," she suggests safeguards for those who study women of the past: "Location" suggests we leave nostalgia at home when we investigate, much as other poems insist we get beyond amnesia in our search. "Burden Baskets" warns against becoming so involved in the artifact that the self of the searcher, and by implication of the searched, is forgotten. "Hohokam" asks that the Indian woman not remain faceless, that she be seen as living, "bringing water to fields of squash."[59] "Self-hatred" suggests that we have mercy for those who have failed, that we see with more than a one-dimensional focus, and that we learn from our past. "Particularity" tells us we must not simplify the meaning of women or see them as mere symbols forgetting their voices, smells, types of work, even their deformities—without these qualities they are kept "helpless and conventional," their true power lost.[60] "Apparition" tells us to look at the woman "closely"; perhaps here in a simple way Rich is underscoring her major theme: draw in your focus and with a clear lens see precisely what women have been and are.

Women and Death: Linkages in Western Thought and Literature has discussed how attitudes have fostered negative associations between women and death. It is hoped that more and more we will see positive writings about women, such as those exemplified by Adrienne Rich and others, only a few of whom are discussed here. It is exceedingly important that our language be in step with the times, for as Rich states: "When language fails us, when we fail each other, there is no exorcism."[62]

NOTES

1. Adrienne Rich, "For the Conjunction of Two Planets," in *Poems: Selected and New, 1950–1974* (New York: Norton, 1975), p. 11.

2. Rich, "The Snow Queen," in ibid., p. 31.

3. Rich, "Letter from the Land of Sinners," in ibid., p. 33.

4. Rich, "Rural Reflections," in ibid., p. 43.

5. Rich, "Snapshots of a Daughter-in-Law," in ibid., p. 50.

6. Rich, "Merely to Know," in ibid., p. 53.

7. Rich, "Marriage of the Sixties," in ibid., p. 59.

8. Ibid., p. 60.

9. Ibid.

10. Rich, "The Roofwalker," in ibid., p. 63.

11. John Donne, "To his Mistress Going to Bed," in *The Elegies and the Songs and Sonnets of John Donne*, ed. Helen Gardner (Oxford: Clarendon, 1965), p. 15.

12. Rich, "The Days: Spring," in *Poems: Selected and New, 1950–1974*, p. 138.

13. Rich, "Planetarium," in ibid., p. 148.

14. Rich, "The Phenomenology of Anger," in ibid., p. 202.

15. Rich, "Shooting Script," in ibid., p. 180.

16. Rich, "Study of History," in ibid., pp. 145–46.

17. Rich, "The Lioness," in *The Dream of a Common Language* (New York: Norton, 1978), p. 21.

18. Rich, "The Fourth Month of the Landscape Architect," in *Poems: Selected and New, 1950–1974*, pp. 224–25.

19. Rich, "Phantasia for Elvira Shatayev," in *The Dream of a Common Language*, p. 5.

20. Rich, *Of Woman Born* (New York: Norton, 1976), pp. 285–86 and elsewhere throughout the book.

21. Albert Gelpi, "Adrienne Rich: The Poetics of Change," reprinted from American Poetry Since 1960, ed. Robert B. Shaw (Cheadle, Cheshire: Carcanet Press, 1973), in *Adrienne Rich's Poetry: A Norton Critical Edition* (New York, 1975), p. 148.

22. Rich, "The Fourth Month of the Landscape Architect," in *Poems: Selected and New, 1950–1974*, p. 225.

23. Rich, "Diving into the Wreck," in ibid., pp. 196–98.

24. Rich, "Waking in the Dark," in ibid., p. 189.

25. Rich, Sonnet XXI, in *The Dream of a Common Language*, pp. 35–36.

26. Rich, "Tear Gas," in *Poems: Selected and New, 1950–1974*, p. 140.

27. Rich, "When We Dead Awaken," in ibid., p. 187.

28. Rich, "The Phenomenology of Anger," in ibid., p. 201.

29. Rich, *Of Woman Born*, p. 55.

30. Ibid., pp. 93–101.

31. Rich, "Sibling Mysteries," in *The Dream of a Common Language*, p. 52.

32. Ibid.

33. Rich, "Natural Resources," in ibid., p. 67.

34. Ibid.

35. Ibid., p. 64.

36. Rich, "Transcendental Etude," in ibid., p. 73.

37. Ibid., p. 75.

38. Ibid., p. 76.

39. Ibid., p. 77.

40. Charles Coffin, ed., *The Complete Poetry and Selected Prose of John Donne* (New York: Modern Library, 1952), p. 441.

41. Rich, "The Images," in *A Wild Patience Has Taken Me This Far* (New York: Norton, 1981), p. 5.

42. Ibid.

43. Rich, "Culture and Anarchy," in ibid., p. 15.

44. Rich, "Rift," in ibid., p. 49. Here Rich's speaker says, "What we're after is not clear to me, if politics is an unworthy name."

45. Rich, "Integrity," in ibid., p. 8.

46. Rich, "Culture and Anarchy," in ibid., p. 15.

47. Rich, "A Vision," in ibid., pp. 50–51.

48. Rich, "Burden Baskets," in ibid., p. 53.

49. Rich, "8. Turning the Wheel," in ibid., p. 59.

50. Rich, "The Spirit of Place," in ibid., pp. 44–45.

51. Ibid., p. 45.

52. Rich, "For Memory," in ibid., p. 22.

53. Ibid.

54. Rich, "For Julia in Nebraska," in ibid., p. 17.

55. Rich, "4. Self-hatred," in ibid., p. 55.

56. Rich, "8. Turning the Wheel," in ibid., p. 59.

57. Rich, "The Images," in ibid., p. 4.

58. Rich, "Culture and Anarchy," in ibid., p. 15.

59. Rich, "Hohokam," in ibid., p. 54.

60. Rich, "Self-hatred," in ibid., p. 56.

61. Rich, "Particularity," in ibid., p. 57.

62. Rich, "Rift," in ibid., p. 49.

IX

AFTERWORD

This study, of course, leaves many subjects relatively untouched or only summarily treated, namely audience response to art dealing with death; poetry versus fiction as a vehicle for perpetuating traditional thinking about women; and the texture of the thinking of past and present women writers on death. Subjects surrounding these like women and suicide; the exploitation of women in time of war; the search for scapegoats; and male dependency might be studied from a variety of viewpoints, including that of the literary artist.

Interesting studies could also be made on the relationships between male and female to determine whether the sympathy of one or both to women's issues would make that person or persons less prone to associate women and death in ways illustrated in this book. This kind of study could cover all strata of society, from the more enlightened to the unschooled. Remarkable unions like those of Mary Wollstonecraft and William Godwin, Elizabeth Barrett and Robert Browning, Mary Ann Evans and George Henry Lewes, Harriet Taylor and John Stuart Mill, or Virginia Stephen and Leonard Woolf might even be studied in this connection.

In addition, certain aspects of the origin of the sex and death association could be studied further. One result of this study has been to allay doubts as to how pervasive this link, as well as that of women and death, has been, but a more complete treatment of the origins of the link might be of interest. Any method that would cause the breakup of the association without consequent distortions in other directions would be of interest, as would evidence of new vigor being infused into the arts by the breakup. Beyond the arts are the actual lives of women on whom change would appear to be of utmost importance, and new evidence of improvement or lack of it needs to be recorded.

This book may help readers understand why unrealistic associations between women and men have continued. It may also anger some readers that the specific artists mentioned here helped perpetuate these associations. Perhaps it will be well to remind persons so disturbed that some of our most notable participants in the arts have espoused highly questionable political systems and that in surveying their careers, we rarely neglect to call attention to such allegiances. Failure to treat certain aspects of writers, especially those affecting such a large portion of the population as women, can result only in an incomplete and misleading treatment. It seems wise to examine language, religion, pictorial representations, poetry, and fiction since these media greatly influence attitude and taste, and in some instances those who work in these areas as, for instance, teachers, are directly responsible for shaping emotional response and comprehension.

It is important to know what is taught, to know what goes into minds that are still supple enough to cast aside what will not make for wholeness and strong enough to grasp what will. This book shows how writers are absorbing tradition uncritically and using it as it fits their needs. It may also show the degree of failure writers have experienced in creating reality and in grasping the extent of the negativism their works give to life.

APPENDIX

Unlike the literature discussed in the main body of this book, the appendix that follows presents a nonfictionalized portion of the actual lives of women. While the literature discussed thus far arises, for the most part, out of the imagination and fantasy of its creators, what lies ahead is factual and therefore representative of that portion of women's experiences that has connections with certain aspects of death.

Since the history at our disposal of women's lives is quite limited, materials on their experiences with death are also limited not only in their variety and scope but also in their dealing in each woman's case with only a part of her life. It stands to reason that a vast amount of women's time, about which we have few records, was spent in areas apart from those related to sexuality or death. Women did not as often face death in war or prove as combative as their mates. Women did care for the young, sick, and dying, but this care was only part of their existence, a great portion of their lives taking place after children were no longer under their intensive care, or in certain other, admittedly limited, roles besides that of parent.

What is striking about the history of women at our disposal is that it, like so much of the literature previously discussed, is overwhelmingly connected with their sexuality. In view of the depiction of women in literature and the general attitudes taken toward them throughout history, the tendency to limit their lives in historical accounts to the sexual should come as no surprise. More surprising is that their involvements with death also almost invariably deal with some aspects of their sexuality and often the most brutal sides of it.

That their personal and private history offers the main basis for the obsession with death found in literature is not a conclusion, however, that anyone looking closely at literature and life would draw. To whatever impetus actual events give to the obsession with death in literature, must be added a complex emotional response to women, a tropism toward death, the desire to conquer, the need to maintain the ego while manipulating others, the satisfaction found by inflicting pain or having it inflicted upon oneself, to say nothing of a vast amount of residual conditioning, peer pressure, and even economic hardship.

For the most part, the experiences which follow describe the reality of the sufferers at given points in their lives; most of the delineations discussed in the main body of this book are by authors experiencing vicarious satisfaction or empathy, and in turn, helping their readers do the same. In contrast to the literature discussed, this appendix is largely removed from the romantic, orgasmic, and stereotypical; this appendix is the other side of the coin, the realistic and experiential side. Occurring as these experiences do in actual life, they are much less exemplary of the irrational aspects of human nature but are rather the kinds of down-to-earth hardships with which women have had to cope.

The conditions under which these events took place are quite different from the quiet, largely unthreatening, study where most of the literature was conceived. It is interesting that childbirth, care of children, and women's work are not overwhelmingly attractive to most of the writers previously discussed; sex or love and death, not as separate entities but when linked, are. In their literary productions sex and love often cannot exist without a large element of cruelty or some kind of activity or aura that presages death.

It needs also to be remembered that art can often have a more far-reaching influence than actual experiences. It is, of course, unfortunate that extreme and unusual events connected with women are the ones that capture the imagination and cling to it whether these events are actual or fictional.

The materials below show women undergoing pain and death or living in the presence of death; men traditionally have to an even greater extent found themselves in predicaments where death occurs or is imminent, but they have escaped having an aura of death hover around them in the excessive and unwarranted ways that women have. This book has underscored a death-oriented perspective held primarily by male writers or by the characters whom they delineate. Should actual female victims speak about their involvement with death, they would tell of their inner responses while undergoing experiences, not of the imagination, but like the ones that follow.

Once it is realized that facing death or the death-producing was not the whole of women's existence, the kind of suffering presented here will be seen in a broader perspective. Once death for women has ceased to be legitimized by overt or tacit acceptance of the part for the whole in much literature and various other walks of life, what follows below will hopefully more certainly become a thing of the past. These occurrences will be put beside all the contributions women have made to life and thus be viewed in the proper perspective—and more rationally.

WOMEN AS EXPENDABLE

Infanticide has always taken its toll of the female population. J. Laurence Angel, who has studied skeletal remains, states that the female in classical Greece had limited chances of survival. The mother, whose average year of demise was 36.2 as contrasted to 45.0 for males, had an average of 4.3 births during her life, 1.6 of the children dying while very young and 2.7 living to average age. The parents, wanting *one* girl to live, consulted the midwife as to whether their first-born female was worth keeping and when found so, they reared her, provided the natural mortality rate or citizenship laws did not interfere. Any other females born were "exposed" or left to die. According to Sarah B. Pomeroy, population statistics in classical Greece did not usually include females, nor did female children receive as much food or have wet nurses that were as expensive as those used for boys.[1]

Infanticide of females occurs in other cultures, and infanticide of both sexes occurs when conquering armies kill the children of the vanquished or when legal sanctions exist prescribing child murder as a means of population control. History reveals widespread instances of killing female infants first in the event of famine. Eighteenth-century France, it is said, had such a "murderous indifference" toward the poor, especially the female, that both the mother and child were disposed of as an "exterminator might dispose of rodents."[2]

The mother, especially if young, meets special kinds of hardships in attempting to dispose of her unwanted infant. Even if she is aware that in many places it has been accepted policy to kill twins, the first born, the deformed, and the female, she is troubled by having to act alone and against society's wishes. Often finding that the father cannot be called to account for his part in her ordeal, she may seek abortion through tonics or unhygienic tools that bring death.

Possibly having a hormonally based readiness to abandon or do away with her child,[3] she may kill not knowing what the reaction of those around her will be. In earlier times, she would be linked with Jews and witches and become the scapegoat or sacrificial beast to alleviate the guilt of whole communities. Her killing became not just a fact of life but a very great need on the part of her people, like confession or the giving of gifts. During the Middle Ages and the Renaissance, she could be condemned to death.

In Brittany, for example, she would die by hanging, after having been broken on the wheel. In 1407, Francesca di Pistoia was condemned, then paraded through the streets with her dead baby tied around her neck, and finally burned to death. The Saxon jurist Benedict Carpzof (1595–1666) boasted that he had assisted in the execution of 20,000 women, most of whom were indicted for witchcraft but a large number for infanticide. He also made it legal that the infanticidal woman sew the sack in which she, a cat, a dog, and a viper were to be drowned.[4] Even as late as the eighteenth century, the condemned woman might be burned alive, impaled, drowned, or decapitated, decapitation being considered by some the most merciful punishment. Suicides were common.

The reader is invited to explore the notion that women have been thought expendable even as mature persons, but infanticide of the female and its consequences are perhaps the most obvious extension of this belief.

BIRTHING AND DISEASE AS DEATH RISKS

Katherine Mayo gives an especially graphic account of what it could be like in India for a young mother of the not unusual age of twelve to give birth. Interestingly, Mary Daly offers the statistics that, in 1971, 48.9 percent of rural births and 33.4 percent of urban births were attended by an untrained *dhai*.[5] This *dhai* is brutal and unhygienic, and stops at almost nothing to extract the infant from the mother's womb. Since many uneducated Indians consider women's sexual functions to be contemptible, this *dhai* is thought to be the proper one to handle the birth, and the mother is believed deserving of her treatment. With labor sometimes lasting three to six days, the attendant gives full attention to hastening delivery rather than to the mother who is provided with no nourishment whatsoever during this time. According to Mayo, writing in 1927, the *dhai*

> kneads the patient with her fists; stands her against the wall and butts her with her head; props her upright on the bare ground, seizes her hands and shoves against her thighs with gruesome bare feet, until, so the doctors state, the patient's flesh is often torn to ribbons by the *dhai's* long, ragged toenails. Or, she lays the woman flat and walks up and down her body, like one treading grapes. Also, she makes balls of strange substances, such as hollyhock roots, or dirty string, or rags full of quince seeds; or earth mixed with cloves, butter with marigold flowers; or nuts, or spices—any irritant— and thrusts them into the uterus, to hasten the event.[6]

In Christian countries during the Middle Ages, if a female child remained a virgin until she was eleven, she might be killed so that her blood could be used by physicians to cure maladies which nothing else would help.[7] Tending the ill and dying adds still another dimension to woman's experience with death.

The cure for many of the so-called women's ailments in much nineteenth-century, and some twentieth-century, medicine centers in the sexual organs. Her "insanity" may be lessened by removal of her ovaries, her masturbation and orgasms may be stopped by a clitoridectomy, her rebellious inclinations (sometimes into feminism) will be blamed on her defective sexual organs, and thus they will be removed. Menopause is something that must be treated. Reactions to rape may be called hysteria.

Puerperal fever in childbirth killed a tremendous number of

women in earlier times. Interestingly, the disease was not prevalent before the seventeenth century when midwives cared for the
mother. In 1861, Igniz Philipp Semmelweis discovered that the
disease was carried by the physician's dirty hands from bed to bed.
Semmelweis made the discovery only to suffer and eventually die,
in part, it is believed from the vilification and outrage perpetrated
upon him for doing so by fellow physicians wanting to protect
their interests and squelch what appeared to them to be nonsense.[8]
Hospitals were also deadly for reasons of hygiene.[9] One source indicates that, as late as 1970, abortions were about four times less
dangerous than childbirth.[10]

Prostitution and venereal disease were the subjects of repeated
parliamentary inquiries in Victorian England. Prostitution was the
fourth largest female occupation in England; the *Westminster Review* reported at one point that 368,000 women were so employed. According to this publication, venereal disease "blights the
infant in the womb, and contaminates the milk drawn by the child
from its mother's breasts. It respects neither virtue, nor purity, nor
innocence, which are alike defenseless against its indiscriminating
and corrupting influence." Attempts to alter the status quo were
"largely unsuccessful, foundering because it would entail some
recognition of a vice, or because the effects of prostitution provided a divinely sanctioned punishment for sexual sin far more
terrible than the law could provide." A woman might be startled
by the accusation against her that she caused the soldiers' death,
by sapping their health; she may have been led to believe that venereal diseases were "the natural and just retribution divinely or-
dained for the punishment of illicit intercourse and that to interfere in any way with its working would be morally wrong."[11]

MARRIAGE BRINGS DEATH

The classical example of the kind of molding that brought extreme pain and suffering to women in preparation for marriage was
the Chinese ritual of footbinding. This effort to keep feet as small
as three inches in length caused women to walk with a kind of
hobble. Some writers report that it was done with the applause of
the males who sadistically, fetishistically, and erotically enjoyed the
woman's suffering. Feet were bound until they were excruciat-
ingly painful, until they smelled and rotted, and circulation vir-

tually stopped. With feet in a semi-amputated state and thighs much enlarged, she was supposedly more erotically enticing.[12]

Child-brides sometimes died from their first encounter with their husbands: "it has been traditional for Hindu men to force intercourse on extremely young female children."[13] One child-bride, aged nine, was brought to an Indian hospital the day after marriage with her left femur dislocated, her pelvis crushed out of shape, and her flesh hanging in shreds; another, aged about seven, died in great agony after living three days; another, aged ten, crawled to the hospital on her hands and knees and has never been able to stand erect since marriage; another, aged ten, very small and entirely undeveloped physically, was bleeding from rectal penetration by a husband forty years of age and weighing over one hundred and fifty pounds.[14] In New Delhi during the spring of 1979, citizens marched to protest the burning to death of Tarvinder Kaur and Kanchan Mala by their in-laws for not being able to produce expected dowry. Their spouses could not remarry with them alive.[15]

In Africa, where women experience genital mutilation, death might also be the result. Three kinds of infibulation, usually referred to euphemistically as "female circumcision," are widely practiced: "removal of the prepuce and/or tip of clitoris, . . . excision of the entire clitoris with the labia minora and some or most of the external genitalia, . . . excision of entire clitoris, labia minora and parts of the labia majora." About the latter, Daly repeats her source: "The two sides of the vulva are then fastened together in some way either by thorns . . . or sewing with a catgut. Alternately the vulva are scraped raw and the child's limbs are tied together for several weeks until the wound heals (or she dies). The purpose is to close the vaginal orifice. Only a small opening is left (usually by inserting a sliver of wood) so the urine, or later the menstrual blood, can be passed."[16] As if she must be made over for the convenience of others, in this setting a woman might expect to have repeated encounters with the knife, for she is sewed up to prevent any "wild" kinds of intercourse (the smaller the aperture the greater her value), cut open to permit the "right" kind, sewed up again for safekeeping, and cut open again for delivery of a child. Her aperture must never be too loose. Opened with a knife upon marriage, she must have intercourse very frequently at first lest the aperture close up again. In Daly's account one girl was reportedly sewed up after being measured to fit her husband's penis; another girl had maggots eating at her insides. In Somali, husbands are known to beat young brides when they first come to their houses until the blood flows and then deflower them with a knife. Men of Bambaras fear death from the "sting" (clitoris) of the nonexcised woman.[17]

The notorious chastity belt was sometimes injurious to a woman's life. Elizabeth Davis writes of one woman who found that the weight of a padlock "her husband had imposed on her was tearing the lips of her vagina and causing her great pain and bleeding." The doctor discovered that the husband had "bored holes in her labia, through which he had inserted two metal rings, similar to curtain rings, which he had drawn together and locked securely with a padlock."[18]

In some cultures, the threat of murder is used to control the wife. When this threat is absent, as in Acan in the Tarascan area of Mexico where it is considered very objectionable to kill a female, women are more outspoken and less passive than in areas where the objection to killing women is not present.[19]

SURVIVAL IN TIME OF WAR: RAPE AND SUBSEQUENT DEATH

Susan Brownmiller gives an account of four small-boned Vietnamese women working in a field when a U.S. buck sergeant and three other soldiers come by and "ball" them in the elephant grass. As the sergeant tells it:

> They were forcibly willing—they'd rather do that than get shot. Then one of the girls yelled some derogatory thing at the guy who'd balled her. . . . He just reached down for his weapon and blew her away. Well, right away the three other guys, including myself, picked up our weapons and blew away the other three chicks. Just like that. . . . Me and this other guy, we got high together in the bunker a lot, and we talked a lot about why we did it. The thing we couldn't understand was that when this other guy shot the first chick, we picked up our weapon without giving it a second thought and fired up the rest.[20]

At home in America, according to the *FBI Uniform Crime Reports* of 1978, there is a forcible rape every eight minutes and a murder every twenty-seven minutes. As Brownmiller states, rape can mean being "subjected at will to a thoroughly detestable physical conquest," and the result of "such brutal struggle might be death or injury, not to mention impregnation and the birth of a dependent child."[21]

Women were victims of mass rape in Bangladesh in 1971–1972: "During the nine-month terror, terminated by the two-week armed intervention of India, a possible three million persons lost their lives, ten million fled across the border to India, and 200,000, 300,000 or possibly 400,000 women (these sets of statistics have been variously quoted) were raped." Some accounts mention as many as eighty assaults on a woman in one night. Eighty percent of those raped were Moslems, and "no Moslem husband would take back a wife who had been touched by another man, even if she had been subdued by force." Other problems include not being able to tolerate the presence of men, gynecological infection, pregnancy and no desire to bear the child, and incompetent abortionists. Brownmiller states that "Dr. Geoffrey Davis of the London-based International Abortion Research and Training Center who worked for months in the remote countryside of Bangladesh reported that he had heard of 'countless' incidents of suicide and infanticide during his travels. Rat poison and drowning were the available means. Davis also estimated that five thousand women had managed to abort themselves by various indigenous methods, with attendant medical complications."[22]

TREATMENT OF THE WITCH AND SOMETIMES THE FEMINIST

Such "aberrations" as the witch and the feminist have been said to arise from carnal lust. In discussions of the witch, we learn that "the church understood that if its control was to be effective, the purge must be extensive and brutal. The insurgents were not easily smashed." Authorities who are willing to cite estimates state that from the fifteenth to the eighteenth century, 9 million witches were executed for their alleged beliefs and crimes. The persecution was especially brutal on the Continent. Torturing and burning destroyed 900 in a single year in the Wurtzburg area and 100 in and near Como. At Toulouse, 400 witches were put to death in one day.[23]

Sheila Rowbotham, in speaking of the sexual revolution in France, states: "It is at the point when the revolution starts to move women out of their passivity into the conscious and active role of militants that the mockery, the caricatures, the laughter with the strong sexual undertones begin." Class hatred, political elitism, and sexual authoritarianism thwarted the feminist's efforts; for example, "A concierge, Louise Noel; a parasol-maker, Jeanne Laymet; a cook, Eugenie Lhilly; the seamstress, Eulalie Papavoine; Elizabeth Retiffe, a cardboard maker; the rag picker Marie Wolff—they were transported, given hard labour and executed"[24].

When the marriage and land laws were passed on May 1, 1950, in China, it was found that when "the women and girls came from the Women's Movement and tried to enforce choice in marriage they met bitter opposition. Some of them were murdered. One father murdered his own daughter."[25]

WOMEN AS SLAVES AND PEASANTS

The Narrative of the Life of Moses Grandy, Late a Slave in the United States of America states:

> Mr. Rogerson was with them on his horse, armed with pistols. I said to him, "For God's sake, have you bought my wife?" He said he had; when I asked him what she had done, he said she had done nothing, but that her master wanted money. He drew out a pistol and said that if I went near the wagon on which she was, he would shoot me. I asked for leave to shake hands with her which he refused, but said I might stand at a distance and talk with her. My heart was so full that I could say very little. . . . I have never seen or heard from her from that day to this. I loved her as I love my life.[26]

The Russian peasant woman of the early twentieth century was said to be particularly passive and fatalistic. The subordination of the peasant woman was so extreme and bound up with backward ways that even with serfdom abolished there seemed no hope for change. Women were still regarded like property, and so it was not surprising "that the physical contempt for all human life general in that society should be acted out almost ceremoniously on the bodies of the women."[27] Russian proverbs proclaimed her deserving of sexual and social flagellation:

> Beat your wife for breakfast and dinner too.
> A wife isn't a jug—she won't crack if you hit her a few times.

The bride's father customarily gave the groom a new whip. Young women in puberty were treated like livestock and were sold to the highest bidder:

> The young girls were soon worn down with work and childbearing. They cooked, carried water, washed clothes in the river, made fires, milked the cows, toiled in the fields, and did the spinning and weaving. In the winter the *moujiks* were often at home with nothing to do but drink vodka and have sex with their wives. There were no contraceptives. Secretly the women went to the local wise woman who operated with nails or buttonhooks or carrots. Childbirth was a kind of nightmare. Infant mortality was high, there were only a few midwives.[28]

THOSE WHO COMMIT ADULTERY OR KILL

The spouse of a woman caught in adultery had the right to kill or punish her severely throughout much of history, for having his "property" violated by another man was thought an extreme infringement upon his prestige. During the later Middle Ages "from Naples to northern Europe, if he caught her in adultery and killed her there and then, he might go free; society encouraged and condoned his wrath. Logically enough, in more ordinary circumstances, he had the moral and legal right to inflict corporal punishment on her: all law systems agreed on this."[29] Divorce is a modern word: "it is agreed that during a space of five hundred and twenty years no marriage was ever dissolved in Rome."[30]

If a woman was implicated in the death of her husband, a most heinous crime during medieval Christian Europe she was burnt alive, for this was thought the "more agreeable" punishment for women. There was a taboo on her blood; as Davis states: "Smother her, poison her, drown her, burn her, or boil her in oil, but do not shed a drop of her blood!"[31] For the middle-class woman in nineteenth-century England, illicit sex was still a far more serious crime for a woman than for a man, but as the century wore on with "the increased opportunities for extramarital sex, made possible by higher standards of living, better transportation, wider circles of acquaintances, and growing leisure and privacy," it was surprising that middle-class women did not commit more adultery.[32] A new distrust of middle-class women who were searching for personal autonomy arose and in the case of Florence Bravo who was accused of poisoning her husband Charles, the prosecution assumed that discovering an adulteress was tantamount to finding a murderess and failed to ask questions exploring any other motive.[33]

According to one study, wives constitute 41 percent of all the women killed and husbands only 11 percent of all males killed. When a man is killed by a woman, the murderer is most often his wife. When a woman murders, she more often kills her mate than men do. One group of statistics shows that 45 percent of female murderers kill their husbands, while only 12 percent of male murderers kill their wives. Males have a much larger orbit than females and therefore kill greatly more outside the home. Husbands provoke wives to murder them more often than wives provoke men to murder them. One factor in producing this pattern is male attention to women connected with his work place, while women have had less chance, at least in the past, to seek out males outside the home. The husband more frequently kills close friends or strangers than does the wife.[34]

In treating male criminals, society tends to view their motivation as economic or social, whereas "women are believed to become criminals because of their menstruation cycle or menopausal symptoms." Rather than objectively treat women along with men, a paternalistic attitude regarding them prevails. Furthermore, "because the life-world of women is said to revolve around securing a mate or living vicariously through their men, the argument follows that the only field of deviance 'appropriate' to woman's role, besides shoplifting, is sexual deviance."[35]

The extent to which women kill persons other than their spouses should not be totally dismissed, however. History reveals that wet nurses, midwives, and girls and women with unwanted babies kill. Wet nursing, like prostitution, was a means of livelihood for poor women who were often responsible for the death of their own children so that they might breastfeed profitable ones. Holding out one's largest supply of milk for the child whose parents paid the most, and thought their babies were being provided with the best, must have resulted in deprivations and miscalculations that meant death to many children. Unlike many unwed mothers who killed their children, the wet nurse could cause the death of her child or someone else's without herself being punished by death. In some places, she was allowed to be the professional killer while, as incidents described above indicate, the unwed mother could be pronounced a witch and made the scapegoat for the community, or in some cases entire governments.[36]

Just as male political leaders have been responsible for inflicting death on a large scale, so women in positions of power have also killed, though, of course, never on as large a scale or as often as men. Queen Elizabeth I and Catherine the Great are only two examples. As mentioned in an earlier chapter, Countess Elisabeth Báthory is supposed to have killed 650 virgins and Empress Theodora had her one-night lovers killed before dawn.[37]

CARETAKER OF THE DEAD

Historically, the care of the corpse has been left to the woman, perhaps partially because washing and dressing it are akin to caring for infants. It has also been suggested that since the child begins in care of the woman, its end should be in her care also. In classical Greece, women also were in charge of the artifacts buried with males, such as spears, shield bosses, and drinking cups, and with females, spindle whorls, cooking pots, and sometimes jewelry.[38] Women have been considered good mourners because they have been thought to be more emotional than men. At wakes women have principal duties.

When Hindu husbands die, wives sometimes are expected to climb on their funeral pyres and thereby commit suicide to preserve their "purity," even though they may be very young, having wed as early as age ten. The Hindu woman, who has been led to believe her sins in a previous incarnation are responsible for her husband's demise, may either go to the fire without being forced, intending to suggest that she knows she is guilty and an agent of her own destruction; or she may be forced there by her in-laws, sons, or other relatives. Refusing would mean she would be hated for the rest of her life. Daly suggests that she could perhaps slip away into the redlight district hoping to disappear, but there she would very probably die at an early age from venereal disease.[39]

NOTES

1. Sarah B. Pomeroy, *Goddesses, Whores, Wives, and Slaves* (New York: Schocken, 1975), p. 70.

2. Marcia W. Piers, *Infanticide* (New York: Norton, 1978), p. 79.

3. Ibid., p. 33.

4. Ibid., pp. 51–69.

5. Mary Daly, *Gyn/Ecology: The Metaethics of Radical Feminism* (Boston: Beacon, 1978), pp. 438–39, n.21.

6. Katherine Mayo, *Mother India* (New York: Blue Ribbon, 1927), p. 95.

7. Gabriel Ronay, *The Truth About Dracula* (New York: Stein and Day, 1972), p. 112.

8. Adrienne Rich, *Of Woman Born* (New York: Norton, 1976), pp. 152–55.

9. Piers, *Infanticide*, p. 67.

10. Robin Morgan, ed., *Sisterhood Is Powerful* (New York: Random House, 1970), p. 560.

11. E. M. Sigsworth and T. J. Wyke, "A Study of Victorian Prostitution and Venereal Disease," in *Suffer and Be Still: Women in the Victorian Age*, ed. Martha Vincinus (Bloomington: Indiana University Press, 1972), pp. 79–93.

12. Andrea Dworkin, *Woman Hating* (New York: E. P. Dutton, 1974), pp. 95–116.

13. Daly, *Gyn/Ecology*, p. 120.

14. Mayo, *Mother India*, Appendix, pp. 411–12.

15. *The Guardian*, July 18, 1979.

16. Daly, *Gyn/Ecology*, p. 156, from Fran P. Hoken.

17. Ibid., pp. 157–67.

18. Elizabeth Davis, *The First Sex* (Baltimore: Penguin, 1972), p. 164.

19. David Lester and Gene Lester, *Crime of Passion: Murder and the Murderer* (Chicago: Nelson Hall, 1975), p. 85.

20. Susan Brownmiller, *Against Our Will: Men, Women and Rape* (New York: Bantam, 1975), p. 111.

21. Ibid., p. 6.

22. Ibid., pp. 81–85.

23. Morgan, *Sisterhood Is Powerful*, p. 543.

24. Sheila Rowbotham, *Women, Resistance and Revolution* (New York: Vintage, 1974), p. 106.

25. Ibid., p. 185.

26. Gerda Lerner, ed., *Black Women in White America* (New York: Vintage, 1973), pp. 8–9.

27. Rowbotham, *Women, Resistance and Revolution*, p. 138.

28. Ibid., pp. 138–39.

29. Julia Martines and Lauro Martines, eds., *Not in God's Image* (London: Temple Smith, 1973), p. 175.

30. Ibid., p. 35.

31. Davis, *The First Sex*, p. 162.

32. Mary S. Hartman, *Victorian Murderesses* (New York: Schocken, 1977), p. 133.

33. Ibid., p. 140.

34. Lester and Lester, *Crime of Passion*, p. 82.

35. Carol Smart, *Women, Crime and Criminology: A Feminist Critique* (London: Routledge and Kegan Paul, 1977), pp. 17–18.

36. Piers, *Infanticide*, pp. 51–54, 73.

37. Denis de Rougemont, *Love Declared* (New York: Pantheon, 1963), p. 152.

38. Pomeroy, *Goddesses, Whores, Wives, and Slaves*, pp. 43–44.

39. Ibid., pp. 114–33.

SELECTED BIBLIOGRAPHY

Alvarez, A. *The Savage God: A Study in Suicide*. New York: Bantam, 1972.

Boase, T.S.R. *Death in the Middle Ages*. New York: McGraw-Hill, 1972.

Brownmiller, Susan. *Against Our Will: Men, Women and Rape*. New York: Bantam, 1975.

Bullough, Vern L., and Bonnie Bullough. *The Subordinate Sex*. Urbana: University of Illinois Press, 1973.

Chesler, Phyllis. *About Men*. New York: Simon and Schuster, 1978.

Daly, Mary. *Beyond God the Father*. Boston: Beacon Press, 1973.

    Gyn/Ecology: The Metaethics of Radical Feminism. Boston: Beacon Press, 1978.

De Beaumont, Edouard. *The Sword and Womankind*. New York: Panurge Press, 1930.

De Beauvoir, Simone. *The Second Sex*. New York: Bantam, 1968.

De Rougemont, Denis. *Love Declared*. New York: Pantheon, 1963.

Dworkin, Andrea. *Woman Hating*. New York: E. P. Dutton, 1974.

Ferrante, Joan M. *Women as Image in Medieval Literature*. New York: Columbia University Press, 1975.

Fiedler, Leslie. *Love and Death in the American Novel*. New York: Criterion, 1960.

Firestone, Shulamuth. *The Dialectic of Sex*. New York: William Morrow, 1970.

Fowlie, Wallace. *Love in Literature*. Bloomington: Indiana University Press, 1965.

Friedan, Betty. *The Feminine Mystique*. New York: Dell, 1972.

Gornick, Vivian, and Barbara K. Moran, eds. *Women in Sexist Society*. New York: New American Library, 1971.

Greer, Germaine. *The Female Eunuch*. New York: McGraw-Hill, 1971.

Hartman, Mary S. *Victorian Murderesses*. New York: Schocken, 1977.

Hays, H. R. *The Dangerous Sex*. New York: Putnam, 1964.

Lerner, Gerda, ed. *Black Woman in White America*. New York: Vintage, 1973.

Lester, David, and Gene Lester. *Crime of Passion: Murder and the Murderer*. Chicago: Nelson Hall, 1975.

Martines, Julia, and Lauro Martines, eds. *Not in God's Image*. London: Temple Smith, 1973.

Mayo, Katherine. *Mother India*. New York: Blue Ribbon, 1927.

Mill, John Stuart, and Harriet Taylor Mill. *Essays on Sex Equality*. Ed. Alice S. Rossi. Chicago: University of Chicago Press, 1970.

Millett, Kate. *Sexual Politics*. New York: Ballantine, 1969.

Morgan, Robin, ed. *Sisterhood Is Powerful*. New York: Random House, 1970.

Piers, Marcia W. *Infanticide*. New York: Norton, 1978.

Pomeroy, Sarah B. *Goddesses, Whores, Wives, and Slaves*. New York: Schocken, 1975.

Rich, Adrienne. *Of Woman Born*. New York: Norton, 1976.
    On Lies, Secrets and Silence. New York: Norton, 1979.

Rogers, Katherine. *The Troublesome Helpmate*. Seattle: University of Washington Press, 1966.

Ronay, Gabriel. *The Truth About Dracula*. New York: Stein and Day, 1973.

Rowbotham, Sheila. *Women, Resistance and Revolution*. New York: Vintage, 1974.

Ruth, Sheila. *Issues in Feminism*. Boston: Houghton Mifflin, 1980.

Smart, Carol. *Women, Crime and Criminology: A Feminist Critique*. London: Routledge and Kegan Paul, 1977.

Sontag, Susan. *On Photography*. New York: Dell, 1978.

Vincinus, Martha, ed. *Suffer and Be Still: Women in the Victorian Age*. Bloomington: Indiana University Press, 1972.

Young, Wayland. *Eros Denied: Sex in Western Society*. New York: Grove, 1964.

INDEX

eator of realistic women, 182; *Diamond Cutters,* 180; *The Dream of a Common Language,* 180, 184–85; feminist, 179; "Frame," 186; "From an Old House in America," 184; going beyond nature poetry, 180; "Hohokam," 187; as innovator, 179; "Integrity," 185; "Location," 187; on male writers, 142–43; *Of Woman Born,* 183; "Particularity," 187; personal poet, 185; "Planetarium," 181; political activist, 183, 185; primitivist, 183–84; reformer of language, 179–87; "Self-hatred," 187; "Snapshots of a Daughter-in-Law," 180; student of history, 182, 183, 184; "Turning the Wheel," 185–86, 187; "A Vision," 185; "When We Dead Awaken: Writing as Re-Vision," 15, 142–43; *A Wild Patience Has Taken Me This Far,* 185–86

Richard, Jean Pierre, on predictions of Emma Bovary's death, 70

Richardson, Samuel, 58–69, 81; his dirge, 61–65; effort to show murderous intent in Lovelace, 64–65; language, 60; readers, 58–61, 68–69; religion, 59. *See also Clarissa*

Richmond, Annie, Poe's association with, 48

Rimbaud, Arthur, schooled on Poe, 47

Roethke, Theodore, 131; "I Knew a Woman" and "Words for the Wind," 131; treats death, 131

Roman Catholic Church. *See* Christianity: female souls in

Romanticizing: the killer, 151; woman, 48, 114, 186

Romantic writers, 45; Edmund Burke, 47; Samuel Taylor Coleridge, 47; John Keats, 47. *See also* Byron, George Gordon, Lord; Keats, John

Rosenberg, Ethel and Julius: Ethel of interest to Adrienne Rich, 187; originals for characters in *The Book of Daniel,* 165

Rossetti, Christine, 140; death not her concern, 140

Rossetti, Dante Gabriel, 47, 133, 140; "The Blessed Damozel," 47; fascinated by dead women, 133; influenced by Poe, 47

Rossner, Judith: death linked to sex, 153; *Looking for Mr. Goodbar,* 153

Rousseau, Jean Jacques, 60; on woman's "natural" position, 24

Rousset, Jean, Emma Bovary's life a prelude to its end, 70

Rowbotham, Sheila, negative responses to feminism, 202

Royster, Sarah, Poe's association with, 48

Rukeyser, Muriel, 140–41; "Ajanta," 140; desirable world, 140–41; seeks peace, 141; seeks realistic approach, 140–41; sees language reviving, 141; sees women beginning over, 140–41

Russ, Joanna, shared sexuality, 153

Russia: peasant woman's life in, 202–3; Poe of interest to, 47–48; society, 89–90, 202–3; Tolstoy's views concerning, 89–90

Sacco, 141

Sadism. *See* De Sade, Marquis; Sado-masochism

Sado-masochism, 151, 194, 198; connections with Christianity, 23,

About the Author

BETH ANN BASSEIN is Professor of English and Women's Studies at the University of Southern Colorado. She has researched eighteenth- and nineteenth-century fiction extensively, and her publications include articles in *Religious Humanism,* poetic and fictional contributions to numerous magazines, two booklets of poetry (*Breaking Apathy* and *Why Did I Laugh Tonight?*), and a bibliography of literature by Chicanas. She has begun a study of John Stuart Mill's feminism.